"A rare book of wisdom. I
me to find the balance of
"normal" in my own life."
Bill Thrall - Author, Leader, Mentor

"This author has truly 'walked the walk,' so there
could not be a more genuine account of lessons
learned – lessons that are so worthy of being
passed on. If a reader wasn't really interested in
the deeper walk, but just happened to open this
book, he/she would still find it hard to put down.
It is inspiring, informative and one of the most
entertaining spiritual truth books I have ever
encountered. A very worthwhile read!"
Barbara Paratore - Editor

"Everyday lessons will jump into your heart
when you read Ken's conversational writing style
on becoming Christ-like. The sound teaching of
Scripture is softened, but not watered down, by
life-story humor. You'll want to buy two books
for a start – one to give away!"
Gloria Graham - Author

Ken Cetton
Essentials

for a deeper spiritual life

To Linda w/ every spiritual blessing & love in Christ,

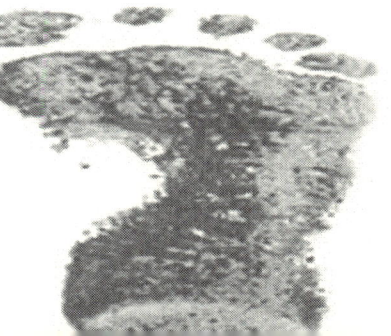

KC
Kenneth Cetton Publisher
Binghamton, NY, USA

Essentials for a deeper Christian life
Published by Kenneth Cetton
© Kenneth Cetton 2013

Unless otherwise indicated, all Scripture is taken from
The New American Standard Bible®
Copyright © 1960, 1962, 1963, 1968, 1971, 1972, 1973, 1975, 1977,
1995 by The Lockman Foundation. Used by permission.

Other Scripture quotations are taken from the following sources:

The Holy Bible, New International Version®
Copyright © 1973, 1978, 1984 by International Bible Society.
Used by permission of Zondervan. All rights reserved.

The Living Bible
Copyright © 1971 by Tyndale House Publishers, Wheaton, Illinois 60187.
All rights reserved.

New King James Version®
Copyright © 1982 by Thomas Nelson, Inc. Used by permission.
All rights reserved.

King James Version. Public domain.

Library of Congress Cataloging-in-Publication Data
Cetton, Kenneth, 1933–
Essentials for a deeper spiritual life / Kenneth Cetton
Includes bibliographical references
To be completed

ISBN 978-0-9898992-0-8

Design: Barry Dunnage FCSD FSTD FRSA, London, England

Printed and bound in the United States of America

To Allen and Ellen Thrall –
without Al's witness and Ellen's prayers,
there would be no book
and no Life.
Thank you, Al. Thank you, Ellen.
Thank you, Jesus!

Think of what you were when you were called.
Not many of you were wise by human standards;
Not many were influential;
Not many were of noble birth.
But God chose the foolish things of the world to
    shame the wise;
God chose the weak things of the world to
    shame the strong.
God chose the lowly things of this world and
    the despised things –
And the things that are not –
    to nullify the things that are.

1 Corinthians 1:26-28 NIV

Acknowledgments

I'm very grateful for the assistance of Mark Winheld whose skill as a former newspaper reporter and author of two books has proven invaluable in helping to overcome my grammatical ignorance. His latest book is "*Open the Sky*" – *The Story of Missionary Pilot Dwayne King*.

I also deeply appreciate the editorial diligence of Kimberly Meeker, an accomplished scholar and musician, who has proven brilliant in her knowledge of writing and research. We look forward to her own literary works someday soon.

My sincere thanks to Barbara Paratore, who kindly read the manuscript for content and line-edited it for the reviewers' edition. And a big thanks to Barry Dunnage, graphic artist from London, who skillfully designed the cover and layout design, and prepared the book for the publisher. Additional gratefulness goes to my faithful prayer partner, Michael Krembs who helped pray this book through labor pains into a live birth.

Not to be forgotten is our Binghamton, New York, Southern Tier Christian Writers Group, which I co-chair with Jean Jenkins, a gifted writer and editor. Participants have come and gone with the passage of time so I cannot list them all, but I am forever indebted to all of them for their patient monthly critiquing. I'm also greatly obliged to the Montrose Writers' Conference under the dedicated guidance of Patti Souder and her caring staff.

All of these dear people and others unnamed are clearly a gift from God, to whom I am deeply thankful. For whatever readability and impact this work possesses, credit goes to them and to Him. For any errors of style or fact, responsibility goes to me.

Kenneth Cetton

About the author

Kenneth Cetton is old enough to have heard a woman share that as a young girl, she saw Abraham Lincoln walk the streets of Springfield, Illinois. Yet he is young enough at heart for his writings to appeal to all ages. "Born again" at age 22, Ken was nurtured among the Plymouth Brethren, a group that has produced such noted Christians as Jim Elliot, George Muller and Harry Ironside. After graduating with a major in sociology, Ken worked with Operation Mobilization for four years, often in Turkey. Many of his stories date from that time. In his writings, he uses his exciting and often humorous adventures in missions to inspire readers and illustrate spiritual truths.

After returning to the United States and marrying a graduate of Moody Bible Institute, Ken led a team of 12 young people across the United States to teach door-to-door evangelism. As his family grew, he continued to preach in churches and also took his witness into the secular marketplace, driving a city bus in southern California. He met many people who needed to hear and see a living testimony of the resurrected Christ. Ken's job also enabled him to practice his faith in the everyday world of those he continued to preach to in churches. Following his years of secular employment and witnessing, he pastored several independent Baptist churches.

Ken is blessed with a keen sense of humor, which he uses in his writings to illuminate the serious subject of the deeper spiritual life, for those desiring to know God and to walk in the steps of Jesus. Ken's articles have appeared in Decision, Moody Monthly and Evangel magazines, as well as in newspapers and overseas publications. Now a writer and occasional preacher, he fellowships with the Plymouth Brethren in Binghamton, New York, where he lives with his wife, Helen.

Kenneth Cetton

Essentials

for a deeper spiritual life

Contents

Introduction by George Verwer

To be supplied

For reviewers and early readers

Thank you for being willing to review this book or purchase an early edition for your own pleasure and spiritual growth. In either case, your endorsement, comments and feed back are very important to us so please take time to get back to us.

While we've made every effort to present this early edition without flaws, if you find any (which seems inevitable), you will do us a great service by reporting them to us. Also. if you have any likes or dislikes about the book's contents and even its layout, we want to hear from you. The final completed edition with it's introduction by George Verwer and comments of both reviewers and readers will be out later this Fall, 2013. By that time we hope to have a study guide available on our website along with any noteworthy changes and additions to this book as well as George Verwer's important Introduction.

In any case, if you truly find the message of what you are holding deeply touching and spiritually uplifting then the greatest service you can do for us (as well as a service for the Lord) is to pass the word on to others so they may be blessed as well. Thanks much!

Blessings in Christ,
Ken Cetton

www.kencetton.com

Understanding this book

If you want to know God or to know Him better than you already do – then this book is for you. The deeper life being written about is actually the normal Christian life that God intended for every Christian to live, about which notable writers have also written in the past.[1] It is not our old life fixed up after we become Christians, but that old life being gradually if not quickly traded for the new one now dwelling within – the life of Christ as Paul proclaims in Galatians 2:20.[2]

To further your understanding, Section I of this book provides material to strengthen the reader's foundation of faith in God and His Word. These are cornerstones of belief that, sadly, have been eroded by the humanistic evolutionary teachings prevalent today. In order to live the Christian life to its fullest, it is important to have a firm and solid faith. In Section 2, the reader will find stories and more illustrations to clarify the Gospel. In Sections 3 through 5, the reader will find truths and insights for entering the exchanged, crucified life by learning to "walk in newness of life" as we are told in Romans 6:4.[3] Also emphasized is the absolute necessity of believing in the sovereign hand of God, who is always seeking to work for our good.

Through the narratives and analogies in each chapter, I have tried to make your reading journey a pleasant one. To that end, hopefully, you will notice that the joy of the Lord is evident through-out this book in spite of the seriousness of the subject matter. However, if you ever find yourself getting bogged down with any chapter that you don't understand, simply skim the material for stories and move on to the next.

Some readers may complain that I did not include other topics that could be considered essentials. Although I have undoubtedly missed a number of them, the ones I have discussed will keep us more than busy for now. Similarly, certain chapters address important themes in a short space. While I apologize for this brevity, the purpose of this book is to stimulate the reader's hunger for a greater personal knowledge of God. Your resulting experiences will provide material to write your own blog, chapter or book on God and His ways.

As for my qualifications for forging this book, I believe that many in God's kingdom, especially those living in areas where the church suffers persecution, understand much more than I do about the subjects addressed. Unquestionably, the spiritual lives of these brothers and sisters in Christ far transcends my own. By comparison, I am a mere dabbler in the deeper life. However, I have been called at this time to craft this book, and to neglect the task would be a failure on my part. I sense the strong "Wind of God" blowing on my back, propelling me to write. But you, my reader, will be the semi-final judge in the matter. Eventually, the awesome final Judge will take His own turn.

Concerning the personal stories of Bible smuggling, arrests and jailings in the Middle East, cross my heart – they are not written to showcase personal heroics . . well, okay let my grandchildren enjoy them that way, but otherwise they are there to hopefully teach spiritual principles. *(Besides, in some situations I was scared to death, so what kind of heroics is that?)*

It is my prayer that this book will lead you to a deeper life with Christ than you ever dreamed existed and that He will richly bless you in the process! May this heartfelt prayer be yours as well.

Kenneth Cetton
July 2013

The chase

The Turkish police had spotted us earlier that evening and their police Jeep was tailing our little French Peugeot. We couldn't seem to shake them. It wasn't that we had broken any laws, but that the police, led by personal preferences, simply didn't appreciate that we shared our Christian faith in Islamic Turkey. Never mind that we were in their country legitimately – that fact was often ignored. As a result, the harassment proved a serious threat to our assisting the Turkish people with our various skills while sharing the Good News of God's love. I was writing a guide to help promote tourism, the three young ladies in the back seat and Dieter seated next to me, often tutored languages. I had to get the girls back to their apartment and we to ours without the police discovering where we all lived. Yet, as I glanced in the rear view mirror into the glare of Jeep headlights, like a predator, it stuck to us as if in tow. What could we do? Minutes earlier, we had left a prayer gathering at the home of an American airman stationed in Turkey. As we climbed into our Peugeot I noticed the canvas-enclosed police Jeep across the street. Once we pulled away, it made a U-turn and we knew we were being followed.

It's hard to shake a vehicle shadowing you in a big city without a wild, Hollywood-style street chase. So after not being able to lose them, an idea came to me. One of the streets I knew was a dead end. But conveniently, it ended at the top of a steep flight of stairs. So I quickly swung and sped the Peugeot down that street and half looking over my shoulder I raised my voice, "When we stop, you girls leap out and *fly down those stairs* and try to make it home on your own." Moments later we braked hard, the doors sprung open, the girls leaped out and ran down the steps muffling their girlish squealing and disappearing into the night. Dieter and I looked back and sighed with relief. The police Jeep had pulled off to the side but they had not followed the girls on foot. *Now*, I wondered as I backed up, hands perspiring, to continue our cat and mouse game . . *what should we do?* Feeling as dumb as ever, I had no ideas. The next plan began to form in my mind as did the first – also from the Lord. "Dieter dear bro", pointing my thumb toward the rear window, "I drove a Jeep in Korea after the war. They're great going up steep hills but they're not built for speed". "So?" Dieter looked at me waiting for an answer. "So simply this pal, since those police Jeeps don't have radios to call in help, we'll try heading out of town and then floor it. Why even this little Peugeot should be faster than that Jeep."

My companion smiled and slapped his knee. "Okay, let's go. If we lose them, we can circle back by another route and go home. Besides," Dieter grinned again, "I'm tired and want to go to bed." Shortly, we found the main highway out of Ankara and as we picked up speed, happily, the Jeep headlights gradually shrunk in our mirror until they were completely gone. With that, we both relaxed, found another road back into Ankara and prayed and praised our way back home – to sleep another night in our own warm beds.

Naturally, this is not written as instructions on how to ditch the police when being harassed and tailed. Rather, as children of God, we all occasionally face personal difficulties in life which loom large, casting their giant shadow across our path. In those times we need to take stock of His majestic power contained within our humble frame – and contrast it with the puniness of whatever is opposing us just as we compared our small but faster Peugeot to a seemingly more powerful Jeep. On life's bumpy highway, nothing we encounter towers more gigantically than God's inner habitation. First John 4:4 says," . . . greater is He who is in you than he who is in the world." So when you feel overwhelmed by adversity, take a fresh look at our adversary's defeat at the cross and contrast him with Christ's actual indwelling, invincible, power. Then simply put the pedal of faith to the solid metal of the truth of that inner residence – and head on Home.

If God is for us, who is against us?
Romans 8:31

Now fasten your seat belt, for more stories and spiritual lessons.

Hide 'n' seek

Our chief goal in life is to find God and come to know Him. But some people think, God hasn't shown up, so why bother? A child-hood game and some lessons from the Bible can help answer that question.

As kids, many of us loved playing hide and seek. One child was "it," and the others hid. Leaning against perhaps a tree, with eyes shut, after counting off the seconds, "it" had to seek and try to find the ones who were hiding. When we grew up, we thought we had left that old game behind us. I've got news for you! We need to become like kids again because God is playing hide and seek – and we are still "it."

He made from one man every nation of mankind to live on all the face of the earth . . . that they would seek God, if perhaps they might grope for Him and find Him, though He is not far from each one of us.[1]

Here we are, leaning against a tree called life, eyes shut, counting off – not seconds but years. Finally, opening our eyes – perhaps at this very moment – we realize that God may not be immediately evident because He's hiding on purpose so that we will search for Him and find Him. Just as in the children's game, He wants us to seek Him. But unlike our former playmates, *He longs to be found.*[2]

The theme of searching for God recurs throughout the Bible. Jeremiah 29:13 affirms, "You will seek Me and find Me when you search for Me with all your heart." You may wonder, Why does God hide if He wants us to find Him? The breath-taking design of creation all around us attests to God's existence. With these wonders, He intends to arouse our curiosity so that by faith we earnestly desire to search for and find Him. If you saw an unsigned note on your door, you would conclude that someone had left the message. You would naturally wonder, *Who put this here?* Nature is God's unsigned note, inviting us to ask the same question and to search for Him. According to Romans 1:20, "His invisible attributes . . . have been clearly seen, being understood through what has been made, so that [those who behold His creation] are without excuse."[3]

We're "it"

God is hiding, and we're "it." He's waiting in the shadows for us to turn the corner and find Him. Jesus instructed His followers, "Unless you . . . become like children, you will not enter the kingdom of heaven."[4] The good news is that God is also seeking us. Jesus said, "The Son of Man has come to seek and to save that which was lost."[5] Therefore, if we're truly pursuing God, we're on a friendly collision course with Him. And this invitation is for all people because even as believers our lifelong goal should be to constantly seek more of Him.

And some reading this might have thought that God hadn't shown up? Worse yet, many people live as though He hasn't, when, in fact, the Scripture informs us, "He is not far from each one of us."[6] All we need to do is look for Him whose handiwork can be seen in all that has been made. And some of you are about to find Him in the person of Jesus Christ.

Seek the Lord while He may be found;
Call upon Him while He is near.
Isaiah 55:6

He counts the numbers
of the stars;
He gives names to all of them

Psalm 147:4

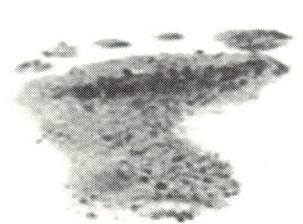

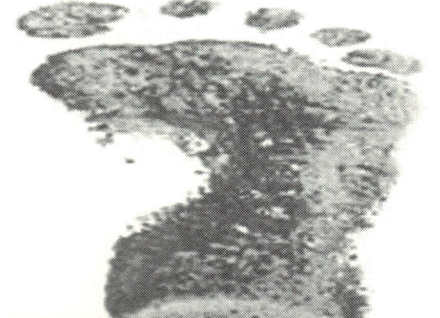

1 Essentials of God
1.1 Is there *not* a God?

The yacht lurched in the violent grip of an angry sea. At times, the hapless craft disappeared, sinking into deep troughs as the ocean dipped and swelled. The crew in an approaching rescue boat saw no one on the deck of the yacht and suspected that the occupants were inside suffering from sickness or coping with engine trouble. The rescuers managed to climb aboard and enter the cabin below, but were shocked to find no one inside. They were even more perplexed to discover a fully set table with a warm dinner. The would-be rescuers must have exchanged puzzled glances and wondered, Where are the people who just set this table and should now be dining? The incident remained a mystery.[1]

The Table Setter

We must ask a similar question as we ponder our existence in the universe. We find ourselves aboard a seemingly aimless craft called planet Earth, drifting through the vast ocean of space called the cosmos. Just as with the yacht's boarding party in the story, the obvious question is, "Where is the Table Setter for Earth's well-designed magnificence amidst the wild tempest called life?" Whether we see Him or not, He must exist because tables do not set themselves – as some would want us to believe. Where can we find Who or what has made this orderly, functioning universe?

We would add a second desperate inquiry: Is the Table Setter friendly, or is He simply toying with us like a child playing with a hobby ant farm? Sadly, faced with such mysteries, many prematurely abandon their pursuit of answers. Some think that if you can't see the Architect of the universe, the Architect doesn't exist. When Russian astronaut Yuri Gagarin, the first human to fly in outer space, looked out the window of his capsule, he supposedly said,

"I don't see God." Gagarin apparently thought that his quick survey dismissed the possibility of the existence of an eternal Creator.

Something rather than nothing

Some people will argue that an almighty God has no need for anything and thus has no need and purpose for Him to exist. For that fact there should be no need for anything to exist and there should be absolutely nothing rather than this vast something. We awaken to life without an explanation for our existence blazoned across the heavens in skywriting. Yet since there is obviously *something* – in fact, a lot of complex things – rather than *nothing*, the most reasonable and logical conclusion, even in the absence of a discernible purpose, is that there is a God.

Multiplied wonders

Some have contended that all the complex wonders of the universe are the result of mindless natural selection. But faith is required for affirming that position, just as is adopting the alternative stance that a super-intelligent Being masterminded the cosmos. This Divine Table Setter's creative hand can be seen in the staggering intricacies of DNA. There is enough data in a single human cell to fill a thousand volumes of an encyclopedia. You wouldn't want to store all those volumes in your house but that information is amazingly stored in a tiny single cell in our bodies. Who encoded the DNA of each cell and enabled it to process the information? If you went to the Smithsonian Library and simply sat in a chair, would you learn much? More than the mere presence of information is necessary for a system to function properly. When we find ancient writings or buried structural foundations, we know they are artifacts of intelligent beings. For every building, there is an architect. For every device – be it a sports car or a hydro-electric plant – there is an engineer and designer. The same logical conclusion should apply to the language of DNA, the building and functional information for all living things. So why do we suddenly depart from everyday reasoning and assume a different explanation for the marvelous world around us?

The precision we find in our world and solar system should make us aware of the Mind behind it. Consider that if the Earth were slightly closer to or further from the sun, this planet would not support life as we know it. The Earth's rotation gives us our days and nights, and the tilt of its axis gives us our seasons which enables the more efficient use of earth's landmass. How can there be physical laws, such as gravity and the fixed speed of light, without Someone to establish them? In calling these phenomena "laws of nature," we are personifying nature while avoiding the concept of God. Yet without a Mastermind, why would the laws be bound to act consistently?

Why do tadpoles turn into frogs? Why don't they just remain tadpoles or start out as frogs? Why do caterpillars turn into butterflies? Why don't they just start out that way instead of going to all that trouble? After living for a time as caterpillars, these insects develop chrysalises and undergo metamorphosis. Like a magician who seeks to make his trick appear even more difficult to perform, the caterpillar completely dissolves into a blob of mush. Then, several weeks later, out comes a butterfly – a totally different looking creature. Why would, and how could, the processes of evolution perform any of these amazing feats? Consider also that there are not just a few species of plants and animals, but an almost endless variety, showing the Creator's amazing ingenuity.

Cells and seeds

Who made plant cells into elaborate miniature manufacturing systems that use photosynthesis to generate energy by taking in sunlight through their leaves?[2] Plants also absorb our exhaled carbon dioxide, manufacture sugar and emit oxygen for us to breathe. A vascular system transports nutrients throughout each plant, which optimizes

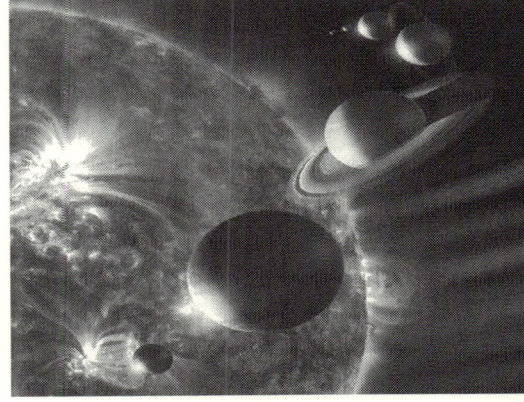

The precision we find in our world and solar system should make us aware of the Mind behind it. © *NASA – National Aeronautics and Space Administration.*

elemental exchange by growing so that the leaves catch the maximum amount of sunlight. According to Duke University Professor of Biology, Dr. Robert B. Jackson:

Trees have sensors that detect light and gravity. From the moment a tree begins its life, it knows which end is up. Trees will generally attempt to grow toward the light and away from gravitational pull. But, as a tree gets older, its branches tend to grow more outwards than upwards. That's so the tree can cast a wider net to catch the light of the sun.[3]

Even more staggering, all the plant's life processes, including bearing fruit, are programmed in the seeds that we typically disregard and walk on. Embodied in each of these tiny capsules, some smaller than a teardrop, are the blueprints for a plant's development. The plan encoded in the magnificently designed, microchip-like seed determines if it will become a scrubby ragweed or a stately redwood. DNA instructions also enable the seed to monitor germination conditions by sensing the temperature and water content of the soil. A single tiny apple seed, for example, contains specifications not only for the future fruit's texture, taste and shape, but also for every last detail of the entire tree, from roots to branches. We rarely think about where the seed gets all this information. It certainly doesn't come from the air or the ground. Next time you eat an apple, look at that small seed with reverence and ponder its awesome Designer. Because the world of nature, from the minute apple seed to the magnificent human body, eloquently declares the existence of a Creator, it seems reasonable to ask, "Is there *not* a God?".

So many of us
The reason we are not overwhelmed by the wonder and design of the human body is because we have become accustomed to seeing so many examples around us every day. When there is only one prototype of a new car, we men often rush out to see it. But once the vehicle is in production and we can see one on every block, we cease to pay attention. Likewise, people have become common place. We living, breathing, self-replicating machines would

be head-turners if we didn't constantly see so many of us. We have grown accustomed to the greatest wonders of the universe – human beings.

Our senses – and more

No end of books could be written on the designs found in the human body, but consider a few that we often take for granted. We have ears located to catch sounds from all directions; Eeustachian tubes to equalize pressure, preventing our eardrums from bursting; brains to help us learn, read, remember, imagine, calculate and invent; and larynxes to sing, make speeches or whisper, "I love you." Do all these features result from the survival of the fittest, or do they reflect the intelligent craftsmanship of the One fittest to design?

Some can tell stories and write poems. Some can paint. Some can compose music. Some can chip away at blocks of stone and carve statues. Some can assemble a variety of food and serve great feasts. To be made in God's image means that, while still His creatures, we can, to a degree, also create.

Our vision is crucial for many of our creative endeavors and for life in a material world. We have two eyes, not one, enabling us to see in three dimensions and thus to maneuver more effectively in our environment. Yet with these two eyes, we perceive only one image, reducing potential confusion. Furthermore, our eyes adjust to incoming light. We experience a world resplendent with color, which our Creator wants us to enjoy.

Our eyes have lashes for protection, tear ducts for cleansing and lubrication, and muscles for opening and closing. Yet all these features would be useless hardware if we didn't possess the ability, through our specialized neurons, to transfer the image from the eye to the brain so that we can understand and remember the objects we are viewing. While it is impressive to have two amazing eyes, it is even more astounding to have a complex system to process the information-bearing electrical impulses coming into the brain. Most people own cameras with lenses, shutters and diaphragms which mimic the eye, but these devices are useless unless you have sophisticated equipment to capture the image. Sadly, some people have eyes, but they are blind. Yet more to be pitied are people who have eyes and can see the world around them, but remain blind to the reality of God.

Without Excuse

Have you noticed that I have put forth evidence for God's existence without using a single Bible verse? Not only does the Bible proclaim an intelligent Designer, but all nature does, as well. His handiwork can be observed in the world around us, which supports the Scripture's testimony to His existence:

For the truth about God is known to them instinctively; God has put this knowledge in their hearts. Since earliest times men have seen the earth and sky and all God made, and have known of his existence and great eternal power. So they will have no excuse.[4]

In the end, belief is not a matter of faith versus non-faith, but simply of where you want to place your faith. All systems of belief – atheism, rationalism and even scientific theory – require faith in their suppositions.

Personal Discovery

When I was 17 years old, I became an atheist – not that I had thought it through. Like many of my friends, I simply followed what the youth culture was promoting, and it wasn't saying much about God. My best friend's stepfather was a prominent, successful businessman and an atheist. I concluded that since his life was on track, why shouldn't I think like him?

But then the day came when my disbelief in God was discarded. As if looking at a photograph, I can remember where I was when a light went on in my mind. I was on the campus of the Milwaukee Boys Technical School, sitting in its oldest building, a structure that had served as a grade school in the late 1800s. I don't know what the instructor was trying to teach, but as he wrote on the blackboard, he glanced over his shoulder toward us students and said, "These people who say there is no God . . " Turning back to the board to write, he added, "Where did everything come from?" It was 1950- and, fortunately, I had not been conditioned to uncritically believe Darwin's theory of evolution. In a heartbeat, I accepted that there is a God. It would be years before I actually began to know Him, but I took my first step that day.

Other people may call this reasoning simplistic, but it makes sense. Someone once pointed out that if you want to believe in God and the validity of Christianity, there is enough evidence to sensibly do so. On the other hand, if you don't want to believe in God, there are enough questions you can create to support that position as well – mistaken though it is.

Like the boat in the raging tempest, our planet is tossed about in a sea of suffering. Yet, as on the yacht, it is undeniable that Someone has set Earth's table – a table of living plants, animals and people, along with countless other wonders. The title of this chapter poses the question, "Is there *not* a God?" I think you'll agree that there is no answer but that – He is

In the beginning God created
the heavens and the earth.
Genesis 1:1

Yours is the day, Yours also is the night;
You have prepared the light and the sun.
You have established all the boundaries of the earth;
You have made summer and winter.
Psalm 74:16-17

1 Essentials of God
1.2 Its a fallen world

The reason for suffering and evil

Supposedly, the first taxicab company in America that equipped vans with wheelchair ramps was started by a Christian, Lenard Lovedol, himself wheelchair-bound. When I attended college I drove for his fledgling Milwaukee company, Handi-Cab.

One Saturday evening when I came in for an assignment, instead of finding Lenard, I encountered a new man and his wife. For some reason, Lenard had hired this rather sleazy-looking couple to run dispatch. Ordinarily, we followed certain procedures, but that night it turned out to be much different. Before leaving for a pickup, I gently informed the new man that he was not doing things the way Lenard normally liked them done and that Lenard might be upset when he found out. As his wife smugly looked on, he arrogantly fired back, poking his thumb into his chest: "Look, I'm running this office, not *Lenard*!" I shrugged and went my way. When I returned Monday morning, Lenard was back – the new dispatchers weren't.

The reaction of that dispatcher pretty much reflects the record of man's responses to God's overtures, through the millennia, in offering us reconciliation through Jesus Christ. In spite of the continuing mess made by our muddy march through the dark swamp of history, we persist in arrogantly poking our thumbs to our chests, as if to proclaim, "Look, we're running this world, not God." Why are we so contrary?

Credit/debit ledger

Most of us at one time or another in our lives have questioned the existence of God, testing His plausibility as if we were figuring a credit/debit ledger. We weigh the possibility of His existence by granting Him credits – the grandeur of a mountain range, the amazing design of an elephant or a dolphin, the wonder of a newborn baby, the manufacturing-like process of photosynthesis that makes sugar from water and CO_2.

On the other side of our mental accounting sheet, we list negative things which seem to scream of His nonexistence: wars, death, murders, sickness, injustice and every sort of abuse Eventually, the ledger on which we're doing the math frequently has God coming out wanting. While not all are driven to atheism by this mental balancing of the books, many end up entertaining doubts as to God's reality, or at least His goodness. But that is the result of our faulty calculations. There is much more that shouts confirmation of God's existence than denies it. We simply have not lain up on God's side of the ledger the entire inventory of marvels that display His incredible, intelligently designed handiwork and there is also an explanation for the existence of evil.[1]

When doing our accounting we repeatedly ask ourselves, why is life so pregnant with evil and suffering? No one escapes. Neither money nor fame keep life's hard knocks from pounding on our door. Some suffer more and others less, but there is no permanent haven of rest, no Shangri-La of escape from our earthly afflictions – only brief respites along the way. Why, from the bassinet to our final breath, are there tears to be shed, hurts that fester,

disappointments and heartbreaks to be borne? Why are there hate, war, murder and greed? Why is there sexual perversion, moles-tation and rape? Why is there sickness and death? Why do people walk away from love and break hearts? Why do people take drugs, drink excessively and spoil their lives and the hopes and dreams of others? Why are we all so very imperfect?

Eventually, the ledger on which we're doing the math frequently has God coming out wanting.

Science marches on . . . to where?

Science prides itself on advancements;- yet, regarding our inner nature, it has accomplished nothing. We remain the same flawed persons our ancestors were – only sporting different clothing and hair styles. Our technology has given us an unending flow of astonishing gadgetry to equip and entertain us, but it only titillates us for a few brief ticks of the clock. Clearly, things do not bring any lasting satisfaction or happiness. If it were so, we in the West should be overcome with euphoria because we have acquired far more than even the super-rich a hundred years ago not to mention monarchs of ages past. Our children have endless toys, games and amusements, but they too become quickly bored and restless, even less content than children of past generations, who had far fewer amusements. My father, born in 1891, said that on Sunday afternoons, lacking toys, he and his friends would make monkey faces in the mirror.

We have microwave dinners ready to eat in 90 seconds. We have dishwashers to clean our dishes, washing machines to do our laundry, automatic transmissions to do our shifting, computers to do our thinking. Yet, apart from possessing more knowledge and possibly being healthier than our forefathers, we remain unchanged. We are not happier and definitely not wiser or more content. We still crave more and have become jaded amidst all of our toys and sexual liberties. In spite of our so-called progress, a world of suffering and discord continues. Why?

The warning and test

The answer to all of these questions comes to us from history recorded in the first book of the Bible, Genesis. The scene takes place after God created the world and placed man in it. It reads,

The Lord God commanded the man, saying, "From any tree of the garden you may eat freely; but from the tree of the knowledge of good and evil you shall not eat, for in the day that you eat from it you will surely die."[2]

Everything in this first-and-only, all-free, fabulous super-market called "paradise" was theirs to enjoy. God warned them not to partake of only one thing. If they did, death would ensue. This was intended to test man's loyalty and obedience to his Creator.

It's standard procedure to test what you've made. Back in the late 1970s, I converted a VW Beetle into an electric car and was hoping to market the retrofit in Southern California. When the car was finally ready, I drove it onto the Garden Grove Freeway to see how fast it would go. The German engineer who had built the electrical components had not installed a governor, which would have restricted the car's speed. There was never any warning not to run the car flat-out because he knew there would be no problem for the motor to handle the high rpm. Had I been warned, I would have been a fool to disregard the instructions of the engineer who designed the system and to have pushed it – as I succeeded in doing, to about 51 mph.[3]

Similarly, man was given free will so that God, who had engineered him, would be honored by man's own initiative to love and obey his Creator. For this reason, God did not install a moral "governor" in Adam but, in this case did give him a strong warning.[4] Unfortunately, our first parents chose to ignore God's dire word of caution, "pushed it" and opted to disobey Him, thereby plunging the human race into spiritual and physical death. There followed a spiritual and moral breakdown. Instead of being guided by an inner connection with God and love for Him, man immediately became preoccupied with himself and his outer physical world. He became sensual, and his love turned into self-love, which turned into lust for sex, lust for possessions, lust for power. Adam and Eve listened to another voice – that of a fallen spirit, Satan.[5] Read what took place as Satan enters in disguise:

Now the serpent was more crafty than any beast of the field which the Lord God had made. And he said to the woman, "Indeed, has God said, 'You shall not eat from any tree of the garden'?" The woman said to the serpent, "From the fruit of the trees of the garden we may eat; but from the fruit of the tree which is in the middle of the garden, God has said, 'You shall not eat from it or touch it, or you will die.'" The serpent said to the woman, "You surely will not die! "For God knows that in the day you eat from it your eyes will be opened, and you will be like God, knowing good and evil." When the woman saw that the tree was good for food, and that it was a delight to the eyes, and that the tree was desirable to make one wise, she took from its fruit and ate; and she gave also to her husband with her, and he ate. Then the eyes of both of them were opened, and they knew that they were naked; and they sewed fig leaves together and made themselves loin coverings.[6]

The great loss

God already possessed angels, awesome creatures programmed to obey Him automatically. But His new creature, man, would be more than simply a servant – he would be a son, made in his Creator's image, a completely new model of God's handiwork. He was designed to obey God – not by being programmed, but out of a loving, obedient heart. When man disobeyed, just as God had warned, on that very day, death entered the world. Physically, Adam and Eve began to slowly die – spiritually, they died instantly. Adam and Eve's sudden awareness that they were naked suggests that they knew things had gone sickeningly wrong. Their sin was disobedience; it wasn't being naked before God. Rather, they lost their inner consciousness of God and became self-conscious instead. Because they were the first couple – our prototypes, as it were – the tragedies they unleashed continued through all generations: sickness, war, cruelty and, ultimately, death; tragedies spawned not by any absence of God's love but by man's wrong choice.

To illustrate, if two General Motor's cars ran a red light and had a terrible collision which killed the occupants, would this imply that GM did not exist and that the automobiles were never a product of intelligent design? Wouldn't we more likely question the skill of the drivers or maybe even that of the engineers at GM? Similarly, we can't dismiss God's existence simply because of the horrendous suffering in the world and we obviously can't even question His creative skills. We can only search for His reasons. God tested us on

His proving ground in Eden, and we failed – not because of a flawed design on our Creator's part but because of a flawed choice on man's. You may protest, saying, "Don't blame me for Adam's folly!" In fact, God ultimately won't blame us if we don't repeat Adam's mistake and instead, choose to obey God through faith in His Son, Jesus Christ.

In addition to the total disconnect from God, disobedience resulted in another great tragedy. The deed to earth fell from man's hand into Satan's. Jesus called this dark foe the ruler of this world[8] and the father of lies.[9] The fall of mankind explains why there is so much evil and heartache on this planet: Satan holds the deed. When he tempted Jesus, he offered Him the world – lock, stock and barrel. We read about it in the following passage: "And he [Satan] led Him up and showed Him all the kingdoms of the world in a moment of time. And the devil said to Him, 'I will give You all this domain and its glory; for it has been handed over to me, and I give it to whomever I wish. Therefore if You worship before me, it shall all be Yours.'"[10]

According to an old hymn it states, "This is My Father's World," and it is, but a temporary dispute is in progress over the title. Until that matter is clearly settled – and it will be shortly – it is up to us to choose which world we desire to belong as citizens. Do we want to continue our loyalty to this decaying material world headed by the prince of darkness, or the eternal one headed by the Prince of Light?

Bad made into good

God has always been able to bring good out of evil, which He accomplished in the fall of man. In His wise providence, He was able to demonstrate, by personal example, what we would otherwise never have fully grasped: The Scripture says, "For while we were still helpless, at the right time Christ died for the ungodly. For one will hardly die for a righteous man; though perhaps for the good man someone would dare even to die. But God demonstrates His own love toward us, in that while we were yet sinners, Christ died for us."[11]

Although God did not prevent the fall He ultimately stepped into the spiritual fray to remedy it. By becoming a man – God incarnate – in the person of Jesus Christ, He took the punishment for all of our sins and suffered the penalty which was due us. The Old Testament book of Isaiah, written seven centuries before Jesus came to earth, prophesied of this event:

"But He was pierced through for our transgressions, He was crushed for our iniquities; The chastening for our well-being fell upon Him, And by His scourging we are healed."[12]

The second birth

Following Christ's death, came His resurrection and the promise of forgiveness and eternal life for all who will believe in Him. Thus, all of our misery and pain serves a purpose after all, if we will permit it to lead us in responding to His amazing love and allow ourselves to be restored. We read of the instrument of this restoration in the words of Jesus:

"Truly, truly, I say to you, unless one is born of water and the Spirit he cannot enter into the kingdom of God. That which is born of the flesh is flesh, and that which is born of the Spirit is spirit. "Do not be amazed that I said to you, 'You must be born again.'"[13]

Besides our entering into this world by physical birth (after our mother's water breaks, i.e. born of water), we need a second birth through which we are spiritually born and once more linked with God. Our first birth made us a child of earth; our second makes us a child of God. By experiencing it, we can actually begin to receive the imprint of Jesus on our lives and become like Him. At long last, we have the power to counter our evil impulses and fleshly preferences – if we as Christians choose to live what the Bible describes as walking in the Spirit and not according to the flesh.[14]

However, just as our first parents chose to follow a different spirit than God Himself, we perpetuate that same disobedience if we persist in unbelief. Isaiah 53:6 states it well. "All of us like sheep have gone astray, Each of us has turned to his own way . . " We may not care for this explanation and be tempted to walk away from it. But that only demonstrates how accurate the Bible is in its assessment that we are fallen beings who remain alienated and "astray" from God by our own choice. Only through faith in Christ, and the subsequent second birth, can we again become completely alive.

Father Dad

Back in the 1920s, when costume parties were the rage, my parents went to one – mom dressed as a Salvation Army Lassie[15] and dad as a Catholic priest. Not having an automobile at the time, they boarded a streetcar for their intended party. Unfortunately, the streetcar came upon a serious accident; a man lay dying on the street. Because of the crowd, the streetcar slowed and stopped. Someone attending the stricken man looked up and saw what he thought was a priest. The onlooker apparently didn't notice that my father had used make-up to enlarge and redden his nose, as if he had been drinking. (On the way home from the party, he would have no need for putty or make-up!) Nor did the good Samaritan notice that the supposed priest was apparently taking liberties and "dating" a female Salvation Army worker. All he knew was that someone was dying on the outside and someone on the public conveyance might be able to help the suffering soul. So he cried out to my dad, "Father, father, this man is dying. Please come and give him his last rites!" No doubt my dad sweated a bit and was very happy when, shortly, the streetcar moved on and took him and my mother to their party.

I'm all for pursuing peace and thereby creating a better world. But man without spiritual rebirth is just as useless in restoring himself and humanity from the fall as my dad would have been in trying to assist a dying man into heaven. No thanks to Adam, we are all fallen and, as a result, live in a suffering, evil world. But thanks to God, we are again offered a chance to choose which spirit to follow. May none of us be like the dispatcher who arrogantly stated, "Look, I'm running this office, not *Lenard*!" True, you may have it your way for Saturday night, but take caution – Monday morning, "*Lenard's*" coming back.

1.3 What is God like?

Oh, the depth of the riches
both of the wisdom and knowledge of God!
How unsearchable are His judgments
and unfathomable His ways!
Romans 11:33

The freshmen at a large Midwestern university were about to take a philosophy exam on arguments for and against the existence of God. They had studied hard and were waiting nervously for the professor to arrive. When he did, he announced that the test would be postponed because of an unexpected faculty meeting. As the classmates sighed with relief, a student in the back pointed skyward and exclaimed, "There is a God!"

In Chapter 1, we examined the reasons why we can believe that God exists. The Bible clearly asserts His existence with authority, yet neither the Bible nor religious beliefs are necessary to reach that conclusion. From birds in flight to flowers in bloom, from cells examined under a microscope to stars viewed through a telescope, from complex human bodies to the laws of physics that govern matter and energy, nature attests to God's existence. An apparently well-designed 'Something-Rather-Than-Nothing' points persuasively to a supernatural Designer.

Because God exists, what is this super-intelligent Creator like? Is He hostile or indifferent toward us? Is He kind and loving? When looking at a suffering world, one might be tempted to see Him as "the dark (and only!) side of the Force," so to speak. But as I explained in the last chapter, God gave human beings free will, and it was our first parents' decision to act independently of God that led to the Fall and all subsequent evil. We, too, have free will and can choose to blame

God for evil rather than ourselves. Nonetheless, something far more compelling indicates that God is anything but indifferent or hostile.

God's likeness

You are a person, so God must be no less than a Person. See Him possessing an energetic, vibrant personality. And because people esteem virtues such as love, patience, mercy and justice, God, as a Person, must value them infinitely more. While we may at times be selfish and evil, we at least want others to practice the noble virtues in their behavior toward us, especially when they exercise authority over us. These widespread principles of conduct can only have their source in God. It is inconceivable that we could be more virtuous than our Creator.

Such conclusions about God's character make logical sense and can be drawn without calling upon the Word of God. Nonetheless, the Bible does state that nature itself helps to reveal what God is like: "Since the creation of the world His invisible attributes . . . have been clearly seen . . . through what has been made" – namely us.[1] The first book of the Bible describes God's original creation of human beings: "Then God said, 'Let Us make man in Our image, according to Our likeness.'"[2] God is like us in our best qualities, and we are a "thumbnail" sketch of Him. Picture the most kind and virtuous person you know in life or literature and you will have some small idea of what God is like.

God is love

In the capacity to love, as with other virtues, God is light-years ahead of us. Yet, due to upbringing and other experiences, some people find it difficult to picture any kind of real love in a parent. Because of the way most of us traditionally envision God, some people are shocked that William P. Young's book "The Shack" depicts God as a very large, joyous African-American woman.[3] However, the unconventional portrayal helps those whose abuse by an uncaring father would make it difficult to identify with the common image of a male, fatherly God.

While God does not have a body and therefore is not fat, female, dark-skinned (or any-skinned), He is exceedingly loving, which is the quality that Young attempts to illustrate. Jesus constantly modeled God's love for us. In one incident He speaks of Himself, likely in a time period before He came to earth, when as the eternal Father He often was like a loving mother hen over Jerusalem. Jesus said: "How often I wanted to gather your children together, the way a hen gathers her chicks under her wings."[4] David's psalms offer a glimpse of God's care for us. In one he wrote: "You have taken account of my wanderings; Put my tears in Your bottle. Are they not in Your book?"[5]

God's justice satisfied

Another divine attribute, justice, at first poses a problem for us fallen beings who find ourselves on the wrong side of God's law. Job's friend Eliphaz observed: "Can mankind be just before God? Can a man be pure before his Maker?"[6] We generally appreciate justice, except when it is applied against us. Justice makes our communities safe. No one wants a lawless society; even outlaws have their own codes and standards. However, because we are all vio-lators of God's laws of perfection, we must be judged. The penalty, according to God's Word, is no mere slap on the wrist: "the wages of sin is death."[7]

Thankfully, God's great love fulfilled the requirement that justice be meted out by providing the antidote: He stepped into human time and paid the penalty Himself in the Person of His Son. Christ died on the cross as punishment for the sins of the world – past, present and future. (This Good News is explained in depth in Section 2.) Not surprisingly, after affirming that "the wages of sin is death," Paul concludes, "but the free gift of God is eternal life in Christ Jesus our Lord."[7] To our amazement, our all-wise God reconciled absolute justice with absolute love. His love satisfied His justice, but He paid a heavy price. However, for our part, we need to ask Christ for "the free gift" of forgiveness and eternal life and by faith thank Him for it. The result will be as the Apostle John tells us: "Whoever believes in Him shall not perish, but have eternal life."[8]

Majestic glory

God's unimaginable glory makes His character far more than the sum of the attributes we dimly reflect. Paul described God as "the blessed and only Sovereign, the King of kings and Lord of lords, who alone possesses immortality and dwells in unapproachable light, whom no man has seen or can see."[9]

God's holy purity is so blinding that we can only behold Him in the Person of Jesus Christ. Describing Jesus, Paul wrote:

He is the image of the invisible God, the firstborn of all creation. For by Him all things were created, both in the heavens and on earth, visible and invisible, whether thrones or dominions or rulers or authorities – all things have been created through Him and for Him. He is before all things, and in Him all things hold together.[10]

God's glory and majesty are innate to His character. The illuminated splendor of God's awe-inspiring, radiant presence is intrinsically Who He is. When gathered before God's throne at the end of time, no one will question His evident grandeur or doubt His competence to rule: "Every knee shall bow . . , And every tongue shall give praise to God."[11]

He Is omniscient, omnipresent and omnipotent

These are big and impressive words which define God's attributes. Let it be suffice to say that He knows everything, is everywhere and is all powerful. Or to make it more personal, He knows us better than we know ourselves, we are always in His sight, and He can do absolutely anything for us if it's in His wise will to do so. David understood these truths:

O Lord, You have searched me and known me.
You know when I sit down and when I rise up.
Even before there is a word on my tongue,
Behold, O Lord, You know it all.[12]

The book of Hebrews confirms that "there is no creature hidden from His sight."[13] Consequently, there is no such thing as a "god-forsaken" place in the entire universe. God is everywhere. As David expresses it: "Where can I go from Your Spirit? Or where can I flee from Your presence? If I ascend to heaven, You are there; If I make my bed in Sheol, behold, You are there."[14] Neither time nor space is of any consequence to God. He was able to create the universe instantly, at a speed that transcends the possibilities predicted under known principles of physics. Because He is the Creator of all natural laws, He is not bound by them. As the Psalmist wrote: "For He spoke, and it was done; He commanded, and it stood fast."[15] Just as He made Adam a mature adult, God may have created the cosmos with the appearance of considerable age. While the newly fashioned Adam may have looked as though he were in his twenties, the universe may seem older than it is. Since the beginning of time, as Job declared, God has done "great things, unfathomable, and wondrous works without number."[16]

God is holy

Likewise, God is holy – absolutely, flawlessly pure, unerring and completely righteous. We may dress to impress, but God impresses all whom He addresses. The four magnificent creatures that reside perpetually in the throne room of His presence "do not cease to say, 'Holy, holy, holy is the Lord God, the Almighty, who was and who is and who is to come.'"[17]

Praise is one response. Speechlessness is another. A famous atheist was asked what he would say if, after he died, he discovered that God was real? Apparently, the skeptic replied that he would ask God why He didn't make His existence more clear. But that question will never arise. According to Romans 3:19, every mouth will be closed on that day – not by compulsion, but because God's antagonists will have nothing to say. Their speechlessness will be rooted in paralyzing astonishment. The day will come when we will all face

Any attempt to define Him would be feebly deficient, like blowing a child's tin horn in the court of the eternal King.

the One whose holy purity is so apparent that those who ignored Him on earth will fall to their knees and feel their hair stand on end.

Indescribable

Our language, which enables us to describe physical realities, is inadequate to explain the Divine. It is impossible to say enough to capture the wonder of God's magnificence. Any attempt to define Him would be feebly deficient, like blowing a child's tin horn in the court of the eternal King. David marveled, "O Lord, our Lord, How majestic is Your name in all the earth, Who have displayed Your splendor above the heavens!"[18]

As we stated in the beginning, picture the most loving, kind and gracious person you have ever known. God is like them, but His goodness and other virtues infinitely exceed theirs. He is resplendent and clothed in unfading majesty.[19] Although a glorious sunset catches our attention for a short while, the brilliant radiance of God is unending. In our new heavenly forms, our awe-struck appreciation of His magnificent grandeur will never diminish. For now, in our fallen state, we are too quickly bored and distracted by things, but then we shall adore Him forever.

A painting of God

I once heard a story about a Kindergarten teacher who was observing her students while they painted pictures. She would walk around the classroom to inspect each child's artwork. As she came to one little girl who was working diligently, the teacher asked what she was painting. The girl answered, "I'm painting God." After a pause, the teacher said, "But no one knows what God looks like." Without missing a beat or looking up from her paper, the girl replied, "They will when I'm finished."

O Lord my God, You are very great;
You are clothed with splendor and majesty,
Covering Yourself with light as with a cloak,
Psalm 104:1-2

1 Essentials of God
1.4 The Son also rises

The storyteller

A little old Jewish gentleman used to board the bus I drove in Anaheim, California, always looking dapper in his freshly pressed suit. After slowly mounting the stairs, he would pause and cheerfully greet me in his slight Yiddish accent. Warmed by his engaging smile, I could not help but beam back. Then he would make his leisurely way down the aisle, causing several of the older ladies to giggle by giving them compliments and kisses.

I liked Sheldon Stein[1] and was fascinated that he claimed to know everybody worth knowing in Hollywood, including Burt Lancaster, Tony Curtis, and Kirk Douglas.[1] Young people today might not recognize those names, but in my day, these movie actors and other celebrities he said he knew were big stars. Sheldon even told me that in the 1950s, he had introduced the harmonizing Lennon Sisters to band leader Lawrence Welk and the girls became a singing sensation and appeared frequently on his popular TV show. Yeah, sure! I thought, but I smiled and said, "That's wonderful!"

I was certain the stories were flights of fancy because I knew where Sheldon lived – in a house trailer owned by his sister in an old trailer park across the street from our upscale mobile-home park. We had a heated pool. He probably had a plastic tub with a hose draped over the side. *But he's a harmless old man*, I thought. *Why not let him enjoy his innocent fantasy*?

Not everyone felt so charitably toward Sheldon, including one we'll call "Scott," a bus driver and close friend of mine who had worked the same route as me months earlier. Scott was a handsome young man with an eye on becoming a movie actor, and with good reason. He had managed to snag some choice roles in local stage productions. With the right break, Scott could finally stop driving a bus and start driving a Porsche. So it must have been extremely irritating for him to hear Sheldon name-dropping, mentioning all the famous Hollywood people he supposedly rubbed elbows with. Besides, Scott also knew that Sheldon lived in a cheap trailer court. As a result, whenever the old man had boarded, instead of happily greeting him, I imagine Scott had rolled his eyes and dryly directed, "Move to the back of the bus, please!" He probably would have wanted to add, "And don't tell us any more of your cockamamie stories. And definitely *no kissing on the bus!*"

One day, Sheldon boarded my bus with a brighter smile than usual and really stretched his already thinning credibility. He announced that he had been invited to Lucille Ball's seventieth birthday party. Of course, everyone who read the newspapers knew that Lucy was having a big birthday bash. I congratulated Sheldon on his alleged good fortune and humored him by asking him to give Miss Ball my personal best wishes. (A few years earlier, I had unknowingly wandered into a Lucille Ball TV rehearsal on the back lot of Universal Studios. I suddenly found myself standing three feet away from her while she was applying her much-needed makeup. Normally, I might have gushed, "Lucille Ball!" However, having heard about her fiery temper, I knew better than to breathe a word. How much less would this poor old man have been included in her circle of friends!) I wondered what kind of made-up tale he would

invent for this occasion. But so what? Sheldon was just a nice old man living out a final dream.

About ten days later, I saw Sheldon again. He was carrying a large grocery bag under his arm and wearing his usual big smile. "How was Lucille's birthday party?" I asked, watching him in my mirror as he made his way down the aisle dispensing his customary kisses. "Wonderful!", he answered, adding, "And if you

Not everyone felt so charitably toward Sheldon, including one we'll call "Scott," a bus driver who had worked the same route as me months earlier.

have a minute, I want to show you something."

Since I had arrived at his stop early and couldn't leave for another three minutes, I engaged the emergency air brake and plopped down next to him. "Whatcha got?" I asked enthusiastically, putting my arm around the top of his seat. By this time, he had taken an old, worn photo album out of the large Vons grocery bag. Quickly finding the middle, he opened it and started showing me pictures of all the Hollywood stars he claimed to know. My mouth dropped open – not because the stars were in the pictures, but because Sheldon was in all of them, too. (This was years before home computers and Photoshop tricks.)

"Lights, camera, action," I blurted out. "You really do know all these people, don't you?" He stopped and looked at me quizzically. "You didn't think so?" "Oh, yes, I believed you," I shamefully lied. "But I'm just so impressed by all your pictures." His smile returned as he eagerly continued to flip the pages. "Wait until I show you this next one!"

As sure as the sun rises in the east, there was Sheldon standing in the midst of the famous Lennon sisters, with his arms around them like a proud father. The next pages showed him with Burt Lancaster doing highflying work for the 1956 film Trapeze. But I was still not prepared for the last picture I saw before I had to start driving. He was standing arm in arm with Lucille Ball at her recent birthday party.

"Beautiful pictures!" I managed to croak while looking at him and patting him on the hand. "Thanks, Sheldon, for showing me them." I never had the heart to tell my friend Scott what had happened. Why tell him that he might have missed the chance of a lifetime – that Sheldon, the man he had so disdained, might have had the influence to place him among the stars of Hollywood?

Sheldon is long gone now, but there is another Person you should make sure you get to know. He, too, was Jewish. Although just a carpenter by trade while on earth, He had previously crafted the entire universe. Don't miss out by being cynical or rolling your eyes about this One who also claimed to know everyone worth knowing – including the eternal Father in heaven.

Jesus: Who is He?

Who is this Jesus who has so greatly impacted the world? The Apostle John, one of the Lord's intimate disciples, wrote of Him:

In the beginning was the Word, and the Word was with God, and the Word was God. He was in the beginning with God. All things came into being through Him, and apart from Him nothing came into being that has come into being. In Him was life, and the life was the Light of men.[2]

In this passage, John uses "the Word" to refer to Jesus, stating that He and God are one and the same. While Jesus was on earth, John knew that his Lord was somehow different. But I believe that it was not until after Christ's return to Heaven that the disciples started to realize that Jesus Himself was the very God of Heaven. Thereafter, the disciples could not help but treat Christ's incarnation with awesome wonder. How can we get our minds around such a concept? Although John believed this truth, he had difficulty describing it, even toward the end of his life. One of his Scriptural letters frames the mystical event of Christ's incarnation in this manner:

What was from the beginning, what we have heard, what we have seen with our eyes, what we have looked at and touched with our hands, concerning the Word of Life – and the life was manifested, and we have seen and testify and proclaim to you the eternal life, which was with the Father and was manifested to us – what we have seen and heard we proclaim to you also.[3]

The Word of God

John's writings seek to demonstrate that Jesus is not simply a righteous man turned prophet, but instead the Creator of the universe Who is one with the eternal Father. John reports that Jesus told His disciple Philip, "He who has seen Me has seen the Father."[4] This relationship is introduced in the beginning of John's Gospel account:

The Word became flesh, and dwelt among us, and we saw His glory, glory as of the only begotten from the Father, full of grace and truth . . . No one has seen God at any time; the only begotten God who is in the bosom of the Father, He has explained Him."[5] Later, John experienced a vision of Jesus in glory: "And I saw heaven opened, and behold, a white horse, and He who sat on it is called Faithful and True . . . His eyes are a flame of fire, and on His head are many diadems . . . and His name is called The Word of God.[6]

In all of these portrayals, John strains to articulate that God had come among us. It was totally incomprehensible that the almighty God would clothe Himself in human flesh, and John must have thought repeatedly, If we had only known! But when the truth did sink in, probably sometime after the ascension, the effect was staggering. Recalling the whole three-year association must have taken John's breath away as he described "what we have heard, what we have seen with our eyes, what we have looked at and touched with our hands."

Who would have known?

Isaiah, inspired to prophesy about the incarnation some seven centuries before, probably didn't understand it, either;- and yet, he was faithful in delivering the message: "For a child will be born to us, a son will be given to us; And the government will rest on His shoulders; And His name will be called Wonderful Counselor, Mighty God, Eternal Father, Prince of Peace."[7] The prophet also foretold that "the Lord Himself will give you a sign: Behold, a virgin will be with child and bear a son, and she will call His name Immanuel."[8] When quoting this verse, the gospel writer Matthew states that "'They shall call His name Emmanuel,' which translated means, 'God with us.'"[9]

In the fifty-third chapter of Isaiah, the prophet foretold that the coming Messiah who would suffer for the sins of the people would not have a charismatic, attention-getting appearance:

For He [Jesus] grew up before Him [God the Father]
    like a tender shoot,
And like a root out of parched ground;
He has no stately form or majesty

That we should look upon Him,
Nor appearance that we should be attracted to Him.[10]

When I was going through Army basic training, I found myself
alone in the barracks one Sunday afternoon with another GI who
also didn't spend his day off drinking. I asked my new friend if he'd
like to go to the rec hall and learn to play the piano. I couldn't play
very well, but I could hammer out a few short pieces of boogie-
woogie music. He said he'd love to learn to play the piano from
me. When we got to the hall, I sat down and clumsily pounded out
the few short chords I knew, looked up at him with pride and said,
"Now, let me teach you the basics of where to put your hands." He
sat down, and I carefully placed his fingers on the right keys and
said, "Okay, now repeat those notes a couple of times." He looked
up at me and asked, "Like this?" Then he proceeded to play like a
concert pianist, fingers flying all over the keys, much to my chagrin
and his amusement. He wore the same plain uniform as I did and
looked like an ordinary dogface. You would never have known just
by looking at him that he was someone very special. That was
apparently also true of Jesus – until He opened His mouth and
spoke like no one had ever spoken before Him. The unique message
of Jesus, and the authority with which He proclaimed it, stood out.

The paramount mission of Jesus, however, was not just to
teach us wonderful moral principles or to wow us with His creden-
tials, but to woo us with His love. He said, "For the Son of Man has
come to seek and to save that which was lost."[11] He accomplished
this goal by dying on the cross, being punished by the Father for
all the sins of the world and rising from the dead three days later.
Peter wrote that Jesus "Himself bore our sins in His body on the
cross."[12] We shall be exploring this subject more deeply in the next
section of this book. For now, let me tell you a story about a man
who made a very wise choice that saved his life, as well as the lives
of those in his family.

The Russians are coming

Dresden, East Germany – World War II was over. The Nazis had suffered their final defeat, and refugees roamed the incinerated, rubble-strewn streets in search of food. The Americans had gained control of this part of the fallen Third Reich but were now leaving. In their place, the Soviet Allies would take over.

For Karl Stecher, it came as a terrible shock that the region where he lived and owned a leather goods and tanning factory would be taken over by the Communists. His factory had survived the war without serious damage, and he had high hopes of resuming non-military business – that is, until he heard the bad news – the Russians were coming.

Herr Stecher knew the Russians did not appreciate free enterprise or those who engaged in it. Obviously, he would lose his factory. Worse yet, he and his family would lose their lives as well.

Stecher saw only one remaining chance for survival. He formulated a bold gamble. When the Russians finally arrived and took possession of the area, he dressed in his best suit and visited the commandant's office in that war-torn city. Stecher enthusiastically welcomed the Russians, putting on the cheeriest face he could muster to congratulate them on their victory and thank them for liberating what was left of the once-great city. Opening his leather briefcase, he pulled out the ownership papers and keys to his factory. Then with a sweeping gesture, he ceremoniously laid them on the commandant's desk. Stecher declared how happy he was that the Russians had come to free the people from the Nazi tyranny and that he wanted the new Communist state to have his factory in its entirety.

Understandably, the commandant was both surprised and favorably impressed. After all, most industrialists had to be hunted down and shot, but here was one who gladly gave the Russians his whole business! Pleased at the accommodating

Dresden, Germany – The Americans had gained control of this part of the fallen Third Reich but were now leaving.

offer, the commandant asked if Herr Stecher would be so kind as to stay on and manage the factory for the state, at a salary. Of course, he humbly agreed to the honor and, greatly relieved, returned home with the factory's keys securely in his pocket, chuckling to himself.

Many years later, I met Karl when I visited Communist East Germany. He had been a friend of my father before the war and now lived well off, with a home in the city and another one I visited on a lake shore. This lifestyle was a testimony to Stecher's wisdom. He saw what was coming; and, instead of fighting and losing, he surrendered everything and won. Of course, secretly he laughed about the whole affair. He had no particular respect for the Communists, but he knew he had to do something to save himself and his family.

There's a lesson in Herr Stecher's story. Just as the Russians came and took over the old city, Christ is going to someday regain control of the whole world. That being the case, wouldn't it be prudent to turn to Him in faith and obedience and, like Herr Stecher, hand over the ownership of our lives now? As it is, we are told that someday, "at the name of Jesus every knee will bow . . . and that every tongue will confess that Jesus Christ is Lord, to the glory of God the Father."[13]

As for my friend Sheldon, he obviously did have friends and influence in the entertainment industry and possibly helped some toward becoming stars. But Jesus' influence reaches far higher. Because if you really do believe and follow this Jewish Man, never mind about being placed among the stars of this world for a mere tick of the clock. Jesus – God incarnate – will place you among the stars of heaven forever.

1 Essentials of God
1.5 You've got mail – from God

Mail call!

The Korean War ended shortly before I arrived in East Asia in the fall of 1953. I fought in only two battle lines: the chow line for seconds and the supply line when the new-style boots arrived. Strangely, the skirmishes in which I felt most endangered involved my duties as the company mailman.

Take note: GIs counting the days before discharge don't take kindly to not receiving letters from their wives or girlfriends. Sometimes I was physically threatened, as though I were responsible for the delayed or missing mail. The reactions got so bad that I would have happily written substitute letters myself. I finally came up with a saying to defuse the situation: "It's not the mailman on this end that's the problem. It's the fe-male on the other!"

These recollections remind me of another batch of letters sent our way. They're in the Bible. Many are love letters from God offering forgiveness, eternal life and directions for getting through this life. Unlike some of the letters that went back and forth between Korea and the States, all of God's mail is trustworthy.

In my experience, the change in me is great evidence for the credibility of Christianity and the Bible. The deeper I go in my walk with God, the more real He becomes and the more His Word proves to be accurate. I can say with the psalmist, "The sum of Your word is truth."[1]

I fought in only two battle lines: the chow line for seconds, and the supply line when the new-style boots arrived.

This chapter is intended to show that God is alive and active in the world and to encourage you to go deeper in your relationship with Christ. God communicates His reality chiefly through His Word, which contains His "love letters" to everyone. But He also reveals Himself in His "personal letters" of communication to individuals. While these drops of mercy must never replace the Bible, they help us in living our faith.

Bible prophecy

The unerring prophecies revealed in God's Word are recorded with confidence and substantiated by historical evidence. Old Testament prophecies with meanings that were often at the time hidden from the prophets themselves; were fulfilled when Christ came. They are like the flowers I used to find pressed between the pages of my parents' large Webster's Dictionary. Paul describes these "pressed flowers," as "the mystery which has been hidden from the past ages and generations, but has now been manifested to His saints."[2] In the Apostles' days, suddenly finding the meaning of prophesies found in the Old Testament was like my suddenly finding beautiful pressed and preserved flowers in an old Webster's Dictionary.

Isaiah conveyed some of the most important messianic prophecies about 700 years before Jesus came. These passages are so accurate that doubters have argued they must have been written after Christ died. That explanation was demolished following the 1947 discovery of the Dead Sea Scrolls because at least some of the 19 copies of the book of Isaiah in this collection of ancient manuscripts predate Christ.

Isaiah 53 makes several astounding prophecies concerning the Messiah:
- God's servant would not be attractive (v.2).
- He would be rejected (v.3).
- Observers would think He was being punished by God (v.4).
- He would suffer for our transgressions (v.5).
- God would lay all our sins on Him (v.6).
- He would not try to defend Himself (v.7).

- He would die (v 8).
- He would be associated with the wicked (Jesus would hang between two thieves) and the rich (Jesus would be buried in a rich man's tomb) (v.9).
- He would be a sin offering, but He would come back to life (v.10).
- Many would be justified by Him (v.11).
- Although He would appear with transgressors, He would bear the sins of many (v.12).

Of course, Isaiah recorded other messianic prophesies as well. Isaiah 7:14 predicts that the Messiah would be born of a virgin: "Therefore the Lord Himself will give you a sign: Behold, a virgin will be with child and bear a son, and she will call His name Immanuel." Matthew quotes this passage and emphasizes that the name "Immanuel" means "God with us."[3] According to the prophecy in Isaiah 9:6, the child to be born will be called "Mighty God, Eternal Father, Prince of Peace." The notion that any human child could be God would have seemed outlandish. But the prophet Isaiah faithfully wrote as he was moved by the Holy Spirit. Without any input from God, Isaiah would not have proposed ideas that were so contrary to the thoughts of his culture. Because the Old Testament contains prophecies that have been fulfilled, as well as passages that are quoted as authoritative by Jesus and New Testament writers, many people are willing to accept the Bible as the Word of God.[4]

The testimony for the resurrection

The four gospel accounts report eyewitness testimony from Jesus' disciples. While not educated men, most of them, like their fellow Jews, were religious. To propagate a gross lie about Christ coming back to life three days after He had been put to death would have amounted to physical and spiritual suicide for His followers. The disciples faced the risk of being put to death in the same horrible way in which their leader, Jesus, had died. It would have been unimaginable to spread a false claim that God had raised Jesus from the dead. One or two disciples might have been foolish enough to be untruthful for some strange, insane reason, but it does not make sense that all 11 would agree to proclaim a lie while earning the disfavor of God and the ostracism of the Jewish authorities. Jesus really did rise from the dead. As Peter preached on the day of Pentecost:

Men of Israel, listen to these words: Jesus the Nazarene, a man attested to you by God with miracles and wonders and signs which God performed through Him in your midst, just as you yourselves know – this Man, delivered over by the predetermined plan and foreknowledge of God, you nailed to a cross by the hands of godless men and put Him to death. But God raised Him up again.[5]

When Peter and John were arrested, threatened and ordered to stop preaching, they told the Jewish leaders: "Whether it is right in the sight of God to give heed to you rather than to God, you be the judge; for we cannot stop speaking about what we have seen and heard."[6] Because the early followers of Jesus had talked, walked and eaten with Him after His crucifixion, they literally bet their lives on the fact that He had risen from the dead.

Historical accuracy

Luke is a good author for skeptics and Bible beginners. His gospel, one of four canonical accounts of Christ's life, includes the Bible's most beloved and best-known Christmas story, and the book of Acts records the growth of the early church shortly after Christ returned to Heaven. In Acts, Luke uses the pronoun "we" 35 times, indicating he was included in the events taking place. He switches to "they" when reporting incidents that did not directly involve him. Referred to as a physician, Luke was a reliable eyewitness whose impressive precision on matters pertaining to geography has won praise, as well as some converts, in the academic world. C. S. Lewis is a notable example.

In the late 1800s, archeologist William Ramsay, determined to challenge the accuracy of the Bible, traveled to the places Luke had described in his writings. Not surprisingly, every place Ramsay stuck his trowel and shovel proved Luke right. As a result of these findings, the archeologist became a believer. Ramsay was respected and honored in his lifetime, and his reputation endures. In the 1960s, a group of archeologists in Turkey told me that they thought he was one of the greats.

Luke's careful scholarship is evident in his gospel. While he was not an eyewitness of these events, the opening of his narrative conveys his respect for research:

Inasmuch as many have undertaken to compile an account of the things accomplished among us, just as they were handed down to us by those who from the beginning were eyewitnesses and servants of the word, it seemed fitting for me as well, having investigated everything carefully from the beginning, to write it out for you in consecutive order . . ; so that you may know the exact truth about the things you have been taught.[7]

When asked to give an opinion of Luke as a historian, a professor of Ancient History at my college answered firmly and without hesitation, "Luke is a very good historian."

Fact, not fiction

Another supporting indication of the Bible's historical accuracy is that its authors mention different people with the same given name. For example, three men named Ananias appear in the book of Acts. The first Ananias, with the collusion of his wife, lied to the Holy Spirit (Acts 5:1). The second Ananias was a believer in Damascus who was called by the Lord to lay hands on Saul to restore his sight (Acts 9:10). The third Ananias was a high priest (Acts 23:2). Similarly, three men called James are mentioned in the book of Matthew. For women, Mary is an obvious example of name recurrence. Anyone writing fiction will almost certainly not resort to that kind of repetition unless it serves a purpose. But because the Bible is written as a true account and not as fiction, this name duplication is not problematic but rather reflects the events of history. The Bible is fact, not fiction.

Word drop

In addition to giving us the Bible, God sends "mercy drops," personal letters that strengthen our faith. During my first year as a Christian, I looked forward to the day when I would be able to preach. So I started to practice preaching dynamically in front of a mirror. While this technique might aid some in learning public speaking, for me, the device was simply vanity. But also, starting from those early days, I constantly prayed, *Lord, please draw me closer!* I was like a baby bird in a nest with my mouth continually open, waiting to be fed. I knew I could experience so much more of the Lord and receive further insights from Him.

One day, shortly after a preaching practice – I remember right where I was sitting – a single word from above suddenly dropped into my mind. I was dumbfounded! In the first place, the word made no sense, and in the second, during my 23 years of living, no thought had ever just "dropped in" on me like that. We all experience times when good ideas pop into our minds, but this event was different. The word that had dropped into my thoughts was "mirror." I pondered, Mirror, mirror? What's that all about? Then it gradually came to me. The Lord was telling me to stop practicing my preaching while standing in front of a mirror. He would teach me to preach in His own time.

I believe the message that "dropped" into my consciousness came from God. His touch surely helped draw me close to Him in those early days. Who knows what He will do for you if you truly hunger for Him?[8]

The stolen bike

God's guiding mercy can also reach out to those who are running from Him, as illustrated by the following letter from a Christian woman in Pakistan:

I pray systematically for my neighbors and friends now, even for some "bad people" living nearby. A few days ago, someone came into my house and stole my brother's bicycle.

When we realized what had happened, we were all very upset and sad, and wondered what to do. Then I said, "Let's pray about it," and so we did. We asked God to bless the thief and give him a chance to hear the Gospel.

An hour later, a young man knocked on our door, bringing with him my brother's bicycle: "I do not know what happened, but I'm not OK. I stole this bicycle but I felt a power moving me to come back and return it." Amazed, we forgave him, shared the Gospel with him and gave him some literature to take away. It was an astonishing and humbling experience. God really does answer prayer![9]

Missionary's prayer

Many Christians who have no regular income, especially those who serve the Lord, can probably tell stories of God's unique, last-minute provision. Carol Terry Talbot, the superintendent of an orphanage in India, narrates one such incident in *"Escape at Dawn"*.[10]

One day, the worker in charge of food supplies reported that unless 300 dollars came in to buy fresh wheat and rice, the orphanage would run out of food in three days. She and Terry recalled that many years earlier, the mission had faced a similar crisis. There was no food, so the founder of the orphanage held a prayer meeting in the church. A short time later, she was called outside to arrange help for a man whose oxcart wheel had broken off in front of the mission. The man was so grateful that he gave her part of the load in his cart: several bags of wheat. The founder sent a message to those in the church: "Stop praying and start cooking!"

But no food-laden oxcart came for Terry, and as the days passed, the mailbag remained empty of the needed monetary support. In the U.S., however, a woman who had heard of Terry's work was sitting up in a hospital bed and writing her a letter. About midnight, Terry Talbot's name had entered the woman's mind and was continually repeated for a while. Later, just before dawn, the message came again but changed to: Carol Terry Talbot – three hundred dollars. Carol Terry Talbot – three hundred dollars. The woman sent a check as soon as she could. Terry was joyfully astounded when the money arrived. As soon as she saw the woman in charge of food supplies, Terry Talbot told her, "Stop praying and start cooking." The most plausible explanation for this answer to prayer is that God had supernaturally intervened by "dropping" a message into the mind of the hospitalized woman.

The dream

"Just as the Lord is working all over the earth," a pastor in Turkey once wrote me, "He is still working in our country." To prove this point, my pastor friend sent me the following testimony of a young woman from a neighboring city relating how she had become a Christian:

I am . . . 25 years old. Believe me, my story is very different – special, I guess – as far as I can tell from meeting other Christian brothers and sisters. On FaceBook [before she became a Christian] I would continually add Christians and talk with them as well as ask for information. I would ask for DVDs, New Testaments and they would send them, God bless them. It had been many years, but for a long time there had been doubts and uprising rebellion in my heart. I was a Muslim and very devout. I read the Koran, prayed five times a day and fasted, and Islamic literature would never leave my hands; I was very sincere in it. My father was an alcoholic, my mother was sick, and I was without a job. I was left in a very bad situation.

One day I got down on my knees in tears and prayed, "Please show me the door and save me. Do you not see how sincerely devoted to you I am and how much I love you? Do you not see me? Mothers love their children one percent but I love you ninety-nine percent. Why don't you love me? Show me the door, save me, or don't hold me accountable for what I will do."

Later I fell asleep and that night I saw Jesus in my dream. He said, "You belong to me." When I got up I sat an entire hour in my bed. My mother thought I had gone crazy. I was filled with so much peace and happiness that I thought

I would lose it if I talked. Later I began to research how to become a Christian. Now I love God so much that I would sacrifice my life for Him.

Do you know what happened? When I began to put my trust in Him and [began] asking with my prayers . . . my father gave up alcohol, my mother's health was restored, and right now I am working the perfect job. I am now His disciple. I am doing and will do all I can so that everyone will hear this gospel.

Please understand that having one's life turn out as well as hers is not necessarily the normal Christian experience. Many people around the world who have become Christians after receiving dreams and visions (which are not uncommon in third-world countries) have subsequently been mistreated, displaced from their homes or fired from their jobs. Some have even been martyred for their faith. But these trials serve a purpose in God's plan for His children. As Paul reassured the believers in Rome, "God causes all things to work together for good to those who love [Him]."[11]

Border crossing

I saw another demonstration of God's personal communication during a Christmas college break in 1962 when I traveled with a group of students who were witnessing in Mexico. Due to local hostility toward evangelical Christians, four guys on one of our teams were arrested for preaching in Guadalajara. The police confiscated their documents pending a court appearance later in January.

However, our friends needed to get back for their classes and couldn't wait for the scheduled hearing. As a result they joined us when we gathered early in January to return to the US. Not knowing if they would be allowed to leave Mexico without their papers, we prayed as our caravan headed north.

We got to the border around 4am on a Saturday. Unfortunately, the four fugitives were called into the Mexican customs office for serious questioning while the rest of us waited outside and prayed. It didn't look good. However, about 25 minutes later, our friends emerged from their grilling, ran to our van, jumped in and said, "Let's go!"

One of the guys added, "They warned us not to let it happen again. They were stern – and not very happy." We gladly thanked God for answering what we thought were our powerful prayers. But had He been responding to "our" prayers alone?

On the following Monday evening, I arrived as usual at the home of an older couple for a missions prayer meeting with about a dozen other Milwaukee-area Christians. Our group included a few who had gone on the Mexico trip.

When I rang the bell, the door flew open. Without even inviting me in, the woman of the house pointed at me and asked in a serious tone, "Were you in trouble Saturday morning at 4am?"

I started to answer, "Yes, we w – " . . She interrupted me, "God woke me up, and for about twenty minutes, I prayed, and about all I could say was, 'Right now, Lord, whatever is needed, do it right now!' Then I had peace and went back to sleep."[12]

As we have said, there is enough evidence to show Christianity is credible for a reasonable person to believe. On the other hand, enough questions might be raised to justify in your mind not believing if you choose that route instead. In order to help you decide between the two paths – since some people think both options weigh evenly – simply picture which one you want to die believing.

You've got mail from God

Read His Word as love letters to you, and experience His personal letters of mercy as you walk in the Spirit.

Your word is a lamp to my feet
And a light to my path.
Psalm 119:105

1.6 Evolution: the sacred cow

It was the early 1940s and on the ground level of an old warehouse, 17 men sprawled on benches and the concrete floor, eating their lunches and trading the usual noontime banter. Suddenly, one man stiffened and looked up, searching the high, crusted ceiling and listening intently. "Hey! That sounds like breaking glass way up there!" His attention was riveted on the faint tinkle of shattering glass somewhere on the five floors above them. With their laid-back lunch now interrupted, some of the men surmised that the numerous neatly stacked cases of empty beer bottles were toppling over, creating a horrendous mess. Turning to a buddy, one man groaned in disgust as he picked up his thermos, taking a swig. Wiping his mouth on his sleeve, he said, "I told you, Charley, not to stack those dag-blasted cases so high!"

Charley, about to bite into his sandwich, quickly raised his eyes toward the ceiling and muttered, "Oooh . . . nuts! What the . . !" But he froze in mid-sentence as the rumbling increased, sending down spirals of dust and paint flakes. Dismissing the falling debris, another man casually remarked, "For crying out loud, it's just a passing freight train, guys." But then Frank, the father of one of my childhood friends, leaped to his feet and yelled, "It's coming down!" He and several other workers quickly scanned the large first floor for the nearest way out.

Although annoyed by the prospect of a huge post-lunch clean-up, most of the 17 men laughed at the few who were panick-ing. Surely, the brewery that had made Milwaukee famous would not permit them to work in an unsafe building. The handful of terror-stricken men had to make a split-second decision: swallow their fears and fall in line with their unconcerned buddies, or run like frightened children. Amid scornful laughter and an ever-increasing rumble, five of them dropped their lunch buckets and dashed to the nearest exit – a window. One man lifted a steel stool and smashed the glass while another quickly knocked away most of the jagged edges with a large file. Hearts pounding, they leaped through the window and dove under a lone adjacent boxcar.

Picture, for a moment, five terrified men finally emerging from beneath their boxcar haven only to find the warehouse still standing. Sheepishly, they re-enter the building – this time through a proper door – and are met by rollicking laughter from their co-workers. Those who had hightailed it will never live this down. They will be the butt of jokes for the rest of their lives.

That's what they might have been thinking, but that's not how the story ends. When the thunderous, earthshaking roar subsided and the choking cloud of dust cleared, Frank and his four companions crawled from beneath their boxcar bunker, shaken but alive. Only then did they realize that 12 of their buddies lay dead beneath a mountain of rubble. The laughter had stopped. Sadly, the disbelieving co-workers got what they wanted – solid, concrete evidence.

Conflicting philosophies

Many people uncritically pay homage to Evolution simply because they were taught – religiously, if you will – to believe it. After all, they think, impressive individuals are among its devotees. These followers are similar to the workers in the story who perished because they trusted a famous company and the majority of voices instead of listening to the few men who carefully weighed the data and fled. The evidence was on the side of the minority who were willing to look foolish and exit the building. In other areas as well, the minority has sometimes been proven right. I am suggesting that that is the case in the study of life's origins.

Regrettably, science, although intended to be unbiased, has been taken captive by an atheistic perspective often called Philosophical Naturalism. This view holds that matter and physical laws are the only realities that exist. Proponents have managed to legislate the suppression of competing theories concerning origins.

Starting with the educational system and extending to those working in scientific fields, these advocates have made Evolution a sacred cow. As a result, many have unknowingly suffered intellectually because of a continual barrage of indoctrination delivered from media and institutions at all levels of society. Even if doubters want to challenge the curriculum, they are denied the academic freedom to do so. It has been said that in China, it is possible to question Darwin, but not to question the government; in the US, it is possible to question the government, but not to question Darwin.

Philosophical Naturalism holds that there is no God, in stark contrast to Biblical Christianity, which states that God exists. Both are philosophical points of view, so neither can claim the exclusive support of science. The rationalist will often maintain that science lacks the tools to investigate non-material or supernatural phenomena, yet that objection should not rule out the possible existence of the supernatural. If those searching for truth are prevented from considering all available evidence, their chances of gaining knowledge will be reduced. The scientific method is limited to using observation and experimentation for understanding reality, but logical thinking can also be an effective means of discerning truth. A detective who rules out the butler from weariness of hearing, "The butler did it," would not be a good investigator. Likewise, the promoters and followers of Philosophical Naturalism have ruled out God because they hate hearing, "God did it!" Maybe the "Butler" really did it after all!

That being the case, in addition to Darwin's theory, (which is based on Philosophical Naturalism) at least one alternative explanation of life's origins should be on the table: the longstanding presupposition that a supernatural Being created all things. Unfortunately, the proponents of Evolution, long ago elbowed their way into the circles of academia and have succeeded in marrying Darwinism to science. Ever since, the two have been inseparable, and woe to anyone who suggests an annulment or divorce.

Strangely, the scientific community has been able to make room for numerous theories in searching for origins including some stating that beings from other planets may have come and started life on earth. Yet at the same time, they dismiss out of hand, the possibility that a Supernatural Being may also have come from another realm and started it. Such lack of logic doesn't make sense. It should clearly warn us that there is a built in bias in many of our otherwise very intelligent scientists and thus a need for us to take caution. If these scientists are so illogical and insistent on leaving God out of the picture, we need to be careful of any other possibly biased dogmatic assertions these otherwise respected men may make. This is especially important for those who are young because, while it may "feel good" to toss aside the concept of God and live as they please now – it will not feel good to die with those convictions.

Nonetheless, Philosophical Naturalism has attracted adherents because its tenets have been repeated so often that, like persistent advertisements, they have thoroughly saturated public thinking. Carrying an aura that inspires treatment as a religious dogma, similar to Papal infallibility, Evolution has managed to escape close scrutiny and has succeeded in forbidding critical examination.

Holy Cow! Look at the King

In "*The Emperor's New Clothes,*" a classic children's tale by Hans Christian Andersen, a vain king is fooled by two swindlers posing as tailors with magical powers. They convince his majesty that the clothes they plan to make for him will be invisible to anyone who is unfit for office or unusually stupid. The king thinks, "If I wore those clothes, I would be able to discover which men in my empire are unfit for their posts. And I could tell the wise men from the fools." As it turns out, no one in the king's service can see the clothes. Even the king himself, who dons the light-as-air garments, can't see them. Yet no one, including the king, will admit to this visual lapse and thereby prove himself unfit for office or unusually stupid.

The tailors in this story could be compared to those who insist on teaching Evolution to the exclusion of all other points of view. Darwin's followers have convinced many that Evolutionary theory has unchallengeable substance, insisting that anyone who does not agree is unfit for office – as an educator or a scientist – or is unusually stupid. Andersen's tale, more than 150 years old, parallels the appalling intellectual limitations forced on us today. This of course is done by eliminating any competing theories – especially those put forth by Christians concerning a creator God.

Returning to this prophetic story, the king has been dressed by the swindling tailors:

So off went the Emperor in procession under his splendid canopy. Everyone in the streets and the windows said, "Oh, how fine are the Emperor's new clothes! Don't they fit him to perfection? And see his long train!" Nobody would confess that he couldn't see anything, for that would prove him either unfit for his position, or a fool. No costume the Emperor had worn before was ever such a complete success.

"But he hasn't got anything on," a little child said. "Did you ever hear such innocent prattle?" said its father. And one person whispered to another what the child had said, "He hasn't anything on. A child says he hasn't anything on." "But he hasn't got anything on!" the whole town cried out at last.

The Emperor shivered, for he suspected they were right. But he thought, *This procession has got to go on*. So he walked more proudly than ever, as his noblemen held high the train that wasn't there at all.

Evolution, the sacred cow, lacks substance

This entertaining story could portray current supporters of Philosophical Naturalism. Many who teach or work in a scientific discipline have been forced to bow down without question to the sacred cow of Evolution in order to keep their positions and not appear "unfit or stupid." Occasionally, a muffled voice, as it were, from the intellectual community will cry, "Evolution "hasn't got anything on!" And as in the dilapidated warehouse in our opening story, there are brave scientists who dare to speak up and shout, "It's coming down!" These scientists can hear the distant breaking of glass and see the spirals of dust descending from the deteriorating ceiling of Evolutionary theory in the light of the discovery of complex DNA. But in the world of academia, these warnings are largely ignored by those defending the decaying structure. Without a doubt, they will ultimately receive, at least in the end, what they are looking for – solid, concrete evidence.

The scientific method is an excellent research tool that can verify observable phenomena. Yet at this time, we do not possess the instruments to test whether Man emerged from primeval soup or was created by a Master Architect Who spoke life into existence. Neither hypothesis can be scientifically demonstrated. Unfortunately, Philosophical Naturalism has kidnapped science claiming it as its own and is playing the kids' game of "King of the Hill" by holding the high ground for as long as possible. But that stance conflicts with a genuine search for knowledge, which seeks truth through numerous available avenues.

Clearly, one need not be religious or believe in the Bible to hold the conviction that a Master Architect designed the universe. The evidence of design in nature is consistent with everyday logic that leads us to look for a Designer. While many, like the workers in the collapsing warehouse, will laugh at this idea, the day will come when the laughter will stop.

Leaving God out of the picture or letting God in, are philosophical positions both of which require faith. To anyone who believes that the eye, the heart or a blossoming flower exist by chance, I say, "Congratulations! You have far more faith than I do."[1]

By faith we understand that the worlds were prepared by the word of God, so that what is seen was not made out of things which are visible.
Hebrews 11:3

Postscript: the spiritual and
social consequences of evolution

During national tragedies, many in our society ask, "Where is God when bad things happen?" This anguished question arises in the aftermath of devastating shootings. These high-profile events also revive the gun-control debate. While one might argue that guns are part of the problem, they are not its root. The danger does not lie in the objects we have permitted, especially in the hands of our youth, as much as in the ideas we have not permitted in their hearts. As a nation, we have excluded God from our classrooms and public life, thereby unintentionally jettisoning moral absolutes as well.

Our predicament as a nation stems from the erroneous idea that to be "neutral" in our thinking, we must not permit students to hear challenges to the theory of Evolution by discussing God as the possible Creator of nature. Suppression of this debate has fostered a lopsided educational system. Creationism – the position that a supernatural Being made the world – is dismissed as a religious viewpoint. But both Creationism and Evolution are legitimate attempts to answer the question of origins.

Atheists have so far succeeded in persuading our judges and elected officials to classify faith in God (theism) as a belief system and therefore a religion. Atheism, on the other hand, is treated as a simple lack of belief, the absence of any formal creed. Yet atheists believe there is no God, so both atheism and theism are philosophical belief systems.

The courts have overlooked the point that laws prohibiting the mention of God as a possible Creator are unfairly favoring the opposite philosophy. Belief in God is a philosophy that may or may not lead to formal religion with prayer and worship. I've met many people who say that they believe in God, but don't hold to any creed and are not noticeably religious. Likewise, atheism is a philosophy that may or may not lead an adherent to become a devotee of an organized atheistic society. Both are systems of belief and faith.

Evolution is a sacred cow and needs to be taken off its lofty pedestal. This theory standing unchallenged has blighted the minds of our youth.

A nation's error: the fallout

Because our courts have ruled a Creator out of the educational curriculum, generations of young people have been left to conclude that there is no Supreme Being to Whom they are responsible, and no absolute moral standards by which they must live. When we forbade speaking of God, we foolishly failed to see that morality was attached to acknowledgment of a Higher Power. Our society's behavior clearly changed after we could no longer mention – you know Who – in our classrooms. As a result, our nation no longer has a universally accepted moral standard.

Evolution is a sacred cow and needs to be taken off its lofty pedestal. This theory standing unchallenged has blighted the minds of our youth. The time has come to make room for Creationism in the consideration of life's origins and to permit open discussion of the possibility that a supernatural Creator exists. And if there is a God (which I do not doubt), a return to Him will likely result in pursuing a superior code of moral and ethical conduct. That high standard, no thanks to atheism and its accompanying theory of Evolution, has been removed from the hearts and minds of our young people, bringing about disastrous spiritual and social consequences. If we will return to academic freedom and the place where we left God out, it is probable that we will find that our schools, our malls and our streets can again become safe for a God-fearing people.[2]

In Him was life,
and the life was the light of men
John 1:4

2 Essentials of the new birth
2.1 Something missing

Prop wash from the revving Northwest Airlines plane at the Mitchell Airfield blew my 18-year-old fiancée's sandy hair around her sad face. I drew her close for one final embrace.

Catching her hair with her hand, she turned and faced me at the edge of the airport's runway. Trying to speak bravely, she raised her voice above the din of the plane's engines:

"I'll be waiting for you at this very spot when you come back."

Clutching her thin waist and gazing at her beautiful face for one long, last moment, I drank in the words of her promise. Our lips gently met. Then I turned into the dark night and walked to the waiting plane.

We were to be married two years later, in June of 1955. To assure her of my constant presence while far away in war-torn Korea, I had written her a short poem before I left:

Face the stars and they will
**   kiss you,**
Face the wind and it will
**   kiss you,**
Face the moon and it will
**   kiss you,**
For I faced them all – and
**   kissed you.**

Over a year later, the cooler tone and decreasing frequency of her letters hinted that she had found someone else.

Romantic, but it didn't work. She would be married in 1955 – but not to me. Time and separation slowly took their toll on our re-

67

lationship. More than a year later, the cooler tone and decreasing frequency of her letters hinted that she had found someone else, but just couldn't bring herself to tell me at the time. The truth is, the lucky guy, Peter, would turn out to be a better husband and provider than I could have been, at least at that point in my life. I was a dreamer with no solid skills, a sure loser unless some sort of miracle occurred.

Back in Korea, I was devastated. I had been faithful to her – not common for the average GI. Longing for solace, I felt like taking up with one of the local women of the night. At least then I might have the brief illusion that somebody cared. I even considered suicide, but I had seen one of my fellow soldiers attempt it with his rifle. It wasn't a pretty sight. Besides, I wasn't sure I'd go to heaven if I died, so neither option seemed like a great choice.

God started yodeling

I had a friend once who told me that when he was a boy, his mother would call for him to come home by yodeling his name out the back door. By applying the technique used for summoning cattle in the mountains of her native Switzerland, my friend could hear the yodel even from a block away. He hated that call, but it got him home.

The first time God clearly "yodeled" for me, I didn't like it, either. The call came during a Christmas Eve service in Korea in December 1954, shortly before I was to return to the States. Those of us who wanted to attend the service piled into trucks and rode to a large tent. The chaplain, a Baptist, preached a Gospel message and called on the GIs to come forward and receive Christ as their Savior. The invitation made me angry. I was accustomed to a more ceremonial approach to religion than taking the "sawdust trail." In the following weeks and months, I mocked that preacher, much to the dismay of even my hardened GI buddies. God had yodeled, but I had yet to come home.

Instead, after some thought, I sought comfort by returning to my formal religious roots, which I had abandoned in my early teens. Ironically, it was a gift from my fiancée that aided my search. The evening before I went overseas, she had reached into her purse, pulled out a small, beribboned package and slipped it onto my lap. I eagerly unwrapped the present. Although I was secretly disappointed to see it was only a pocket New Testament, I did my best to look pleased. Now, desperate for solace, I opened the little book and read it nightly. Sadly, my reading was mostly intended to defend myself in religious discussions. I would be able to say, "I've read the Bible. You can't tell me anything." As a result, a dark cloud of despair continued to hang heavily over my heart.

Arriving home a few months later, I rushed from the North Shore Commuter Station to my fiancée's home on Milwaukee's North 32nd Street, hoping against hope that my suspicions were wrong. They weren't. It was over. Her eyes no longer spoke of the adoring desire she once held for me. There was only one thing to do. I needed to forgive her new beau. After all, I thought, it's the Christian thing to do if I want to get to heaven. The next Sunday morning, I met him on the front steps of the church. Instead of duking it out – probably much to the pastor's surprise – I shook Pete's hand and told him that I forgave him.[1]

Religious but empty

I became active in that church, the same church in which I had been confirmed and that my ex and her future husband attended. The pastor, impressed by my show of piety, appointed me chaplain of the College and Career group and suggested I attend seminary and enter the ministry. But I confided to him, "There seems to be something missing within me, and I don't know what it is." He didn't know, either. I had been confirmed in his church and was properly religious. What more could I add? I wondered.

That summer, I started dating another girl from the church. We often concluded our dates with prayer. However, when we both began college in the fall, she joined a sorority and wanted to start partying, which meant taking up drinking and smoking, activities I had avoided up until then. I was naively afraid those behaviors would disqualify me from heaven. Of course, I didn't get that idea from the Bible. As I tell people now, drinking and smoking will not keep anyone out of heaven. In fact, considering cirrhosis, car accidents and lung cancer, drinkers and smokers may get there a lot sooner. But back in college, my concern over this issue heightened the tension with my girlfriend, and I had to find an answer if I wanted to keep dating her.

My dislike of drinking was the result of my father's habit of drinking too much, especially at Christmas, spoiling what should have been a happy time of year. I desperately wanted to do only what I thought was good – I didn't want to miss out on heaven! I thought one had to be perfect to enter God's Kingdom. What I didn't realize was how very imperfect I was, even without alcohol and nicotine.

Tormented by the fear of dying unprepared, I approached one of my junior college teachers, who constantly spoke of her religious faith. After class one day, I asked her, "Is there anything in the Bible that says smoking and drinking are wrong?" Her bright expression quickly darkened, and I realized that I had asked the wrong person. I made a hurried exit.

Al, my classmate

Then I remembered Al Thrall, a student who was in a couple of my classes. He seemed like a regular guy, was well-liked and my fellow classmates said he really knew his Bible. So one day, I asked him the same question. Instead of answering, he invited me to his home to talk about it. This time, I thought, maybe I'll get the answer I so desperately need.

The entrance to Al's second-floor flat could be reached only from the back of the house. He and his wife lived in a cubbyhole apartment that must once have served as an attic. The dimly lit, creaky stairs I mounted didn't look at all like the stairway to heaven. I had no expectation of encountering the God of the universe that night. If someone had told me that this was where I would become wealthy beyond my wildest dreams, I would have scoffed, "Not at this place, I won't! Maybe in a grand cathedral with streams of light beaming through stained-glass windows while a sonorous organ plays in the background, but not here. This place is too ordinary, too mundane, for a meeting with God."

But Al's mission in life was reaching people like me. He had not signed up for junior college simply to get a degree, but to be God's instrument in leading others to find a far more important piece of knowledge. Three months after he began the fall semester, he was still praying to discern whom God was softening up to receive the Good News of Jesus. Al told his wife, Ellen, he knew of several promising possibilities. So why, he must have thought, is the least likely prospect showing up at our door tonight?

As Al waited for me, he may have thought about the darkness from which God had rescued him. He had grown up in "Pigsville," a poor section of Milwaukee near the river and railroad tracks. One day, at a wholesale food market, he saw an expensive car pull up. A well-dressed man puffing on a cigar stepped out and started barking orders that sent people scurrying. Al asked a friend, "Who is this guy?" The answer came back, "A local gangster." Instantly, Al decided he would be like him – a prosperous mobster. While Al was not a violent person, he eagerly sought every way possible to achieve his new goal. He developed himself physically by boxing, and he did well in Golden Gloves tournaments for young people.

On the dark side, he became involved in burglary. Shortly before he would have likely been arrested, his father finally realized what was happening and quickly took Al to Texas in hopes that he would turn his life around. But the young man could not easily abandon his dream. One night, while casing a possible place to burglarize, he was spotted by a police patrol and trapped in a darkened parking lot with no way out. Three sides of the lot were blocked by buildings and a fence too high to scale. While one police-man stayed with the patrol car and aimed the searchlight on the only exit, the other officer carefully examined every car, opening doors and shining his flashlight under each vehicle. Al was sure he would be found as he lay under one of the cars. When the officer approached, Al pulled his body up against the chassis with all his strength. He was not discovered.

Thoroughly shaken, Al staggered with wobbly knees back to his cheap rooming house. He had heard the Gospel of Christ previously from a man named Gus who sought to evangelize street kids. Al's

younger brother Bob had become a believer then, but Al had rejected salvation, preferring his dream of power. However, after his
near arrest, his attitude changed. He fell to his knees by his bed
and cried out to Christ for forgiveness. Al told me later that upon
rising to his feet, he had been amazed that he felt like a completely
different person – so new and clean. He had burst out of his room
looking for someone to tell, but no one nearby could be found.

Arriving at Al's flat

Now at the top of the stairs, I knocked on Al's door. Opening it, he
greeted me warmly as I stepped into his clean, but very modest,
flat. We sat and chatted together while Ellen served cookies and
punch. But I hadn't come for small talk, and I wondered if we would
ever get around to discussing my freewheeling girlfriend. I finally
broke in and asked, "Al, is there anything in the Bible that says
drinking and smoking are wrong?"

Al looked intently at me and said, "Ken, you're trying to work
your way to heaven. It's not smoking or drinking that will send us
to hell, but all the other sins we have committed." From a nearby
table, he took his well-worn Bible, opened it and said, "Listen to
Romans 3:10: 'There is none righteous, no, not one.' That means,
even though we may try to be good, we never can be good enough."

What are you talking about? I thought. *How can a guy who
forgives the theft of his fiancée like I did not be good enough for
heaven? And what does this "righteousness" stuff mean?* After all,
while I was not perfect, no one made more of an effort to be sinless
than I did. Not only did I not smoke or drink, but I never used a
word of profanity, either.

Al continued building his case, now speaking even more
emphatically, "We are justified by faith, not by the works of the
law." *Justified, righteousness!* I wondered, Who does he think he's
talking to, Martin Luther? I didn't understand any of it. Observing a
cloud of confusion slowly descending on me, Al continued, "That's
why God offers heaven as a gift to be received." He then read
Romans 6:23: "For the wages of sin is death, but the gift of God is
eternal life through Jesus Christ our Lord." He looked up at me and

tried to explain, "According to the Gospel, when Christ died on the cross, He suffered for all the sins of the world – including yours. All you need to do now is simply believe that He did this for you." Al searched my face for some sort of light to go on, but I was still tangled up in theological terms – "righteousness" and "justification" – and couldn't get past them.

Trying a different tack, Al closed his Bible. He leaned forward and asked deliberately, "Ken, did you ever receive Christ as your Savior?" Al stopped and waited for an answer to the most important question ever put to me.

His words shocked me. In a flash, I thought, *I've received everything the church ever offered – baptism, confirmation, comm-union, free candy at Christmas. If the church offered it, I lined up for it. But I have never received Christ as my Savior.* I knew that He had died for the world, but until that moment, I hadn't understood that He had suffered for me personally. "No," I answered truthfully, feeling a bit uneasy, "I never did that."

God yodeled again

With an earnest gaze and a firm voice, Al asked, "Do you want to do that now?" What I wanted to do right then was to get out of there. This is too scary for me, I thought. At the same moment, it dawned on me that the Christ Al was speaking about was living, while the one I believed in was just a picture on the wall over the altar. I was transfixed by that thought, and I couldn't help but say, "Yes, I would like to do that now." Al bowed his head to pray and suggested that I pray, too. A few halting, but sincere, words tumbled from my lips: "Thank You, Jesus, for dying for me and giving me eternal life. Help me to live for You. Amen!"

I was stunned as we stood up and faced each other. I had come for an answer to a girlfriend relationship question, but I left with the answer to life's biggest and most important relationship question. We shook hands, and Al said, "If you believe what you just prayed, you're now a child of God." It was eleven o'clock at night, early December 1955. As I descended the stairs, Al called out after me, "Let's meet for Bible study, okay?" Still stunned, I agreed. When I reached the bottom step and opened the door to go outside, I remembered a scene from the movie "*A Man Called Peter*" portraying the conversion of Peter Marshall, the former chaplain of the U.S. Senate; in typical Hollywood style, images of angels were singing gloriously in the background. At the same time, I recalled reading in Luke that there is great joy in heaven when one sinner repents.[2] Smiling to myself and nodding toward heaven, I thought, Well, I don't hear you rejoicing, but I know you are. That night, God flooded my heart with great joy and peace.

God had again yodeled, only this time, I had come home. And yes, I would lose another girlfriend, but that would be of little consequence. For that night, in a humble little house with only a back door for a front door, I became wealthy beyond measure. There I discovered that the missing "something" in my life was really a missing Someone Who would fill my empty heart with His peaceful presence forever. But what's that I hear? God is yodeling your name, too – so why not answer?

A prayer
Thank You, Lord Jesus, for dying on the cross for all my sins. I trust You from this moment on to be my Savior. As a result, I boldly thank You for Your promise of forgiveness and eternal life. Amen!

These things I have written to you who believe in the name of the Son of God, so that you may know that you have eternal life.
1 John 5:13

2 Essentials of the new birth
2.2 Accept no substitutes

On a Saturday afternoon in 1959, I was minding my own business as I briskly walked down Milwaukee's busy Wisconsin Avenue. When I passed under the marquee of a theater premiering the new Marilyn Monroe movie *"Some Like It Hot"*, I was suddenly accosted by a portly, cigar-smoking man in a business suit. Without a word, he grabbed my arm, turned me around, walked me back a few steps and placed me next to a curvaceous blonde. Startled, I looked at her, but she was staring straight ahead, smiling at the photographer who was about to take our picture. Meanwhile, the fellow with the cigar had found another young man and was escorting him to the other side of this petite beauty. I abruptly turned back to her and stammered, "What's this all about?!" She glanced over at me and whispered that she had just won the local Marilyn Monroe lookalike contest sponsored by the theater chain. Then she quickly faced the front again and smiled at the camera.

I tried to digest this sudden burst of information. Looking at the cameraman, I realized that the other guy and I were supposed to be gawking at the shapely Monroe lookalike. It also dawned on me that if the photographer was working for the Milwaukee Journal, my picture might appear on the front page of the Sunday morning edition. In a flash, (no pun intended) I imagined my Christian friends picking up the

Looking at the cameraman, I realized that the other guy and I were supposed to be gawking at the shapely Monroe lookalike.

newspaper on their way to church the next day and seeing my photo. Undoubtedly, they would ask each other, "Isn't that Ken Cetton, the one who wants to be a missionary, ogling that . . . that blonde?" Panic came over me as I wondered how I could buy all the papers in the stores around the church and steal the copies from my fellow congregants' front porches. (As my wife can tell you, it takes me a while to process things.) Nonetheless, while some may like it hot, I don't. So just before the picture was snapped, I turned and bolted, much to the consternation of the portly businessman. He stared after me, momentarily baffled, then shifted his cigar to the other corner of his mouth and quickly snagged a more willing candidate as I made my swift exit.

The lookalike gospel

Lookalikes, attractive as they may be, are always second best, or worse. This principle is especially true for Gospel "lookalikes." Unfortunately, many people have settled for these imitations instead of swiftly walking away. The Apostle Paul faced lookalike Gospels in his day. Scolding the church in Corinth, Greece, he wrote: "You seem so gullible: you believe whatever anyone tells you even if he is preaching about another Jesus than the one we preach, or a different spirit than the Holy Spirit you received, or shows you a different way to be saved. You swallow it all."[1]

Paul similarly reproved the churches in Galatia for being lured toward accepting substitutes:

I am amazed that you are so quickly deserting Him who called you by the grace of Christ, for a different gospel; which is really not another; only there are some who are disturbing you and want to distort the gospel of Christ. But even if we, or an angel from heaven, should preach to you a gospel contrary to what we have preached to you, he is to be accursed! As we have said before, so I say again now, if any man is preaching to you a gospel contrary to what you received, he is to be accursed![2]

The Apostle could have saved himself the expense of extra ink and parchment by not repeating the curse in the last line, but the reiteration underscores how serious he was about preserving the one true Gospel. His warning should alert us to be careful to believe only the complete original Gospel and not accept the superficial concoction of some person or church that presents just parts of the original message. The Gospel, which means "Good News," is God's instruction on how we can be forgiven and assured of heaven.

The true gospel

When I was standing next to Marilyn's lookalike, I could tell she was not the real Marilyn, but only because I had a good idea of what the actual movie star looked like. Similarly, you can spot a false Gospel by knowing the true one, which is repeated throughout the New Testament and presented very clearly by name in one particular passage. To test yourself, stop reading, grab a piece of paper and write down what you think the authentic Gospel of Christ is, in twenty-five words or less.

Naughty, naughty! I can see, even from here, that some of you have not bothered to write it down. Yet by doing so, you can know for sure if what you believe matches what God tells us. (Okay? Got it down? Good!) Now, compare what you've written to what the Holy Spirit tells us through the Apostle Paul in 1 Corinthians 15:1-4. Please note that I have underlined a portion showing that the Gospel can be narrowed down to just fifteen words.

Now I make known to you, brethren, the gospel which I preached to you, which also you received, in which also you stand, by which also you are saved, if you hold fast the word which I preached to you, unless you believed in vain. For I delivered to you as of first importance what I also received, [here it comes now] that **Christ died for our sins** according to the Scriptures, and that **He was buried,** and that **He was raised on the third day** according to the Scriptures."

How did the real Gospel compare with the one you wrote? Aren't you amazed that the most important news for all mankind to know and believe – the very heart of God's message – can be boiled down

to what I have underlined? "Christ died for our sins . . He was
buried . . He was raised on the third day." God has taken something profound and made it succinct and clear for us to understand.
Obviously, it's not good enough for our personal version of the
Gospel to come close to looking like the real thing. Ours must be the
same as the one God states in his Word.

Furthermore, Paul points out that as long as you believe
this Gospel, "you are saved." (No wonder it's called Good News!)
Starting at age 12, I took confirmation classes for two years to
memorize creeds and church doctrine. As good as those teachings
were, all I would have needed to really confirm my faith would have
been to truly believe the fifteen words of the Gospel. Thankfully,
I eventually did. Lamentably, it took eight more years.

A different Jesus

You may also have noticed that in 2 Corinthians, Paul claims some
were preaching a different Jesus. You might think that a church
that teaches about a person called Jesus is teaching about the
real Jesus. But Paul states that this assumption is not necessarily
accurate. Some churches preach Jesus as a wonderful teacher and
a fine example to follow. But they downplay His death on the cross,
His suffering for the sins of the world and especially His resurrection
from the dead. To omit or merely symbolize the sufferings and
resurrection of Christ is to preach
a different Jesus.

. . . but the real Jesus is not just another god. He's the God above all gods. It appeared that she believed in a different Jesus.

Years ago, I was going from
house to house in India selling
Bibles. At one home, the woman
who met me at the door smiled
broadly when she heard what
I was doing and said, "Oh, I
believe in Jesus!" She opened
the door, revealing an entryway
covered with about fifty different
pictures of gods. Looking at them,
she pressed her fingers to her

lips, puzzled for a moment and then brightened, pointing to one picture. "Ah, there He is! There's Jesus!" Indeed, there was a picture of a man labeled Jesus, but the real Jesus 's not just another god. He's the God above all gods. It appeared that she believed in a different Jesus.

Despite what you may think, I'm not stretching things by insinuating there are churches that preach a different Gospel and a different Jesus. When I was a young Christian, a college classmate invited me to a Sunday evening gathering of students at his church. His pastor was to lead a discussion on "What Is a Christian?" I gladly went but was immediately appalled to find that I was the only one who had brought a Bible. Even the pastor didn't have a Bible. During the meeting, everyone gave a personal definition of a Christian. Between the comments. I couldn't keep from interrupting, "But the Bible says . . " Some students leaned back and looked up at the ceiling as they gave their answers. I looked up, too, thinking, Maybe this place is like some great European cathedral with Bible verses on the ceiling. But it wasn't. I truly was unable to grasp how a building with stained-glass windows and a cross on the steeple could be a meeting place for worshipers who did not revere the Bible as the authority for their faith. At last, perturbed by my appeals to the Bible, the reverend turned to me and coldly said, "Why don't you dry up!" (Honest!) Then, resuming his holy smile, he continued listening to the absurd answers of those without Bibles.

To think that there are churches that teach about a man named Jesus but fail to emphasize His suffering for our sins, His resurrection and our need for salvation through faith in Him! The Jesus they preach may be wearing a white robe and holding a lamb in His arms, but if he never hung on a cross and died to save us, he's just a lookalike – a different Jesus. The Bible warns us to watch out for such substitutes.

Good works plus

While many people may believe Christ died for their sins, they might also believe they must do good things to get into heaven. They assume that God will someday weigh their good deeds against their bad deeds, and knowing that they never did anything really bad, they reason that they will merit heaven. Sorry to burst your bubble, but no one gets into heaven by good works. As Paul instructed Titus: "He [Christ] saved us, not on the basis of deeds which we have done in righteousness, but according to His mercy."[3] Mind you, the Bible does speak at length of good works and sincere dedication. (That's what this book you are reading is largely about.) However, God intends that after we are saved, we respond by doing good, sacrificially loving and helping others in gratitude for the free gift of salvation.

Other churches insist that we must be baptized or become members in order to go to heaven.[4] The consequences of mixing the true Gospel with these added beliefs remind me of an incident from one of my favorite college classes: chemistry lab. My lab partner, Harry, who also enjoyed the lessons, never threw away any of the chemicals we had used. Instead, at the finish of the lab class, as I rushed off to another class, he'd pull out a beaker and add our latest concoction to the previous experiment.

One day when I bumped into him between classes, he was coughing violently. I asked, "Harry, why are you coughing so badly?" Between hacks, he hoarsely grunted, "You know how I pour the chemicals together after each experiment?" I frowned and said, "Yeah, I sure do know that." He answered, "Well, when I did it this last time, some dark green vapor came out of the beaker – cough – and I've been like this ever since." I was stunned. "Harry! You're lucky you didn't blow the whole school to smithereens along with everyone in it!"

Similarly, it is deadly to adulterate the Gospel of grace with requirements for good works, baptism and church membership. Although being baptized and going to church are great, they're not needed to experience a spiritual rebirth or to become a child of God. Such extras create a lookalike Gospel, not the authentic one from God. How would you respond if someone were to ask you right now, "What must I do to be saved?" When that question was put to the Apostle Paul in the Book of Acts, he replied, "Believe on the Lord Jesus Christ, and you will be saved."[5] The faith that saves us is as easy as looking into the face of God in prayer, humbly asking Him for His free gift of grace and forgiveness and then thanking Him. The following story provides an analogy for the accessibility of grace.

The gentle touch of faith

In some of the older city buses I once drove, passengers had to work hard to open the rear doors, getting a good grip on the rectangular door handles and pushing vigorously. Then new buses arrived, equipped with rear doors that opened easily by pressing a narrow "touch strip" on the rectangular door handles.

Shortly after the new buses were introduced, a young outlaw-biker type rang the bell to get off at the next stop. His ragged shirt revealed tattoos and chest hair, as well as plenty of muscle. As the bus slowed to a stop, he grabbed the rear door handles but missed the touch strips. The doors failed to open. He then leaned into them with all his might, fighting the bus hydraulics that kept them tightly shut. (Had he been Superman, the bus company would have lost two good doors that day.) Beads of perspiration popped out on his forehead. If he had been sporting a tattoo of a Hawaiian woman in a grass skirt, she would have been doing the hula on his bulging, quivering muscles. Still the door did not budge.

Behind him stood a white-haired little old lady with a flower in her hat. After patiently waiting while he struggled, she said, "Excuse me, sonny, but I've gotta get off this here bus." Looking at her in bemusement, he stepped aside, probably thinking, *Go ahead, lady. You try it.* Approaching the doors, she reached out with her frail, white-gloved fingers and ever so gently pressed the touch strip. With a loud **swoosh**, the doors opened, and she disembarked, followed by the astonished dude with the strained muscles.

Many fight the hydraulics of God, which are intended to regulate the passageway to heaven. These people either entirely ignore His Word, or they seek to enter His kingdom by their noble works, baptism and church membership. But these efforts are all wasted and will not open heaven's gates. Jesus said, "I am the door; if anyone enters through Me, he will be saved."[6] As it turns out, nothing can get us into heaven but faith in Christ's death and resurrection. Carefully read Ephesians 2:8-9: "For by grace you have been saved through faith; and that not of yourselves, it is the gift of God; not as a result of works, so that no one may boast."

Christ's death paid for our salvation – completely – because He took the punishment for all our sins. We insult God when we try to add anything other than a thankful heart. If you and I want to be sure of heaven, just touch the faith strip, and the doors will open. No amount of effort can substitute for following God's design.

The lookalike revisited

As for my close encounter with the Marilyn Monroe lookalike, I have to confess that if she had been the real Marilyn Monroe, it probably would have taken me a bit longer to get out of there. Hopefully, however, my church friends would still have seen my picture as only an unrecognizable blur in the Sunday morning paper. But don't walk away from the real Gospel. Don't appear as a mere blur on the pages of history. Accept no substitutes. Memorize the fifteen words of 1 Corinthians 15 that condense the Gospel: "Christ died for our sins . . He was buried . . He was raised on the third day." Simply reach up by faith and thank Jesus for what only He could do for you, and the doors of heaven will **swoosh** open for your arrival.

... she reached out with her frail, white-gloved fingers and ever so gently pressed the touch strip. With a loud **swoosh**, the doors opened, and she disembarked.

If you confess with your mouth Jesus as Lord, and believe in your heart that God raised Him from the dead, you will be saved.
Romans 10:9

A prayer

Thank You, Lord Jesus, for paying for my salvation. I reach up now with the touch of faith and accept Your forgiveness and thank You for the new birth.
Amen!

2 Essentials of the new birth
2.3 Forgiven

Lessons from a banana leaf

Thirsty and covered with dust after many hours of driving India's jungle roads, I wearily seated myself in a thatch-roofed, roadside restaurant. The accumulated grime mingled with perspiration on my face, and I welcomed the glass of water my waiter brought me. He also placed a fresh banana leaf in front of me as a dinner plate – typical in a rural Indian eatery. However, I immediately noticed a problem. The leaf, like my face, was soiled with dirt. "Sir," I said, pointing to my biodegradable dinner plate, "my banana leaf is dirty."

Waving away persistent flies, the waiter leaned forward, peering closely at my green leaf dinnerware. Perhaps he considered turning it over and using the other side. However, since we were surrounded by banana trees, I hoped for a new leaf. Instead, after a thoughtful pause, he looked up, smiled confidently and, in his best English, said, "I fixy problem, Sahib!" Dipping his fingers into my water glass, he promptly washed the dirt off my leaf, beaming proudly at his efficient solution.

I sat, stunned. I now possessed a cleaner banana leaf, but my water was undrinkable. Speaking slowly through parched lips, I managed to ask, "Now . . . may I have a clean glass of water?"

Obviously disappointed, he gazed at me while wiping his hands dry on his stained apron, probably thinking, What a strange fellow this is! But bobbing his head from side to side, Indian fashion, he picked up what he thought was a perfectly clean glass of water, disappeared behind a worn kitchen curtain and returned with what I hoped was a different and cleaner drink.

I can laugh now about this event, but there is a disquieting similarity between the hygiene of that rural diner and our own careless imperfections before an absolutely impeccable God. His

Word says that although God is holy, He loves us so much that He "has sent His only begotten Son . . . that we might live through Him."[1] Nonetheless, before we can appreciate that Good News, we need to grasp the bad, yet fixable, news: we are terribly flawed in His sight.

God is holy – we are not

Like the waiter with my leaf and water glass, we have no concept of how the stains of our sins offend a faultless God. We think that if we simply "turn over a new leaf," as my waiter might have thought of doing, our spiritual problem will be solved. Or we might consider cleaning ourselves up by going to church, by applying a splash of charity like a cancer walk or by attending a candlelight vigil, hoping these actions will make us acceptable to Him. But, sadly, the Bible informs us, "All of us have become like one who is unclean."[2]

The Bible proclaims that God is faultless: "Holy, Holy, Holy, is the Lord of hosts."[3] One of the marked differences between our own character and God's is that He is pure beyond all measure. Clearly, we are not. We might think the air around us is clean until a shaft of sunlight suddenly exposes the many floating dust particles. Similarly, a shaft of His pure light across our souls will reveal our own countless inner impurities. The Bible states, "All have sinned; all fall short of God's glorious ideal."[4] (Emphasis added.) Most of us object to God's dark assessment of our sins because we prefer to compare ourselves with people who seem much worse than we are. But in doing so, we are looking in the wrong direction. We fail to compare ourselves with God and His high and holy standard of perfection.

I can laugh now about this event, but there is a disquieting similarity between the hygiene of that rural diner and our own careless imperfections . . .

When I left home for college I started doing my own laundry, I knew that, as an Army veteran, I was a better launderer than most of the younger college guys. I was pleased with my skills until I came home on a weekend break. As I proudly put away the white T-shirts I had washed, laying them next to the ones my mom had cleaned, I noticed something greatly disconcerting. I suddenly saw that there is "white," and then there is really white. We may not feel very sinful when comparing ourselves to others, but how do we look compared to God?

When dyeing almost killed a date

During my last summer before finishing college, I was interested in a young lady who also planned to be a missionary. I called Elaine and arranged to take her to the Wisconsin State Fair the next afternoon for a date. However, in the morning, I discovered that my only casual pants were badly faded, and I was too broke to buy a new pair. So as my mother was on the way out the door leaving for work, I asked her what I could do. She said there was a package of green dye in the laundry room and to simply follow the directions. Down to the basement I went with pants in hand. I found that the dye was the exact shade of green I needed.

Following the directions on the box – well, as a guy almost follows them – I dyed my pants a very nice green. Unfortunately, I also dyed my hands a not-so-nice green (the result of not reading the part of the box with the skull and crossbones and other boring warnings). Now I needed to find something to clean my hands. First, I tried Duz, the laundry detergent that, according to the old commercials, "does everything" – everything, that is, but remove green dye from hands. Then, I used a bar of Lava soap – still no "volcanic eruption" of the dye. Finally, I used 20 Mule Team Borax, which had often removed the tough grease stains acquired when working on my car engine. Grease, it could remove; green dye, it couldn't. So I doubled the amount, hoping its power would increase to 40 Mule Team, but that didn't "pull it off" either.

As a last resort before calling Elaine and canceling our date, I went red-faced and green-handed to my dad and showed him my predicament. He put his newspaper down and ran his hand over his bald head, which always seemed to make him think better. After pausing to study my hands, he got up without a word motioned me to follow him down to the basement. As I meekly trailed after him, I tried to keep up my spirits by acting cool. While descending the basement stairs,

I told him that if he was thinking of using Duz, it doesn't; Lava is a laugh; and ax the Borax. And I added that if he thought I should just go out with my hands in my pockets, that would appear dumb – although it would be an appropriate look.

In the laundry room, he again ran his hand over his bald head – more thinking needed. He surveyed a shelf of miscellaneous bottles and selected one bearing only a pasted-on, homemade label. Uh oh! I thought. What strange, powerful solution is this? Then he motioned me to place my hands over the laundry tub. (At times, he was a man of few words.) With trepidation, I obeyed and held up my green hands. Dad poured out a generous amount of the mystery liquid. Instantly, my hands were clean – and, thankfully, still there. I was amazed! I rinsed off and went out on my date. Elaine was none the wiser.

As for your sins, you may have tried everything. You may have spent your life praying and going to church every day or working in a soup kitchen or just trying to be nice. Perhaps you attempted to turn over a new leaf, as my waiter in the banana story may have contemplated. While all these activities are virtuous, nothing will remove our sins except the blood of Jesus, which cleanses instantly through our faith in His death and resurrection.

It is not merely sentimental to speak of Christ shedding His blood for us. Similarly, we might say we are thankful for the soldiers who spilled their blood so we could be free. They died to save us, and that's exactly what Christ's bleeding and dying on the cross was all about. He was actually being punished by God the Father for all the sins of the world. Scripture says, "The Lord has caused the iniquity of us all, To fall on Him."[5] As a result, we are assured that "the blood of Jesus His Son cleanses us from all sin" and that "if we confess our sins, He is faithful and righteous to forgive us our sins and to cleanse us from all unrighteousness."[6]

We all have a date with God – either with sin on our hands and in our hearts, bringing us eternal banishment from His presence, or with clean hands and clean hearts, bringing us eternal life. No matter what we try, nothing will remove our sin stains and make us clean except faith in the blood and sufferings of Christ. To this day, I have no idea what my dad used to clean my hands. But in the spiritual realm, you can accept a detergent that is even better than his mystery chemical. When you believe Jesus shed His blood for your sins, you can be made fit for heaven.

So by faith, place your sinful hands under the fountain of God's solution, the blood of His Son – the only cleansing agent on the Father's shelf that will make you as pure as Himself – and confidently look forward to your eternal date with God.

A prayer
Thank You, God, for loving me so very much
that You left Your judgment seat
and took the punishment for my sins
by shedding Your blood
in the person of Jesus Christ.
Thank You for forgiveness.
Now help me to follow You with all my heart.
Amen!

2 Essentials of the new birth
2.4 Heaven is out of this world

I often criss-crossed Turkey on long bus trips. In the process I frequently became exhausted from not being able to sleep well on the bus. One such evening, I asked the bus driver to drop me off at the next town in order to stay at a cheap hotel. He obliged but when the bus had pulled away, I instantly realized that I had been dropped off about a mile outside of the town and stood in complete darkness.

At first, I attempted to walk the road looking down at my feet using a very dim flashlight. City folks like me, have no idea of how pitch black it can be on a starless night in the middle of nowhere. So after several tumbles into the roadside ditch, bag and baggage, (and I almost wanted to stay there and just go to sleep) I got smart and located the best I could, the middle of the road. Them looking straight ahead to the distant lite up town and ignoring where my feet were I walked straight toward the light. In doing so, I eventually reached my destination for a good night's sleep.

Our trip to heaven is somewhat like that. Often as pilgrims we get so occupied with the earth we're walking through that we lose sight of the our real goal at the end of the road – heaven and frequently keep ditching ourselves along the way. Instead, we need to focus on that heavenly city "whose architect and builder is God." (Hebrews 11:10) In so doing, we'll arrive with much fewer spills into life's gulleys on our record and will look much less disheveled when we enter the gates of that great City.

The promise of Heaven
The coming of Jesus pulled up the shades in the darkened rooms of this world, throwing open the curtains to let the light of Heaven pour in. Jesus said in John 14:1-3:

Do not let your heart be troubled . . . In My Father's house are many dwelling places; if it were not so, I would have told you; for I go to prepare a place for you. If I go and prepare a place for you, I will come again and receive you to Myself, that where I am, there you may be also.

Christ brought "immortality to light through the gospel."[1] The Apostle Paul describes this Good News as "the mystery which has been hidden from the past ages and generations, but has now been manifested to His saints."[2] Contrary to what many Christians believe, the people of the Old Testament did not have an assurance of Heaven or eternal life – only occasional glimpses of the future promise.

Israel did not have this assurance

Instead of the sure hope of eternal life that is offered us today, the people of Israel were promised orly earthly prosperity and longevity if they loved the Lord and obeyed His commandments. "If you keep the commandments of the Lord your God and walk in His ways . . . The Lord will make you abound in prosperity."[3]

Jews of the Old Testament era believed in Sheol, the place of the dead that is mentioned in several of the following texts. "Whatever your hand finds to do, do it with all your might; for there is no activity or planning or knowledge or wisdom in Sheol where you are going."[4] Concerning the inactivity of those who had died, Isaiah the prophet adds, "Sheol cannot thank You, death cannot praise You; those who go down to the pit cannot hope for Your faithfulness."[5] King Solomon, who prospered and abounded in riches and pleasures but unfortunately he had no hope beyond them, said near the close of his life, "The living know they will die; but the dead do not know anything, nor have they any longer a reward, for their memory is forgotten."[6]

Yet we read of one glimpse of Heaven from the Old Testament in what is probably the oldest book in the Bible, Job:

As for me, I know that my Redeemer lives,
And at the last He will take His stand on the earth.

Even after my skin is destroyed,
Yet from my flesh I shall see God;
Whom I myself shall behold,
And whom my eyes will see and not another.[7]

Most of us remember that David wrote in the beloved twenty-third psalm, "Surely goodness and lovingkindness will follow me all the days of my life, and I will dwell in the house of the Lord forever."[8] Yet David also wrote, "There is no mention of You in death; in Sheol who will give You thanks?"[9] Nonetheless, elsewhere some light does seep in through the drawn curtains of the Old Testament. According to the prophet Daniel, "Many of those who sleep in the dust of the ground will awake, these to everlasting life, but the others to disgrace and everlasting contempt."[10] As a result of accumulated revelations given in Scripture, by the time Jesus arrived on earth, most Jews believed in a final judgment and a resurrection to eternal life. Of course, members of the Jewish sect of the Sadducees strongly disagreed.[11]

Jesus brought us a sure expectation

This historical perspective should help us appreciate the astounding message Jesus brought and the reason the hope of the Gospel is so comforting. It adds fresh meaning to the words of Christ's disciple Peter who said, "Lord . . You have words of eternal life."[12]

Not only did Jesus offer the promise of Heaven for all who believe, as declared in John 3:16, but He upped the ante and said our bliss would start at the very end of this life. Jesus told Martha, "I am the resurrection and the life; he who believes in Me will live even if he dies, and everyone who lives and believes in Me will never die."[13] He also said, "Truly, truly, I say to you, if anyone keeps My word he will never see death."[14]

The Bible speaks of Christians who have died as being asleep. This description more likely characterizes what those living on earth see rather than what those who have died experience. They are, apparently, living as disembodied spirits in the heavenly Paradise. According to 1 Peter 3:18, Christ was "put to death in the flesh, but made alive in the spirit." Paul teaches that when we die, we go to be with Christ even though our bodies go to the grave. At the resurrection, our bodies will be raised and instantly changed while being united with our spirits coming from Heaven.

Paul, said, "For to me, to live is Christ and to die is gain."[15] While wanting to remain on earth to serve the church, Paul struggled with his longing to go to be with Jesus. "I am hard-pressed from both directions, having the desire to depart and be with Christ, for that is very much better."[16] Paul also said in 2 Corinthians 5:8 that he preferred "rather to be absent from the body and to be at home with the Lord," making clear that upon death, Paul knew he would become a conscious, disembodied spirit in Heaven.

All the above mentioned truths should open our eyes in wonder and our mouths with praise for what Christ has brought us, a gift far better than anything ever offered before.

What is Heaven like?

As for a description of Heaven, anyone who has been a parent has experienced the frustrating task of attempting to explain something complex to a child. A youngster once asked his father why his sliced apple was turning brown. The father, knowledgeable about the chemical processes involved, rattled off a scientific explanation of oxidation. When he finished, the child looked around and asked, "Daddy, were you talking to me?"

For similar reasons, God limits the information He provides us about Heaven. He frames the language in the simplest terms – streets of gold, walls of jasper. Like children, we lack the under-standing and the specialized vocabulary needed to comprehend things so remote from our everyday existence. Paul tries to convey this concept in 1 Corinthians 2:9: "Eye hath not seen, nor ear heard, neither have entered into the heart of man, the things which God hath prepared for them that love him" (KJV). Much of what is to come is unexplainable. Paul said in 1 Corinthians 13:12 "For now we see in a mirror dimly, but then face to face; now I know in part, but then I will know fully." However, we do know from descriptions in Revelation that our future dwelling place will have cities and that it will be on a completely new earth. We read in Revelation 21:1-2, "Then I saw a new heaven and a new earth; for the first heaven and the first earth passed away . . And I saw the holy city, new Jerusalem, coming down out of heaven from God."[17] On the other hand, Jesus said in John 14:2 "In My Father's house are many dwelling places; if it were not so, I would have told you; for I go to prepare a place for you." As a result, not all that God has planned for us may be confined to the new planet alone.

Still, when you picture the new earth, don't think of earth as we know it in its present size. The new one may be as big as our whole solar system. When you think about this new creation, think big and glorious, with all the beauty of mountains, lakes, streams, forests and ever-blooming flowers, along with gentle animals and much more than we could ever guess. How would you like to pet a tiger and have it purr like a kitten, or stretch out and lean your head on a resting lion without fear? Heaven on the future earth won't be just an improved version of what we now enjoy, but one that is radically enhanced and marked by overflowing love, complete happiness, security and freedom from the consequences of sin. We are limited in envisioning the unspeakable future that awaits those who love God.

We are limited in envisioning the unspeakable future that awaits those who love God. Try to imagine contacting members of a friendly, isolated aboriginal tribe. Assuming you could speak their language, how would you explain automobiles, airplanes or cellphones?

"An airplane is like a big bird that you ride on," you might say. "Huh?" your tribal friend says, wrinkling his brow in bewilderment. "Well, that's not exactly right, either," you say, scratching your head while searching for a better description. You try again.

How would you like to pet a tiger and have it purr like a kitten, or stretch out and lean your head on a resting lion without fear?

"It's more like a big bird that you ride in." By the time his laughter stops, you've given up.

The best way for us to understand Heaven is not so much by physical descriptions of what it will be like, but rather, by considering what we will be like when we get there. In Revelation 21:4, we read, "And He will wipe away every tear from their eyes; and there will no longer be any death; there will no longer be any mourning, or crying, or pain." That promise would be extravagant by itself, but Heaven will be much better than even our most elated moments. There will never be any pining for the "good old days" on the present earth. Heaven will be better than drugs, better than Christmas, better than sex, better than anything anybody has ever experienced on this planet. Here, nothing is secure but our faith. There, all that we cherish will be safe.

According to a parable Jesus told, when He comes into His kingdom, He will reward his faithful followers by appointing them to privileged tasks in His royal service (Luke 19:17-19). These occupations will bring us great fulfillment. I believe that our fallen nature causes our boredom and restlessness in this life. In Heaven, we will no longer have that sinful nature but instead the very nature of God Himself, delighting in all that brings Him pleasure as we bask in the glory of His presence and abounding love for us. We will be treated to scenes of mind-bending beauty.

Do we have your eyes on that Eternal City or have we fallen in a ditch and gone to sleep? Hebrews 11:16 tells us, "But as it is, they desire a better country, that is, a heavenly one." And Ephesians 5:14 admonishes us, "Awake, sleeper, And arise from the dead, And Christ will shine on you."

2 Essentials of the new birth
2.5 The other place

It was the mid-1960s. Earlier that day, that the police had arrested
Dieter, my German brother in Christ, and me, for what they considered a serious crime: mailing invitations offering a Bible study
course by correspondence. Now both of us – and possibly a few rats
– were residents of a filthy cell. Despite some trepidation, we made
the cell a sanctuary for prayer and praise to Him.

That evening, a guard opened our door and ordered us into the
adjacent holding area. The stern-looking man in charge read aloud
a document we were to sign, confessing that we had committed the
crime of attempting to proselytize. When he finished, he held the
papers toward us and arrogantly demanded, "Sign these!" He drew
on his cigarette and added expressionlessly, "And you'll be free."
But we objected and insisted we were not guilty of any crime and
had not violated the laws of Turkey. "Sign," he sneered angrily,
raising his voice while flicking his cigarette ashes onto the already-
littered floor, "or you will not be released!" But we were not guilty of
any wrongdoing, and we were not about to sign a false confession
just to breath fresh air.

Knowing what we must do, Dieter and I traded glances, turned
simultaneously and stepped back into our dark, smelly prayer
chapel. Before closing the door, I repeated, "We are not guilty of
any crime, so change that document to simply state the facts of
our arrest." And Dieter added firmly, "That we can sign." Then with
a loud clang we pulled the cell door shut. It was all a matter of
principle. The police had been acting on their own personal feelings
without regard for the freedoms stated in their laws and in the
Turkish Constitution.

Through the blue haze of his cigarette smoke, the astonished
jailer stared in disbelief at the closed cell door. None of his prisoners

had behaved like this before – singing happy songs, praying endlessly and then refusing release except on their own terms. He returned within the hour with a document written as we had demanded. We signed and went home.

In this we are looking at Hades, a terrifying abode of suffering for unbelievers after death. If Dieter and I had been locked up in that "holding tank," we would have signed anything to get out. In Old Testament times the spirits of the dead occupied a place called "Sheol," the word used in Old Testament Hebrew, or "Hades" in New Testament Greek. (In my remarks in this chapter, I will mostly use the term Hades. The word Hell as explained later, is the term used when referring to the place of final judgment which is the Lake of Fire.)[1] Respected Bible teacher, William MacDonald, author of Believer's Bible Commentary, remarks that Sheol "was spoken of as the abode of both saved and unsaved" in the Old Testament period.[2]

The First Book of Samuel illustrates the Old Testament perspective on life after death. King Saul sought a medium to summon the prophet Samuel from the dead to give advice. Saul made this request despite God's prohibition on consulting mediums (or witches), possibly because the only things they might be able to conjure up would be evil spirits. The story unfolds as follows:

Then the woman said, "Whom shall I bring up for you?" And he said, "Bring up Samuel for me." When the woman saw Samuel, she cried out with a loud voice.... The king said to her, "Do not be afraid; but what do you see?" And the woman said to Saul, "I see a divine being coming up out of the earth." He said to her, "What is his form?" And she said, "An old man is coming up, and he is wrapped with a robe." And Saul knew that it was Samuel, and he bowed with his face to the ground and did homage."[3]

After rebuking Saul, Samuel adds: "Moreover the Lord will also give over Israel along with you into the hands of the Philistines, therefore tomorrow you and your sons will be with me."[4] Some Bible scholars believe the woman only faked Samuel's appearance but the Bible says that Samuel spoke to Saul. Fourth and that "Saul knew that it was Samuel." Therefore, it seems that this apparition truly was the prophet Samuel. Note that he comes up out of the earth and not down from Heaven. Note also that Samuel says that Saul, the king, would be joining him the next day. We can conclude that when people died in Old Testament times, they went to Sheol, (Hades) the place of the dead.

Two sections

Jesus gives us further insight into the after-death state in the story of Lazarus and the rich man. Lazarus was a destitute, sickly beggar who was laid daily at the rich man's gate, longing to receive even the crumbs dropped from his table. Unfortunately, there is no record that Lazarus received much, if any, help. When he died, he "was carried away by the angels to Abraham's bosom."[5] In time, the well-to-do man also died. Since he was still under the Law (this took place before Christ's death and resurrection) and failed to love his neighbor Lazarus as himself, (which is the second most important commandment) he was apparently condemned to Hades. Continuing the story, Jesus says:

In Hades he lifted up his eyes, being in torment, and saw Abraham far away and Lazarus in his bosom. And he cried out and said, 'Father Abraham, have mercy on me, and send Lazarus so that he may dip the tip of his finger in water and cool off my tongue, for I am in agony in this flame.' But Abraham said, "Child, remember that during your life you received your good things, and likewise Lazarus bad things; but now he is being comforted here, and you are in agony. And besides all this, between us and you there is a great chasm fixed, so that those who wish to come over from here to you will not be able, and that none may cross over from there to us."[6]

Many Bible commentators believe that because Lazarus is mentioned by name, Jesus is recounting an actual event. MacDonald writes "This is not spoken as a parable."[7] This account shows that before the resurrection of Christ, all but three people went to Hades, when they died. [8] We can conclude from the story given by Jesus that Hades contained two sections: one a place of terrible suffering and the other, called "Abraham's bosom," a place of peace and rest. (Scofield Reference Notes.)[9] Those residing in the blissful section, apparently under the care of Abraham, were in a first-class waiting room of pleasant repose and probably in deep sleep, unconscious of their surroundings. So while both the rich man and Lazarus were in Hades, they were in two distinct parts.

In describing the terrifying holding tank of the suffering side of Hades as well as even the wonders of Heaven, the Bible often uses earthly symbolism because our languages are too limited to describe spiritual realities. Jesus Himself makes this point when He says to Nicodemus, "If I told you earthly things and you do not believe, how will you believe if I tell you heavenly things?"[10] So Heaven's "streets of gold" may simply stand for the most glorious and precious materials imaginable and much beyond that. Similarly, fire and brimstone may possibly be used to represent the horrible section of Hades because no human description can depict the great terror of hopelessness and the pain of deep remorse for having permitted oneself to be blinded to the truth of God.

Where did Jesus go after He died?

On the cross, when Christ said, "It is finished!" He died and completed His suffering for the sins of the world. The early church fathers sought to codify this event and what followed in the Apostles' Creed.[11] In Scripture however, we read of Christ's trip to Hades in a prophecy given by David and quoted by Peter in the Book of Acts: "He [David] looked ahead and spoke of the resurrection of the Christ, that He was neither abandoned to Hades, nor did His flesh suffer decay."[12]

In asserting that Christ was not "abandoned to Hades," Peter simply meant that Jesus was not left there like all the others who had previously died. Instead of immediately going to Heaven, as is our privilege, Jesus, when He died, went in His Spirit to the part of Hades cared for by Abraham. When the dying thief on the cross was assured that he would be with Jesus in Paradise, the Greek word for

Paradise means an enclosed park or garden. This sheds new light concerning the mysterious section in Hades where the believers such as Lazarus were residing. For the first time now, when Jesus spoke to the repentant thief, He used this term, Paradise. It's used again when Paul tells of his near death experience saying that he "was caught up into Paradise . . ."[13] Shortly, we'll learn more about what happened to Paradise itself.

The Bible states that when Jesus went to Hades, He also had a word for those lost souls on the other side of the chasm. The following helps us to understand what happened:

For Christ also died for sins once for all, the just for the unjust, so that He might bring us to God, having been put to death in the flesh, but made alive in the spirit; in which also He went and made proclamation to the spirits now in prison, who once were disobedient, when the patience of God kept waiting in the days of Noah, during the construction of the ark, in which a few, that is, eight persons, were brought safely through the water. [14]

It appears that the people to whom Christ was proclaiming resided not in "Abraham's bosom" but across the fixed gulf along with the former rich man. Possibly He explained that He represented the Ark, which many of them had missed boarding in Noah's day. Perhaps they scoffed, seeing that Jesus was no longer alive on earth. Little did they know that He was also a representation of Jonah. Jesus tells us in Matthew's Gospel: "Just as Jonah was three days and three nights in the belly of the sea monster, so will the Son of Man be three days and three nights in the heart of the earth" (emphasis mine). [15]

What happened at Christ's resurrection?

Three days later, Christ not only fulfilled His promise to leave Hades, but, according to Paul, did something else as well.

Therefore it says, "When He ascended on high, He led captive a host of captives, and He gave gifts to men." (Now this expression, "He ascended," what does it mean except that

He also had descended into the lower parts of the earth? He who descended is Himself also He who ascended far above all the heavens, so that He might fill all things.)[16]

By what was just quoted, Paul confirms that Jesus had gone into the lower parts of the earth where the spirits of the departed dwelt in the non-suffering part of Hades. Jesus apparently emptied that part, also called Paradise, of all who had been waiting there, from Adam onward, including its caretaker, Abraham. That part of Hades held all who had died before Christ's resurrection but who believed in and obeyed God. Some may wonder how they could have been saved, since they had not known and thus not believed in Christ's atoning sacrifice. But the author of Revelation states that Jesus is "the Lamb slain from the foundation of the world."[17] That means that the sacrifice of Christ was as good as done even before it was accomplished on earth, and thus God could apply it to anyone of His choosing who obeyed Him and did what was right. (God still exercises this prerogative. Most Christians believe that young children and the unborn who die are saved apart from having any faith.)

Early on the morning of the resurrection, Mary Magdalene saw Jesus in the garden, but she did not see the great spiritual host that He was leading to Heaven. We read of this imminent rising toward Heaven which would take place after He meets Mary: "Jesus said to her, 'Stop clinging to Me, for I have not yet ascended to the Father.'"[18] When Jesus died, His physical body lay in the tomb, but His Spirit went to the Paradise side of Hades until the resurrection. According to Matthew, a number of tombs in Jerusalem were opened, and many of the spirits whom Christ led were apparently given permission to reenter their bodies. One might think this incident occurred at the time that Jesus died because of its location in the text. But a careful reading clarifies that the sightings took place when He arose and likely while leading the host to the new Paradise in Heaven: We read in Matthew 27:52-53, "The tombs were opened, and many bodies of the saints who had fallen asleep were raised; and coming out of the tombs after His resurrection they entered the holy city and appeared to many."

Where do unbelievers go now when they die?

Although Paradise has been emptied and obviously relocated, (Paul was "caught up into" it, not down to it.) the suffering part of Hades is still open for business. At the end of the ages, however, Hades will give up its prisoners to be judged. Then those whose names are not recorded in the Book of Life will be cast into the Lake of Fire, which is Hell and will also consume death and Hades.[19] There are a small minority of Christians who believe that at the final judgment, those who are thrown into the Lake of Fire will be destroyed. Proponents of this theory cite the Scripture that calls the Lake of Fire the second death (Rev. 2:11). However, most Christians conclude that the Scripture gives more weight to the teaching that Hell is everlasting. And even if the destruction argument were correct, unbelievers will still face an unknown span of years of horrific suffering separated from God in Hades until that destruction takes place.

The dreadful section of Hades and the Lake of Fire exist not because God is cruel, but because He is a righteous judge Who must punish sin. The safety and comfort of our earthly societies depend on maintaining standards of right and wrong and on punishing negative behavior. If your neighbor tried to murder you and was sent to prison, no one would fault the judge. God applies a similar principle when judging our sins.

To a person imprisoned even for a short time, freedom appears sweet.

The Turkish jail cell I shared with my friend was a five-star resort compared to Hades. Don't let that latter place of distress be your destination. Commit to believe and follow Jesus Christ, starting right now. John 1:12 says, "As many as received Him, to them He gave the right to become children of God, even to those who believe in His name."

2 Essentials of the new birth
2.6 Jesus buys wrecks

There's a church in our town with a lit-up "Jesus Saves" sign. Before I was captivated by the love of God, I made fun of that sort of thing. Such garish displays with the words, "saved" and "salvation" seemed antiquated to me. I thought they belonged in an antique shop next to high-button shoes and red Victorian sofas. But that's because I had failed to comprehend how accurately they describe our peril-filled situation and what it took for Jesus to step in and rescue us from our human sinful wreckage.

One way for us to understand salvation is to consider the meaning of the closely related word "salvage," which is: "Something saved from destruction or waste and put to further use."[1] This definition portrays perfectly God's actions in making us fit for His heavenly kingdom. With no apologies, the Scripture repeatedly uses these "salvage" terms. For example, in the Book of Acts: "And there is salvation in no one else; for there is no other name under heaven that has been given among men by which we must be saved"[2] (Italics added).

Years ago, I was often com-pelled to frequent auto salvage yards. There I would see a vast array of vehicles, all of which were unfit for their originally intended purpose of proudly conveying people to their destinations. Instead, these vehicles were good only for salvageable parts and an ultimate meltdown. Similarly, we too, are spiritual wrecks in the fallen junk yard of humanity. But like the junked cars, we also likely have some good, usable parts. One person can play the piano or perhaps create sculpture. Another does works of charity. Still another designs buildings or develops a new medicine. Nonetheless, God does not save us from the wrecker's ball of judgment because we possess any "good parts" or manage to do some commendable things. In fact, He doesn't even choose us because we look promising. We are told in God's Word: "Consider your calling, brethren, that there were not many wise according to the flesh, not many mighty, not many noble; but God has chosen the foolish things of the world . . the weak things . . the base things . . [even] the things that are not . . "[3]

Obviously, God seeks after any rusting human hulk He can find who will awaken to His whisper and loving touch. When we are aroused from our spiritual deadness and respond to His Gospel invitation, we are purchased by our new Owner – Jesus really does buy wrecks – and retitled under His name. He redeems us from Satan's wrecking yard in order to restore us to God's original intention. That purpose, as the Westminster Shorter Catechism so succinctly states is "to glorify God and to enjoy Him forever."

Still, you might wonder about people who not only show creative skills, but also possess varying degrees of god-like characteristics such as – love and kindness – but are not Christians. The reason for the existence of these traits is that man was originally made in God's likeness, just as we read in the creation event in the first book of the Bible. "Then God said, 'Let Us make man in Our image, according to Our likeness . . '"[4] So even though we are fallen and wrecked by sin, we still retain some glimmer of God's similitude within us.

An acquaintance of mine once showed me a photograph of Adolf Hitler smiling down at a little girl. The photo was given to my friend by an older German whom he had met after World War II while serving overseas in the U.S. military. His German friend had taken the picture when Hitler had visited his village before the war. Although most of Hitler's actions were evil, there is a possibility that, just for a moment, the Nazi dictator might have displayed a

Years ago, I was often compelled to frequent auto salvage yards.

tiny speck of the warmth that God had originally implanted in all mankind. (Satan and his demon spirits do not have even a trace of kindness in their fallen condition because they were never made in the image of God. (You'll never find a demon-possessed person full of love – only evil.)[5] Because God's faded image is found in some measure in all, one occasionally may catch a small glimmer of His goodness and creative ability even in the worst of us. Likewise in a salvage yard, some of the junk may possibly look pretty good from one angle, but when we see another side, we understand the reason it's on the scrap heap.

It's obvious then, that God does not save us because we possess any good within, but simply because He lovingly desires to restore us to our originally intended condition, and to eventually make us infinitely better. The moment He buys us back from Satan's worldwide wreckage yard through the redemption of the cross, a new person is birthed within us. We do not have to wait until we are cleaned up and brought back to our original intended luster. The Apostle Paul wrote, "Therefore if anyone is in Christ, he is a new creature; the old things passed away; behold, new things have come."[6] This promise gives followers of Jesus full assurance that a makeover has begun and its grand completion will finally take place in heaven. The Apostle John tells us of that magnificent event: "Beloved, now we are children of God, and it has not appeared as yet what we will be. We know that when He appears, we will be like Him [Jesus], because we will see Him just as He is."[7]

The remake process

When we are "saved" by Jesus, the Holy Spirit begins the long process of returning us, as close as we will permit, to God's original intent and likeness while we remain on earth. The Apostle Paul wrote that Jesus "gave Himself for us to redeem us from every lawless deed, and to purify for Himself a people . . zealous for good deeds."[8] However, this spiritual repair does require our sincere and earnest cooperation. Paul is not speaking here about what we will be like in heaven but about what God wants us to be like while still on earth. As a result, because we're not yet in heaven, our next step, if we are "salvaged" people, is to become part of a Bible believing church.[9] If you were to buy a wreck from a salvage yard, you wouldn't park it in the woods or way out in a field. A car sitting alone in the boondocks will never be restored on its own. Rather, you would take it to a garage that specializes in restoring wrecks or you would become part of a club that has this same intense interest.

Likewise, unless one has a last-minute conversion as did the thief on the cross, Jesus does not take us directly to heaven but instead, places us in His mystical, earthly church, which is called the Body of Christ. (This title indicates an intimate and close relationship with Him and is also called His Bride.)

The church is not a building, but a world-wide body of believers with whom we are commanded to be tangibly linked, especially in a local fellowship. We are told in the Book of Hebrews: "And let us consider how to stimulate one another to love and good deeds, not forsaking our own *assembling together, as is the habit of some* . . "[10] (Italics added). God intends to use the church as part of His restoration process while we patiently wait to be transported to heaven. During this interval, He seeks to start working on our flaws by knocking out our dings and dents and helping us to clean out all our inner muck and mire. The Apostle Paul admonished: "That in reference to your former manner of life, you lay aside the old self . . and put on the new self, which [is] in the likeness of God . . "[11]

The church is not a building, but a world-wide body of believers with whom we are commanded to be tangibly linked.

Don't drive a jalopy

If we can help it, few of us, will drive an old backfiring wreck with missing fenders that looks and sounds like it should be returned to the junkyard. So we shouldn't expect God to be content to have His "fleet" of children on the road of life acting as if they still belonged in the

Devil's scrap heap. The ones still held captive by our prior owner are unaware that they are under the watchful eye of Satan's mean junkyard doggies, ignorantly awaiting the giant trash compactor and ultimate meltdown. But thankfully, through faith, you and I have been saved from that ignominious end.

So the terms "Jesus Saves" and "salvation" are neither archaic nor inaccurate after all. Instead, they give us a good picture of what Jesus had to go through to ransom us. As a result, as His salvages from the spiritual wrecking yard, we can rejoice deeply in the personal meaning of salvation, "saved from destruction," and gratefully allow ourselves to be "put to further [good] use."[12] But just in case you're still in the "junk yard" why not by faith move your location and ownership right now.

A man once asked Apostle Paul this question:
"Sirs, what must I do to be saved?"
and Paul answered,
"Believe in the Lord Jesus, and you will be saved."[13]

2.7 Where is God when bad happens?

Where is God when bad happens? For all of us the answer may be different, but find out what this woman learned, when she asked that very question and the miraculous way God brought the answer.

When my wife, Helen, attended Bible college before we were married, she was good friends with "Lydia."[1] Both were zealous for Christ and Lydia wanted to serve Him boldly as a missionary in a foreign country. While in school, the two friends took every opportunity to make the Gospel known wherever they went. Then Lydia met "Tim,"[1] a nice young man who was a professing Christian. He was training for a lucrative profession that would enable his family to prosper. However, as I saw it, while Tim would be considered a good catch for most typical young women, his evangelistic goals in life were not compatible with Lydia's. I could not help but warn her of what appeared to be a looming danger: failure to fulfill the purpose God had put on her heart. At her graduation, I confronted her, looked her in the eye and declared, "Yes, Tim's a great guy, but don't marry him because you may not get to fulfill your life's dreams!"

They married anyway, and I regretted having spoken so emphatically. Years and distance separated Lydia and Helen, but they kept in touch by mail. As predicted, Lydia never got to a foreign field to serve Christ. She seemed to have become sidetracked by the excitement of married life and was not following any part of her evangelistic dream. But, I also reflected, Which one of us lives so perfectly before God as to earn the right to fault others? We all fall short.

Then one day, a letter arrived telling of a tragic accident in which Lydia had lost a limb. We were devastated and prayed for her recovery. A few years later, she flew across the country to Southern

California to visit us for a week and re-connect with my wife. They had a great time together touring D sneyland and seeing the sights of Los Angeles. One evening near the end of Lydia's stay, I asked her, "Lydia, how are you doing spiritually?"

Lydia is a strong person, intelligent and not easily intimidated. She had attained a high position in a large company. Tapping her fingers on the table and leaning forward so I would clearly see her anger, she looked at me and asked bitterly, "Where was God when I was in all that pain in the hospital after my accident!?" I gulped and tried to form words, but she broke in and demanded, "Where was He in all my pain!?"

Now I was speechless. I could only look at her and try to understand how deeply the ordeal had affected her. A flippant response would not do. What could I say in God's defense? Finally, I answered softly, "I don't know where God was, Lydia, but I'll ask Him, okay?"

At our Garden Grove home, I spent less time swimming in our pool than I did walking around it and praying. That night as I paced, I took Lydia's question to Jesus. I don't use flowery words when I speak with God. I probably said, "Lord, you know her question. Where were you in all her pain . . . huh? Why weren't you there . . . where did you go? She'd like an answer, Lord Jesus." I repeated my question in different ways as I slowly circled the pool. Although I know God is all-wise and makes no mistakes, even I was still curious to learn why He seemed to have hidden Himself from Lydia in her great need. After a period of discussion and entreaty with Him, I went to bed.

Many of my years in Southern California were spent in secular employment, which was my ministry as well. For a long time, I was a city bus driver. (I had wanted to be a missionary

If you want to meet and get know a lot of people, there is no better way to do that than working in mass transit.

in a foreign country, but God had other plans, so I decided to be a missionary at home. If you want to meet and get know a lot of people, there is no better way to do that than working n mass transit). I met many needy folks who liked to sit up in the front of the bus and pour out their problems as they might to the guy serving drinks at the corner bar. I served no tangible drinks, but I did dispense the Water of Life, the ultimate solution. I also shared Christ with my fellow drivers, and for a while, was the Union Chaplain.

I remember distinctly the supernatural response the Lord gave me the day after I had asked Him about His divine whereabouts during Lydia's distress. While driving my bus, I wasn't thinking about the question but was focused on the traffic. As I was turning at the corner of Tustin Avenue to go west on Katella toward Disney-land, the message dropped into my head like a prompt card from Heaven. I was dumbfounded.

You might assume that my subconscious mind had mulled over the problem and, like a computer, finally downloaded the answer. We all have those moments, but this one was different. My Pente-costal friends would call this profound realization a "word of know-ledge" (1 Corinthians 12:8). In my life, such experiences of under-standing have happened only twice, so I can distinguish them from the more common variety of sudden insight. The Holy Spirit had unmistakably given me the answer for Lydia.[2]

As I sat across the table from Lydia that evening after the dishes had been cleared, I spoke up. "Lydia," I said with a bit of trepidation, "I have two things to tell you from the Lord as to where He was when you were going through all that pain." She looked at me thoughtfully, then sat back and said, "Okay, what are they?"

This time, I was the one who leaned forward and said, "First of all, He told me . . . that He was right where you had left Him." I paused, looking into her eyes. "Now He says, come back to Him in faith, love and the deep devotion you once had, and He'l be there." That was all I had to say. I wished her goodnight, got up and left.[3]

Shortly afterward, Lydia excused herself and slipped into her room. She then lay on her face before God, finally realizing that she was the one who had moved away from Him – not the other way around. Confessing her sin and need, she returned to the joyful presence of the One Who still loved her. She did what many who are still adrift need to do right now, come back home to Jesus – right to where they left Him. What about you?

So he got up and came to his father. But while he was still a long way off, his father saw him and felt compassion for him, and ran and embraced him and kissed him. And the son said to him, "Father, I have sinned against heaven and in your sight; I am no longer worthy to be called your son." But the father said to his slaves, "Quickly bring out the best robe and put it on him, and put a ring on his hand and sandals on his feet; and bring the fattened calf, kill it, and let us eat and celebrate; for this son of mine was dead and has come to life again; he was lost and has been found." And they began to celebrate.
Luke 15:20-24

My soul thirsts for God,
for the living God.
Psalm 42:2

3 Essentials of a deeper life
3.1 The deeper life – what is it?

Beneath the magnificent vaulted canopy of stars, I took a meditative stroll across the UW- La Crosse football field behind my dorm. It was 1959, my first year on campus. Although an air of stillness prevailed, the next evening; the stands would be filled with boisterous students, led on by noisy bands and energetic cheerleaders. The floodlit field would hold determinec, clashing players – but now it all lay in darkness, awash in silence as I walked and prayed.

Suddenly, like a gust of cold, chilling wind, there arose across my inner being, ghost-like memories of former feelings. They reminded me of lonely melancholy walks long past, before I knew God. While thankfully this momentary swell no sooner came than left, it jolted me to a stop mid-path. How different those old feelings were from the light-filled ones of my new life.

Like a child playing the old-fashioned statue-maker game, I stood frozen in my steps and struggled to compare these two incompatible sensations, past and present. What was the difference between them? True, many changes had taken place in my life. I was no longer the person I once was. Yet the contrasting feelings between how I used to feel as a non-Christian, compared to now, demanded a deeper explanation.

Then, like a giant wave crashing upon a beach, the answer came to me. That's it! I suddenly realized. Relieved, I again gazed into the heavens and whispered. "That's it! . . I'm no longer alone – not anymore."

Deeply moved, I breathed a sigh of relief. I had just discovered that I had been taking God's presence for granted as if I had always possessed it when I actually hadn't. Now, contrary to the fact that I stood solitary under only the light of distant, silent stars, the realization came afresh. The emptiness I had formally experienced had since been replaced by the very peaceful presence of God Himself and – I was simply no longer alone.

What is the deeper life?

A W Tozer argued that the word "mystical" succinctly describes the deep spiritual life that God has called us to enter. Because of our second birth, the sense of God's abiding presence which I just illus-trated has become His intention for every one of us to enjoy. That's why this book was almost titled, "The Deeper, Yet Normal, Christian Life." If we live in the supernatural dimension, as Jesus Christ intends, then we will have a spiritually richer, deeper life than many Christians in our Western culture are experiencing. On the other hand, we call this the "normal" Christian life because deep spirituality is exactly what Jesus called His followers to normally experience.

In this new life, a believer discovers the ability to do by the power of the Holy Spirit that which would otherwise be difficult or even impossible to perform. Instead of just memorizing Philippians 4:13 "I can do all things through Him who strengthens me." we find that we actually can forgive, pray, turn away from sin and calmly take even the harshest criticisms. Yet we do so not simply because it's our duty, but of having learned the meaning of Colossians 3:9-10, of having " . . laid aside the old self with its evil practices, and have put on the new self . . " The deeper life turns out to be one of inner confidence, of "joy unspeakable" and of grace and peace in the most difficult circumstances. In the chapter titled, "Overflowing Grace And Peace," I'll share how by God's grace I was able to forgive the teenage murderer of my sister and her unborn baby. Paul des-cribes this life best in Galatians 2:20: "I have been crucified with Christ; and it is no longer I who live, but Christ lives in me; and the life which I now live in the flesh I live by faith in the Son of God, who loved me and gave Himself up for me."

Jesus spoke of this deep communion with Himself in the Gospel of John, saying, "He who believes in Me, as the Scripture said, 'From his innermost being will flow rivers of living water.'"[1] This river represents the overflowing presence and power of the Holy

Spirit of God. Whatever spiritual closeness to God we may have thought belonged only to the first Christians and the psalmists is potentially ours. However, it is something that we have to go after by faith.

Godly mentor and friend, Theo McCully, the father of Ed McCully, one of the five missionaries martyred in Ecuador in 1956, often said, "Determination, not desire, determines destiny."[2]

Stuck between floors

Unfortunately, many Christians remain stuck near the level where they first entered the faith. Similar to a freight elevator caught between floors, we've been stuck there so long, we think that after our initial spiritual rise, our present immobility represents the normal life for God's children. The Apostle Paul reprimands us, that most have remained spiritual babies when we should be fully mature grown-ups.[3] Our walk is merely a crawl; or at best, we are tottering unsteadily.

To raise our spiritual condition we will find it helpful to start using the "lift buttons" God has given us and stop looking upon His commands as mere decorative plaques on the walls of our stationary elevators. There's a button marked "love," another "prayer," and still another marked "forgiveness of enemies."

We may tend to think of these and other Christian virtues as means of gaining extra credit. But God intends them to be part of our normal, everyday activity. When we learn how to start practicing these cardinal principles we'll be amazed to eventually hear the hum of the spiritual "lift" and see the doors springing open on a floor we didn't know even existed. It turns out that Christianity will produce as much spiritual reality in our lives as we will permit. Woven into the fabric

. . Many Christians remain stuck near the level where we first entered the faith. Similar to a freight elevator caught between floors . .

of our Christian faith is a dimension that transcends simply learning Biblical facts. Instead, the teachings of the Bible are to be learned so that we can know and experience their very Author.

Commenting on Acts 2:42 "They were continually devoting themselves to the apostles' teaching and to fellowship, to the breaking of bread and to prayer." A W Tozer said:

In the Book of Acts faith was for each believer a beginning, not an end; it was a journey, not a bed in which to lie while waiting for the day of our Lord's triumph. Believing was not a once-done act; it was more than an act, it was an attitude of heart and mind which inspired and enabled the believer to take up his cross and follow the Lamb whithersoever He went. A W Tozer "Faith Is a Journey, Not a Destination"[4]

The transfer

Though most of us know we've been spiritually reborn through faith in Christ, we have yet to digest this marvelous truth so that it changes us internally. If the new birth has taken place in your inner life, you have a brand-new "you" alongside an old "you." Picture the new person with hands folded in prayer and the old person, with arms folded in defiance. The Father wants us to transfer the core of our life to this new person.

To use another image, when an airport gets a new control tower, the air traffic controller moves from the old tower to the new one. Here the former tower represents the old, sinful human nature that you and I were born with. Even the best people have this inner twist of fallen character. The new tower represents the new, born-again you. God's Word says, "If anyone is in Christ, he is a new creature; the old things passed away; behold, new things have come."[5]

Sadly, most of us Christians in the Western world, even very religious and active ones, largely operate out of the old "control tower." Either we don't know how to make the transfer, or we don't even know there is such a thing as a "new" tower. Worse yet, some believers love their old tower – the self-centered not God-centered life – so much that they don't want to make the transfer.

But ultimately, those who work at moving from old to new find the shift deeply rewarding. They learn the secrets of becoming more Christ-like in character and practice. They start delighting in spiritual things. They'll not only find they've stopped hating people who have wronged them, but will also observe with sincere wonder that they've begun to love and forgive them. They will want to pinch themselves to see if they are still alive! Grace will become not just a word, but their actual experience. Back in 1992, how else could I walk around with a smile radiating from my face after receiving the news that I had cancer and had about three to five years to live?

Note however, that these godly qualities such as genuine love and forgiveness originate in the new person and are obtained only by transferring control from the old self. These spiritual virtues clearly aren't to be found innately in any of us. But the Bible tells us to imitate Christ and "put on the new self, which [is] in the likeness of God."[5] How to implement this elementa truth, will be discussed in the chapters to come and will be based solidly on the Word of God and not on personal theory.

Lounging at the base camp

As much as we claim to love the Bible, we often overlook the important obligation to obey it. God has intended His Word to lead us to the Spirit-filled life. But we have more often focused on simply acquiring knowledge. In so doing we rob His promises and instructions of their power. We are like would-be mountain climbers who, upon arriving at the base camp, see no further need to scale the steep crags. We are content to be sheltered in a tent (seated in church) at the edge of this spiritual "Mount Zion." We'd rather not labor (hungering for God in prayer) through the low-hanging clouds to greater heights and promised brightness.[6] We cannot see the sunlight from the base camp, so we think, *Who knows if that promised brightness of "joy unspeakable" really exists? Why bother if I'm not sure it's all that great?*

I had an experience like this in my college days when I spent several weeks at Bear Trap Ranch, high in the Colorado Rockies.

Some of my friends occasionally made late-evening climbs up the higher peaks to view Colorado Springs all lit up like a sparkling diamond -. I chose the less-risky path and stayed at the base camp. Come on! I thought. The view up there can't be that spectacular can it?

To this day, I regret not having taken the risk. Similarly, we will regret if we live and die at the mere base of this mystical, holy mountain of God's promises – God's Word in our laps but not in our hearts. Instead God intends for all who are reborn to be spiritual mountaineers with climbing sticks in hand.

As a young Christian, someone close to me observed my spiritual restlessness and asked me, "Kenny, what more are you searching for?" At the time, I couldn't give an answer. I only knew that because of the awesome, mind-bending God with Whom I had been linked, there must exist abundantly more. Possessing Biblical knowledge about His ways was by itself insufficient. Instead, I wanted to know Him much deeper based on His precious truths being taught.

Back in the mid-1960s, I smuggled some Bibles into then-communist East Germany. The pastor who received them asked, "You know that we believers here are more spiritual than those of you in the West, don't you?" "Yes, I'm sure you are." I replied softly. Though his question may have sounded prideful, I knew that he was right. The severe persecution they had suffered either drove them away from God or drove them into a deeper relationship with Him. Therefore, if we lack the pressures of persecution to drive us to this deeper life, that life may only come by a determined effort of faith to claim the higher ground through prayer and Christlike living.

The proper spiritual mix

What we may discover is that we have not been putting in all the ingredients necessary for the deep mix of true spirituality. Any cook can tell you that when you leave a vital ingredient out of a soup, you will be greatly embarrassed if your guests discover the omission before you do. In the same manner, ignoring key ingredients to becoming a spiritual man or woman can result in a bland and tasteless dish for the One we serve. In so doing, we may carelessly serve God a lesser life, one that lacks the deep, rich ingredients of patience, love, forgiveness, humility, persistent prayer and optimistic trust during trials. Little wonder then that the Scriptural "recipe book" should tell us, "But I say, wa k by the Spirit . . . [for] the fruit of the Spirit is love, joy, peace, patience, kindness, goodness, faithfulness, gentleness, [and] self-control."[7]

Lacking these qualities make us spiritually anemic compared to so many believers in the suffering church, who likely comprise the majority of Christ's bride around the world As one Chinese Christian said, "Don't pray that we will no longer be persecuted, but rather that we will stand firm and grow by it." Because you and I don't feel forced to commit ourselves to Christ-like behavior, we treat the vital ingredients as mere options. As a result, we choose the components we fancy. We have settled for a sp r tual drink that could easily be labeled "Christianity Lite," which will add spiritual weight to no one.

Price tag

What will it take to possess the deeper life? Some years ago a restless, troubled college girl deve cped a close relationship with a godly older woman. Looking into the elder's peaceful, shining countenance, the younger woman said, "I'd give everything to have what you have!" "Dearie," the older woman replied looking into her young friend's face, "that's exactly what it cost me."

Though the deeper life is as free as our salvation, the process might cost us dearly: doing by faith what we should do, even though at the moment we may not feel like doing it. Amy Carmichael put it this way: "Doing that which I would not choose, but which Thy love appoints." For us this says that we are to ignore our inner lack of enthusiasm. Instead we are to anticipate by faith that God's Spirit will eventually change us, leading us to revel in the unseen. That's transferring from the old control tower to the new. Even in suffering, if we have a positive expectation of final good from God, we're laying footings for spiritual growth. *Spiritual optimism is the key to the deeper Christian life!*

If we couple that with a deep belief in the absolute sovereignty of God in knowing, as we read in His Word, "that God causes all things to work together for good to those who love God."[8] our foundation will go down deep. God desires for us to take our hands off the steering wheel of our lives and let Him take control as we trust Him for positive spiritual outcomes. As we transfer our center of operations to the new control tower, a joyful fresh and invigorating life will gradually awaken within us.

Similar spiritual reality can be ours

One time on a Bible smuggling trip to Bulgaria, I was walking in downtown Sofia with a godly Bulgarian Christian who was to receive the Bibles. "The secret police called me in this past week," he said. I looked at him with a mixture of pity and admiration. He turned his gaze into the distance. "They said to me, 'Stanislaus![9] Vhenever vee fint Bibles in Bulgaria, vee know *you're behint it!*'" Then he heartily slapped me on my back and smiled broadly exclaiming, "Isn't dat vonderful?"

Our brother Stanislaus obviously possessed the deep joy and reality of faith through suffering. Isn't that we want for ourselves? We can start possessing that joy if we are willing to learn to make the spiritual transfer to leave our old, self-centered habits behind and "put on the new self." In so doing, we'll all eventually discover afresh as I eventually did that we're no longer alone anymore.

3 Essentials of a deeper life
3.2 I could've had a V8!

Nuts! Arrested again – just when I thought I was going to leave this Black Sea city of Samsun unnoticed. As I had been traveling throughout Turkey, I had collected phone books so that my friends and I could use the addresses to send people offers for a free Bible correspondence course. I had a problem, however, and I just couldn't help myself. It was like having a shoplifting addiction, only in reverse. Instead of taking things, I had a compulsion to give – in this case, Gospel tracts.[1] That morning, I had just given one to the Muslim proprietor of a cheap hotel as I was checking out.

I am not exaggerating when I say that I stayed in the cheapest of cheap hotels. These days, there are many travelers who won't even use the freshly changed linen and blankets for fear of con-tamination. In cut-rate hotels in the Middle East, the sheets were changed once a week whether they needed it or not – no matter who had slept in them the night before. (I used to carry an extra T-shirt to use for a pillow case.) In the Western world, a hotel owner might be arrested for running such a hovel. In Turkey, I was the one who was arrested – for giving out a single life-saving Gospel leaflet to a poor lost soul. This gesture was not illegal in Turkey in 1964, but the average Turk didn't know that, and often the police didn't know it, either. The innkeeper had called the cops.

The restaurant

When you are jailed in Turkey, you are usually responsible for provi-ding your own food yourself or through your relatives. You wouldn't want to serve a life sentence there if you were an orphan or short on relatives. Probably because the police were not apprehensive that I would escape, one of them took me to a nearby restaurant later that day so I could order my own evening meal.

The cafe, like most Turkish eateries, had a window display with some of the lip-smacking items on the menu. I lingered at the entrance. Before my eyes were mouth-watering shish-kabobs rotating on skewers. The aroma was tantalizing. I stood mesmerized, staring at the juices dripping from the revolving chunks of meat. Nearby were pieces of flaky, honey-sweetened baklava. With my appetite kindled by this exhibit, I empathized with Esau, who bartered away his birthright to satisfy similar cravings. Turks have an annual "Sugar Holiday" in which they lavish visiting friends with unlimited amounts of sweets and desserts. I always made sure to visit all my Turkish friends on that holiday.

I snapped out of my reverie, however, reminding myself that my desire to help the Turkish people was being underwritten by ordinary, self-sacrificing folks back home. So I never felt at liberty to indulge in extravagances - (Once after buying candy at a London sweet shop, I had been guilt-ridden for months).

Sitting down and quickly glancing over the menu, my eyes fell on the cheapest item, biber dolmasi – stuffed green pepper. I hated it. (I had found a dead fly in this dish once.) But I ordered the cheap meal anyway, adding a small glass of highly concentrated Turkish tea for a penny and a half and, as always, a slice of bread on the side, which, by this late hour, would be as dry as toast.

The Turkish policeman sat next to me, and we chatted as I ate. When I finished, having passed up his courteous recommendation that I indulge in a dessert (which would have cost more of my benefactors' hard-earned money!), I got up to pay my meager bill. As I arose, however, much to my consternation, the amicable policeman put up his hand like a traffic cop to stop me while nodding his head back, which in Turkey meant a definite

Finally, eying my empty tea glass on the counter, I miserably thought, "Why, I could've had a . . V8!"

"No!" Then he stepped up and paid my bill for me. I stood, jolted, mentally swaying as if on a small craft in a rough sea. Did I actually just order the cheapest meal on the menu, and the local police department was paying for it? I was numbed by the thought. You mean, I pondered, glancing at the display window, I could have had shish-kabobs dripping with gravy over rice garnished with vegetables?

I stared at the meat so temptingly displayed, still rotating on skewers, and inhaled its beckoning aroma. I pictured myself drawing up to the counter, but stopped short and stood in utter disbelief. You mean, I brooded on, I could have had deliriously sweet baklava for dessert? My eyes darted back to the other window display. Finally, eying my empty tea glass on the counter, I miserably thought, "Why, I could've had a . . V8!"

Nathan and David

Pathetic soul that I was, my predicament reminded me of an incident in King David's life when he, too, was "arrested," so to speak – by God's prophet Nathan, as recorded in Second Samuel.[2] The prophet sternly rebuked David for the wickedness of his adulterous liaison with Bathsheba and the murder of her husband, Uriah. Nathan listed everything God had done for David, including anointing him king and delivering him out of the hand of his chief enemy, Saul. Then the prophet brought to light some intriguing and hitherto unknown information. Speaking for the Lord, Nathan said, "And if that had been too little, I also would have given you much more!"[3] (Emphasis added.) David must have been staggered by the impact of those words, just as I had been shocked that evening in the Turkish restaurant when I discovered too late that I could have freely had much more.

The divine card game

God's revelation of what was potentially in His hand to further enrich David reminds me of a card game my folks used to play with another couple on Saturday nights.[4] Each couple played against the other pair, although no one player knew what was actually in any of the other three hands. However, by watching the cards the partner played, one could gather clues about what was in that person's hand and what to play to win points as a team. The trouble was that when each round was over, the losing couple would argue over each other's mistaken plays. With the cards now face-up, my dad would often chide my mom, saying something like, "You should have known that I had the queen of hearts when I played the jack." And mom would retort in disgust, "I thought you were getting rid of hearts and playing diamonds!" Likewise when Nathan confronted David, the game was over. God was laying down His cards face-up, revealing His hand. Surprisingly, He was potentially far more generous than David had ever thought. As richly blessed as he was, God was telling David that he could have had more – if only he had played his cards right and asked.

Truly we can never ask too much from God because we are actually never asking enough in the first place. God will never run out of rich blessings to give to His children. You can ask the wealthiest men in the world for billions; you can't ask them for trillions. But you will never bankrupt God's incalculable spiritual treasures. To be sure, there are things God does not want us to have. Yet there will always be a bountiful cache of gifts and grace that He earnestly desires for us to acquire from His more-than-willing hand. As Jesus Himself said, "Ask, and it will be given to you; seek, and you will find."[5] Our problem is that we do not take the time in extended prayer to press in on God, begging Him to open the windows of heaven. For this slackness, He scolds us through James, saying, "You do not have because you do not ask."[6]

More than can Be imagined

Incredible as it may seem, it has been said that in 1899, the Director of the U.S. Patent Office stated that everything that could be invented had by then been invented.[7] So many new patents had been put forth in the preceding years that nothing new could be imagined. Yet radio, television and computers had not been conceived, not to mention a multitude of other inventions still to come – some of which would even place men on the moon.

This supposed lack of foresight typifies the way most of us think spiritually and should make us appreciate all the more what Paul wrote to the Ephesians: "Now to Him who is able to do far more abundantly beyond all that we ask or think . . ."[8] We come to God as if He were a pushcart peddler with a meager supply, when He in fact has an unlimited department store of treasures to shop from. There is so much more to be asked for and possessed beyond the veil of our clouded envisioning. As John Newton, the author of "Amazing Grace," writes in the wonderfully worded second stanza of another hymn:

Thou art coming to a King,
Large petitions with thee bring;
For His grace and power are such,
None can ever ask too much.[9]

While all of us need to seek more, even outside the limits of our imagination, God wants to fill our cups to overflowing, and for that to happen, we need, by faith, to become spiritually proactive. Since we are approaching the God of the universe, there is always more for us to have of His endless treasures that we need to seriously seek with earnest, persevering prayer and even fasting. What do you want that will bring glory to Christ and great satisfaction to yourself? Special enduring graces or the spiritual gifts He promises? Asaph declared in a Psalm, "But as for me, the nearness of God is my good."[10] Do we think God runs a fixed carnival game with glittering prizes that only a few can win? The Holy Spirit is waiting for each of us to step up and claim His prizes and gifts. Still we must "play the game" God's way and understand that, as we read in James, "The effective prayer of a righteous man can accomplish much."[11] (Emphasis added.) Holy living, love for those who hate you, and purity of heart are qualities that count greatly with God.

Cards face-up

The late-nineteenth-century evangelist D. L. Moody said, "If there are any tears in heaven, it will be when God lays down the plan that He had for my life next to the way I lived it." With mixed feelings, I sometimes visualize that at the end of this life and the beginning of the everlasting one, God will finally lay down His cards face-up for me to see. It will become clear that He was playing as a partner with me in this game of life. I will then fully realize that I could have enjoyed a far greater abundance of His enabling graces and gifts, both the imaginable and the inconceivable. Searching my face, He'll look at me intently and lovingly ask, "Ken, why didn't you play your prayer card?" Nodding toward my laid-out hand, He'll add, "You should have known that I held the trump card to win our game."

And me? I'll feel as dumb as I did after I had ordered the cheapest meal on the menu – and the Turkish police paid for it. Instead of stuffed pepper, I could have had shish-kabobs dripping with gravy over rice garnished with vegetables. I could have had seductively sweet baklava for dessert (pass the insulin, please)! Why, I could've even had a . . V8![12]

And we'll all feel dumber yet when Christ shows us all the things He held in His nail-pierced hands to freely give us and then adds: "And if that were not enough – I would have given you more."

3 Essentials of a deeper life
3.3 Out of luck, into grace

"The Lord has established His throne in the heavens,
and His sovereignty rules over all."
Psalm 103:19

Pow! A rear dual tire blew and shook the cross-country Turkish bus
– and me. Like a giant wounded beast, it heaved and swerved,
but kept on charging. The driver did not even slow. Early evening
was approaching and changing a tire at dusk meant unpleasant
work. Let the people in the garage do it, he likely thought. We'll be
there in an hour or so. Tired from the long trip, he just wanted to
get home to his wife's hot dinner, put his feet up and relax. So he
simply continued to press toward Izmir.

Bit by bit, however, the blown tire began to unravel, and
increasingly loud banging emerged from inside the wheel well
beneath my seat. The tire next to it was probably heating up and
would soon burst into flames or blow like its partner, sending us
into an inescapable, fiery crash. I
started to pray.

Middle Eastern people believe
in kismet, which means that your
fate is irrevocably written on your
forehead and can't be changed.
This belief may have motivated
the fierce Turkish fighters I met in
Korea in the 1950s just after the
war there. They likely concluded
that if their fate was death on the
battlefield, nothing could change
the outcome, so they gave no

Early evening was approaching and
changing a tire at dusk meant unpleasant
work. Let the people in the garage do it,
he likely thought.

thought to reckless actions in combat. I saw these warriors drive their Jeeps and trucks with just this devil-may-care attitude. In areas where Turkish troops were stationed, I would often encounter a vehicle in a ditch with a grinning Turk sitting on top of it. If I had stopped to ask what happened, he might have replied with a smile, "Kismet!" Years later in Turkey, I once saw two out-of-town buses that had collided head-on, telescoped together and burned. One driver had tried to pass a slower vehicle on the road when he met the other bus coming at him out of the fog. Kismet!

As my bus continued into the sunset toward Izmir the banging inside the wheel well grew intolerably louder, and even my fellow Turkish passengers murmured in agitation at the driver's refusal to stop. Finally, over the din of the disintegrating tire, they cried, "Durma! Durma!" (Stop! Stop!) They apparently concluded that the kismet written across the bus driver's forehead was not necessarily written on theirs. Hearing the loud chorus of protests, the driver reluctantly pulled over. In the glow of flashlights held by the relieved travelers, he got down in the dirt and replaced the shredded tire.

The Sovereignty of God is not like Kismet

Thankfully, kismet is not written on the forehead of a child of God. The outcomes of our lives are written – if anywhere – on the hands of God, through which all things must pass. Nothing escapes His notice or potential control, and if we trust Him with our lives, the results will always be positive for us—either here on earth or, at last, in heaven. The Bible implores us to surrender to the sovereign, loving care of God. The Apostle Paul wrote, "I urge you, brethren . . . to present your bodies a living and holy sacrifice, acceptable to God . . . "[1] That includes our will and our intellect as well.

Amazingly, the God of the universe has given us free will to choose whether or not we want to believe the Gospel and ultimately go to heaven. Likewise, He has given us free will to choose whether we want a measure of heaven to come down into our daily lives while on earth. We respond to His call to surrender not simply by saying "yes" or "no," but by granting or withholding trust in Him for the day-to-day events that take place in our lives. If we blame others, or even God, for our calamities or give in to depression or bitterness because of our circumstances, we are not yet surrendered to His personal sovereignty over us. I have found that those who are resting in God's control in some measure radiate joy and peace. We are privileged to be so positive because we can claim this key promise in the New Testament: "We know that God causes all things to work together for good to those who love God, to those who are called according to His purpose."[2]

I heard Joy Ridderhof, founder of Gospel Recordings, express this attitude of optimistic trust: "When we rejoice in adverse circumstances, we are taking the situation out of Satan's hands and placing it into God's." Just as believing in the cross of Christ is the foundation of our salvation, so is letting God take responsibility for the outcome of our lives, while, at the same time, anticipating ultimate good, is the foundation of successful Christian living. This principle forms the basis of the following chapters.

Peace in a jail cell

The Bible tells us that, sooner or later, God will bring good from everything that comes our way if we count on Him and are willing to wait. In 1964, I was arrested for giving out a single Gospel tract in Samsun, Turkey. Following my exoneration at a brief court trial, I was re-arrested and escorted by the police a long distance to Istanbul and its large metropolitan jail. That night, I lay down with only a newspaper separating me from the filthy plank of the jail bed. No one knew my whereabouts, and because my arrest was illegal, I wondered if I would ever be able to contact my friends and family again. But when the lights were turned out, it suddenly became evident that God was in that cell. His perfect peace rolled over me like a placid tide sweeping a moonlit beach. I drifted easily off into a tranquil sleep. The consciousness of God's presence was more than worth the inconvenience of arrest and incarceration in a grimy jail cell. I was released in the morning.

As demonstrated by many of the difficult events in my life, even if God does not always change the circumstances, experiencing His undergirding grace is always more than sufficient.

Our sufferings are due to the Fall

Because of Adam and Eve's sin in disobeying God, the world has been subject to suffering, tragedy and death. In choosing to obey Satan rather than God, Adam unwittingly caused the control of mankind to shift to the domination of evil. In John 14:30, Jesus calls Satan "the ruler of the world." John states in his first letter, "We know . . that the whole world lies in the power of the evil one."[3]

As a result, even when we become God's children, our lives are still subject to our own mistakes as well as to the seemingly random, senseless events of the fallen world where we live. After all, when we're born again, we do not receive a trouble-free life of health, wealth and constant happy circumstances. But as children of God, all that touches us must first pass under God's scrutiny before it can enter our lives. While He does not always prevent us from suffering, He may use adversity to burn away our sinful dross and refine us. Yet the results are always worth it. Even in the worst situations, if we trust God and rest in His personal love, good will ultimately come. That's His promise to us. Before there was recycling, there was God Who could produce beauty out of garbage. We read of His tender care in Jeremiah: "'For I know the plans that I have for you,' declares the Lord, 'plans for welfare and not for calamity to give you a future and a hope.'"[4]

A classic example of trusting God's control is found in the life of Joseph, who lived in and around Egypt about 4,000 years ago. The story, which I have summarized in my own words below, covers 14 chapters in the Book of Genesis (37-50) and spans about 14 years. This abridged account focuses on the power of God's sovereign design to bring good out of evil.

From riches to rags to riches

Many years ago, there was a large family of 12 young men who lived in the Middle Eastern land of Canaan. Their father, Jacob, doted on his young son, Joseph, loving him above all the others. To show his favoritism, Jacob gave Joseph a special, colorful coat. Joseph should have known better than to parade his fancy clothes in front of his brothers and boast about his night-time dreams of prosperity and family leadership. (Teens will be teens, even four thousand years ago.) As a result, when his jealous brothers found Joseph alone a good distance from home, they decided to kill him. Fortunately, they changed their minds and sold him to slave traders bound for Egypt – if you think becoming a slave is better than dying.

Although cast off and forgotten by his brothers, young Joseph was not forgotten by God. He found favor with the Egyptian official who had bought him and appointed him head over all his property and possessions. Unfortunately, being a handsome young man, he found too much favor with his master's wife, who attempted to seduce him. A principled young man, Joseph resisted her evil advances. But as spurned lovers often do, she got upset and lied - to her husband, that Joseph had tried to seduce her.

Finding favor as a prisoner

Joseph, far from home, was now thrown into prison. But God had a plan for him, and Joseph again found favor, this time with the head jailor, and was entrusted with the care of the other prisoners. Sometime later, Pharaoh had a disturbing dream that no one could interpret until God revealed the meaning to Joseph, who informed Pharaoh that a great famine would afflict Egypt and the surrounding lands. Joseph also suggested a way that Pharaoh could prepare for the coming shortage and make a great deal of money in the process. As a reward, the former prisoner was made second in command to Pharaoh himself. Joseph built storehouses so that when the famine arrived, Egypt was stocked with more than enough food.

Because the famine reached Canaan, Jacob, who thought his beloved Joseph was dead, sent the other sons to Egypt to buy food. Joseph eventually revealed himself to the astonished and fearful brothers who had almost killed him. Now it was his chance to get back at them, and who wouldn't have wanted to even the score with those troublemakers? But Joseph didn't make use of his position to exact revenge. Instead, as they trembled before him, he told them not to fear and said, "It was not you who sent me here, but God."[5]

Imagine! For all the misery he went through, he could have sent them to the rack and made them a few inches taller! But Joseph had matured. He didn't blame his father for imprudent favoritism. Joseph likely regretted his adolescent arrogance toward his brothers, but he got over it. And impressively, despite his suffering, he didn't even blame his brothers. Although pointing out that they had done wrong, he concluded by saying, "As for you, you meant evil against me, but God meant it for good in order to bring about this present result, to preserve many people alive."[6]

. . Joseph, who was sold as a slave. They afflicted his feet with fetters, He himself was laid in irons; until the time that His word came to pass, The word of the Lord tested him. Psalm 105:17-19

Making it all practical

So Joseph avoided bitterness and revenge – although he did play a cat-and-mouse game with his brothers before he revealed his identity. Scripture does not depict Joseph as a plastic-figure-on-the-car-dashboard type of saint. He is shown as a sympathetic person having a bit of fun at his rascally brothers' expense, but not intending to do them great harm. In the end, he was more than kind and forgiving, no doubt experiencing great contentment as a channel for God's blessing. The teaching of God's personal, sovereign care becomes very practical here. Accepting whatever comes our way as His permitted plan for each day will bring us peace.

I've lost a loved one through violence, so at such times we may be tempted to say, "Well, if everything comes through the hands of God, then God took the life of my loved one." But in His sovereign control, He may permit death to occur for our good – and even for the good of those taken. Understandably, when the tragedy involves those we cherish, we may be tempted to hate God for permitting accidents and terrible crimes. But we must keep in mind that horrible deeds are committed not by God, but by a world degraded by Satan. If God intended to prevent all tragedy, He would have shut down the world a long time ago, but then you and I would never have had the privilege of knowing Him. Instead, because of our relationship with Him, we are entitled to do what the lost world cannot do: anticipate that good will eventually arise out of evil. However, we must not expect to be able to predict positive results in advance. In our dark hour of grief, we can seldom imagine any shining outcome.

Years ago, a godly woman I knew told a story that illustrates the dangers of trying to micromanage God's response. A certain family had a young boy who became seriously ill. Naturally, the family pleaded desperately with God to spare his life. While there was nothing wrong with that desire, instead of asking for God's will to be done, their prayers bordered on demands and threats. God finally granted their request, but as the boy grew up, he was not an easy person to live with. So while it is important to pray in the midst of difficulties, we must seek to trust that no matter what happens in life, God sees the whole picture and knows what is best for all concerned. This approach does not mean we should stoically accept everything, saying, "What will be will be." That's kismet. Instead, we are to trust that the loving hand of God will intervene on our behalf in a fallen world while we humbly and patiently wait for a positive outcome. The Apostle Peter wrote, "Therefore let those who suffer according to the will of God commit their souls to *Him* in doing good, as to a faithful Creator."[7]

God's purpose

As we've seen in Romans 8:28, God intends to make good out of all things in the lives of "those who are called according to His purpose." The verse that follows, verse 28, tells us that purpose: "For those whom He foreknew, He also predestined to become con- formed to the image of His Son."[8] God's plan is for us to become like Christ. While the process is not always comfortable, there can be no greater comfort than to be like Him. Because we will share in the perfect love, peace and joy of Jesus forever when we become like Him, it seems sensible that we should start letting His life be lived in us right now, realizing that this is God's purpose for us.

Optimistic faith in God's sovereignty

I have found that even the most horrible events in my life, such as my battle with cancer and the murder of my sister and her unborn child, have eventually brought about good that I would not want to give up. The Word of God tells us, "Rejoice always,"[9] and adds, "In everything give thanks; for this is God's will for you in Christ Jesus."[10] While we may not be able to give thanks for everything, we are told to give thanks in everything. That's why we can say with Joseph regarding the trials in our lives, "God meant it for good." For the Christian who is abiding in the love of God and His sovereign care, there is no such thing as disappointment with God, only disappointment with ourselves when we fail to trust Him.

Elisabeth Elliot, wife of martyred missionary Jim Elliot, said, "The sooner we subject ourselves to the Lord of Life and to those He puts over us, the sooner we will find our freedom and joy." As we can see, our destinies are neither written on our foreheads, as in kismet, nor controlled by anyone but God alone if we will surrender all our circumstances to Him. While we ourselves or others may have caused our problems, God directs the outcome. Thankfully, we're truly out of luck and into grace. Our responsibility is to trust Him to work everything for good by His loving, sovereign hand, as He did in Joseph's life. As Peter says, "Therefore humble yourselves under the mighty hand of God, that He may exalt you at the proper time, casting all your anxiety on Him, because He cares for you."[11]

3 Essentials of a deeper life
3.4 No more Mr Nice Guy

A look at the believer's crucified and risen life

Many Middle Eastern taxis, like buses, follow a predetermined route and are shared by perfect strangers who ride together. Passengers can board or get off anywhere along the way, paying only for their part of the trip. While these convenient conveyances travel primarily within cities, some offer town-to-town service. In Turkey, such a taxi is called a *dolmush*. Most are standard automobiles, although some are quite upscale. (The only time I ever rode in a Mercedes was during a shared taxi trip across a desert in Syria. In spite of the uneven roadbed, I felt like I was riding on a cloud.).

While smaller capacity makes the price a bit more expensive than a bus fare, the *dolmush* is still the transport of choice. You're guaranteed a seat, at least when you can find a taxi that isn't full, and the ride is fast – sometimes too fast. (Check your life insurance policy for exclusions that probably also include hang gliding and bungee jumping.) By taking a *dolmush* in rural Turkey, you can avoid intercity buses carrying sick cows and crates of squawking chickens headed for the market and dinner table.[1] So a *dolmush* is the way to go if available, especially when you're in a hurry.

Consequently, a friend of mine, we'll call Jack, who was on a trip in eastern Turkey, was pleased to find that he didn't have to take the bus because he was on a *dolmush* route.[2] As he flagged down a taxi, he observed that while the front seat was full, there were only two passengers in the back, and the man who would end up in the middle appeared to be dozing. Jack happily hopped in.

Anyone who has traveled outside his or her native country encounters cultural differences. When the man in the middle leaned heavily on Jack's shoulder, he simply tried to ignore it as just another Turkish habit, like male friends holding hands. Occasionally, the sleeper would lean so far forward that his head would hit the back of the front seat. Yet he still didn't wake up, and Jack concluded that the man must be drunk or on drugs. Even more disconcerting, he almost ended up in Jack's lap. The passenger seated on the other side promptly jerked his troublesome companion back, while Jack helped with a not-too-gentle shove. At that point, having finally had enough, my friend turned to express polite, but firm, disapproval. Only then did he realize that the man who was leaning and falling all over him was not asleep. He was dead.

In those days, if a relative died in a hospital in rural Turkey, the family's challenge was to quickly transport the deceased home for a proper Islamic burial before the setting of the sun. Draping the body over the back of a slow-moving donkey simply would not do. In this case, the fastest way for the next of kin to convey the body was to pay the dead man's fare in a *dolmush* for a final trip into the sunset.

Jack frantically jabbed the driver's shoulder and shouted above the Turkish music blaring on the radio, "Pardon, efendim! (Excuse me, sir!) I would like to get off here!" The driver looked around at the open farmland with no village in sight, turned down the radio and twisted to face the backseat. Still speeding, with one hand on the wheel, he asked Jack in astonishment, "*Burada mi!?* (Right here!?)" "*Evet, efendim, burada!* (Yes, sir, right here!)" Jack answered. When the car stopped, my friend got out, quickly paid his fare for the shared hearse – I mean *dolmush* – and waited for another taxi. This time, Jack would make sure none of its occupants were . . sleeping.

Body and spirit

Strange as it may seem, something inside every human being is also as dead as the man in the shared taxi. Our bodies enable us to live in the material world and interact with other people who are alive. Our spirits were created to allow us to interact with God. Jesus said, "God is spirit, and those who worship Him must worship in spirit and truth."[3]

The problem is that Adam's sin brought death not only physically but also spiritually, severing the original connection between God and Man. We are told in Scripture, "Through one man sin entered into the world . . and so death spread to all men."[4] From then on, all humans would be born with their two-way sensory channel to God offline and down. Only occasionally, at His own choosing, did God waken certain individuals to seek Him. In Old Testament times, people experienced deep spiritual stirrings only because God reached out first and made their spirits alive to Him. The Word is clear concerning our alienation from God:

There is no one who does good.
The Lord has looked down from heaven upon the sons of men
To see if there are any who understand,
Who seek after God.
They have all turned aside, together they have become
    corrupt;
There is no one who does good, not even one.[5]

This spiritual disconnect left us like an airplane without wings. We were meant to soar but instead can only taxi the runways of life. Many feel that something is wrong and lacking but have no idea what it is. Just as the man in the cab was dead to communication with other people, so at birth we are dead to spiritual communion with God.

New birth

That's where the importance of the second birth becomes clear. Jesus told a very religious man in John 3:7, "Do not be amazed that I said to you, 'You must be born again." Paul wrote, "When you were dead . . . He made you alive together with Him . . ."[6] The Bible is not talking about our physical bodies but is referring to the wonderful event that our disconnected dead spirits have been livened again, and the connection restored when we first believed. We may or may not have noticed it when it happened because it's a mystical experience.[7] God meant for us to be "spiritual" in our thinking and acting – not living by the impulses of our fleshly minds and feelings, but under the influence of the Holy Spirit. We are told, "Walk by the Spirit, and you will not carry out the desire of the flesh."[8] Mere religion is like decaffeinated coffee. You may enjoy it, and it may even be good for you, but it won't wake you up. Compared to religion, the second birth is the real stuff.

As born-again people, we now have a new nature as sinless as Christ. If we could live in that new person 24/7, we would never sin. But life is like a football game. We receive the kick, catch the ball and run for a touchdown. Regrettably, many determined players on the other team keep getting in our way, trying to pull us down. Sometimes we're tackled by our own bad habits and old desires, at other times by the deceit of the enemy of our souls. But no one gets a clear run from one end of the field to the other. We all get roughed up, or even dragged through the mud, at least a few times - (I know what you're thinking: someone who has a last-minute conversion, like the thief on the cross, may live a sinless life for the final moments. However, that person won't have any eternal rewards waiting on the other side.).

The Christian life is a tough ball game, but God wants us to win. While we may never succeed at being sinless, hopefully we will sin less and less. The key to spiritual victory is to live in the confidence of the Bible's declaration that "if anyone is in Christ, *he is* a new creature."[9]

Life is like a football game . . . many determined players on the other team keep getting in our way, trying to pull us down.

Crucified life

Paul exhorts us, as born-again believers: "Consider yourselves to be dead to sin, but alive to God in Christ Jesus."[10] This is based on the facts explained in Romans 6, that when Christ died on the cross, we died with Him. And when Christ rose from the dead, we did also. This is what the symbol of baptism is all about. So when Paul tells us to consider ourselves dead, that's good advice, of course, but it doesn't really tell us in practical terms how to apply our union with the death and resurrection of Christ. In Galatians 2:20, Paul gives us more specific teaching for living that life:

I have been crucified with Christ; and it is no longer I who live, but Christ lives in me; and the *life* which I now live in the flesh I live by faith in the Son of God, who loved me and gave Himself up for me.

According to Paul, we are to visualize our old self as dead: "I have been crucified with Christ." But that step is not enough. Next we are to realize that Christ Himself lives within us: "it is no longer I who live, but Christ lives in me." Finally, we are to live a godly life through our faith in Him: "the *life* which I now live in the flesh I live by faith in the Son of God." Memorizing that verse and reviewing it often will pay dividends in spiritual maturity.

During World War II, English civilians were trained to be airplane spotters. They carried cards showing the shapes of Allied and Axis planes and had been instructed to phone in an alert if an enemy aircraft flew overhead. Similarly, Paul gave the Galatians contrasting lists for spotting carnal and Christ-like conduct.

Now the deeds of the flesh are evident, which are: immorality, impurity, sensuality, idolatry, sorcery, enmities, strife, jealousy, outbursts of anger, disputes, dissensions, factions, envying, drunkenness, carousing, and things like these . . . But the fruit of the Spirit is love, joy, peace, patience, kindness, goodness, faithfulness, gentleness, self-control; against such things there is no law. Now those who belong to Christ Jesus have crucified the flesh with its passions and desires.[11]

The whole New Testament abounds with examples both of fleshly and of spiritual behavior.

No more Mr. Nice Guy

There came a point in my life when I had to say, "No more Mr. Nice Guy." I had been a fine example of patience, but my apparent goodness was achieved by my own effort with little of God's power. At long last, circumstances tapped out all there was of my natural virtue. If I was going to make it in the world, in my marriage, in my job and through all the other pressures of life, I had to change from Mr. Nice Guy to *Mr. New Guy*. That New Guy in me is Christ. We are to simply relax and let Christ live His life through us. Whatever is Christ-like, let it out, and whatever is not, swat it like a bug; crucify it. Consider yourselves dead to that behavior, and focus on His life within you. Mr. Nice was running on empty, and Mr. New is running on an endless supply of grace. Not a bad trade-off.

But beware. When the enemy sees that he has failed to prevent us from going to the cross to "die in Christ," - he tries to get us off the cross to walk in the flesh. Loud criticism may come against us as we seek to live this crucified yet risen life. Like Jesus when He was on the cross, we will be strongly challenged to step down and set a few people straight. The enemy longs for such angry responses. People will appear to be trying to get us off the cross by tempting us to live again in the old nature instead of through Christ. However, Satan is the real instigator of their attacks. Stay put and let them rail on. To take a line from the cinema, "live and let die" as you learn to live and walk in "newness of life" according to Romans 6:4, and die to the old life of sin.

Imagine Jack turning to the supposedly slumbering man in the taxi and saying, "Look, you stupid jerk, watch what you're doing!" Would the man have retorted with an equally angry reply? No, because he was dead. If Jack had waved money in front of his seat-mate's face and said, "Here's a hundred bucks. Go grab another *dolmush*," would this man, in his seeming stupor, have accepted the offer? No, because he was – you know what.

If someone had shown him pictures of scantily clad dancing girls, would he have bought them? You get the idea. Nothing could have gotten the dead man's attention because he was now in a completely different world. So it is with us as we learn to abide in Christ's death and resurrection. We read that God "raised us up with Him, and seated us with Him in the heavenly places in Christ Jesus."[12] This verse does not suggest that we can't be tempted, but rather that, as we seek to walk in newness of life, we are to "put on the Lord Jesus Christ, and make no provision for the flesh."[13] This experience is our privilege as believers.

The Pastor

For example, I know a pastor who had faithfully served in a small church for years. One Wednesday night, he arrived expecting to lead a Bible study as usual. Instead, the deacon board read him a list of grievances and gave him two weeks' notice. True, every church should have the right to change pastors, but the deacons were letting him go without any thought of severance pay to provide for him and his wife while he looked for a new pulpit. Moreover, only one small item among the complaints had any validity, and that problem could easily have been corrected.

The pastor could have called for a church vote because most in the congregation supported him. Yet a winning vote for the pastor would have been a hollow victory, causing the church to split. So, while trying to negotiate better terms, he agreed to leave quietly for the sake of this beloved church for which he had labored. Nonetheless, close to a third of the attendees, (counting their children), later left the congregation because the adults suspected their pastor had been railroaded.

But a wonderful thing happened that evening as he drove home: he felt no bitterness or animosity toward those who wanted to quickly remove him without any recompense. He knew that he and his wife were in the care of a sovereign God. The pastor later said he had actually pinched himself to make sure he was still alive, hardly believing he could feel only compassion for those who had so inconsiderately dismissed him. Better yet, after having spent many years diligently seeking to live the crucified and resurrected life, he felt the reality of the Spirit-filled existence as never before. Until that night, the pastor did rightly practice being Christ-like. Now it was easier. His attitude no longer came from faithful obedience but now from deep conviction of Christ's Spirit who was living and confirming it within him. That kind of experience is available to every one of us.

As Augustine said, "It's Not Me!"

The ability to live as a new person in Christ is illustrated by a story that has been passed down about Augustine, a man of God in the early church. After becoming a Christian, Augustine was revisiting his home in the ancient Egyptian city of Alexandria and happened to be walking along a street near one of his old haunts. He was surprised by a former girlfriend who called out to him, "Augustine – Augustine – it is I!" As he continued walking away, Augustine called back, "Yes, but it is no longer I!"

The coming chapters in this book will discuss how to walk in the Spirit in a practical way. As we have seen, we have a sinless new nature, as a result of our second birth and our spirit has been reconnected with God's Spirit. Yet we still have our original sinful nature that competes for our attention. Paul wrote: "Walk by the Spirit, and you will not carry out the desire of the flesh. For the flesh sets its desire against the Spirit, and the Spirit against the flesh; for these are in opposition to one another."[14] To deal with that conflict, we need to be like the man in the Turkish taxi – dead to this world. But in our case, we can also declare, "Nevertheless I live; yet not I, but Christ liveth in me: and the life which I now live in the flesh I live by the faith of the Son of God, who loved me, and gave himself for me."[15] Like Augustine, we can say, "It is no longer I."

3 Essentials of a deeper life
3.5 Love is number one

In Germany during World War II, a family whose apartment had been bombed moved next door to a Christian family. The believers helped their new neighbors by inviting them to dinner, giving them towels and bedding and making other sacrifices for them. As it happened, the man they helped was a high Nazi official. A short time later, a Christian woman who lived in their city was called in for questioning because she refused to join the Nazi party. Her neighbors hated her for this stand, and it seemed likely that she would go to prison. But when the Nazi official who had been helped so much found out she went to the same church as the family that had aided him, he freed her. He even made sure she got her much-delayed allotment checks. You may never know until eternity the ripple that the pebble of your love makes when dropped into the pond of humanity.[1]

Love and care for others should abound in our lives. In fact, a Christian should be in the habit of doing random acts of kindness. When we see things lying on the floor at a department store, we could stop to pick them up. I can't picture Jesus walking by and ignoring disorder. This practice also applies in our homes. Remember, "love is kind."[2] Acts of kindness, patience, forgiveness and extra assistance should pervade our lives. Even if you're a guy and think you're tough or macho, love should be at the core of your Christian character.

One day, when I opened a can of pork and beans that I had bought, I had to strain my eyes to find the meat. The pork consisted of two small pieces of fat that together were as small as the nail on my pinky. On the can's label, "pork" appeared near the bottom of the ingredients list, alongside other trace additives. When God checks the ingredients list of our lives, how far down does He have to look before He finds "love"? Would it be listed near the end?

Our main ingredient

The New Testament stresses that love should be the first ingredient in the lives of Christians. The Bible's "love chapter" confirms that "faith, hope, love, abide these three; but the greatest of these is love."[3]

Faith in Christ is the only ingredient that God seeks in those who have not yet believed. But once we have become followers of the Lamb, love should be our number one characteristic, followed by hope—our sure expectation of eternal life in Heaven—along with faith. We may think we're doing a great deal for God. We may be teaching Sunday school, tithing, preaching and evangelizing, but if we are not showing compassion, forgiveness and kindness, God's Word asserts that we are nothing. Hope and faith are extremely important; yet love *must* be number one.

Our love should be like His love

The Savior practiced what He preached, and He wants us to practice what He preached as well, by loving others, whether they are deserving or not. We are instructed to "be imitators of God, as beloved children; and walk in love, just as Christ also loved you and gave Himself up for us, an offering and a sacrifice to God as a fragrant aroma."[4] Love does not draw a line in the sand or set limits: "Love never fails."[5] It usually costs something to give love, but this investment pays back more than any other.

As long as our lives are dominated by our fallen nature, we cannot love as God wants us to. Through the second birth, He makes each believer a new person. When Jesus spoke about patches for wineskins, He supplied a metaphor for our new nature:

No one sews a patch of unshrunk cloth on an old garment; otherwise the patch pulls away from it, the new from the old, and a worse tear results. No one puts new wine into old wineskins; otherwise the wine will burst the skins, and the wine is lost and the skins as well; but one puts new wine into fresh wineskins.[6]

Rather than patching up the old, sinful "wineskin" we were born with, God has given us a new nature that connects us with Him. In addition, He has filled us with the "new wine" of the Holy Spirit. When the Holy Spirit was poured out at Pentecost, the disciples were so ecstatic that others taunted, "They are full of new wine."[7] Most Christians who lack love are still living in the old wineskins of the fallen nature. We are admonished: "Lay aside the old self, which is being corrupted in accordance with the lusts of deceit, and . . be renewed in the spirit of your mind, and put on the new self, which in the likeness of God has been created in righteousness and holiness of the truth."[8]

Each day as we practice stepping into the new person and ignoring the loveless impulses of the old one, our walk with Christ will eventually become second nature. We will be able to be kind and compassionate, gentle and patient, to a degree we previously thought impossible.

Even if your spouse is arrogant or moody, or simply uses you to satisfy needs selfishly – food, sex or a paycheck – we ought to model the patient love of Christ. Naturally, we should seek counseling because we might be partly at fault. Regardless, we are to express love and compassion. In doing so, we will find that we are starting to inhabit the God-given, born-again life.

As those who have been chosen of God, holy and beloved, put on a heart of compassion, kindness, humility, gentleness and patience; bearing with one another, and forgiving each other, whoever has a complaint against anyone; just as the Lord forgave you, so also should you. Beyond all these things put on love.[9]

Some Christians will excuse themselves from the responsibility of being charitable by saying, "I can't help having a temper because of the Irish (or whatever) in me." Wouldn't it be better for them to say, "I can't help but love others because of the Jesus in me"? As we have seen, in our old selves, we are not capable of displaying God's love. But as we learn to turn our backs on our fallen nature and to practice the distinguishing virtues of our new nature, we will be able to say, "It is no longer I who live, but Christ lives in me."[10] That will happen if, in each moment of temptation, we make a practice of choosing to walk in the Spirit instead of in our fallen flesh.

The practical side of love

As we enter this deeper life of love, we will be amazed to find that caring for others becomes almost effortless, even if the object of our love hates us. To be honest, most of us would admit that it's not "natural" to show kindness to those who don't care for us. However, God promises, "Walk by the Spirit, and you will not carry out the desire of the flesh."[11] The Bible does not berate us into loving but urges us joyfully to "put on love" like a coat. In doing so, we'll find that we are putting on Christ.

Most of us agree that we should love others – that is, we agree until someone mistreats us. Then we're faced not only with the struggle to love but also with the temptation to hate and retaliate. I knew a young man who smiled and nodded enthusiastically while I spoke to him about the love of God. However, one day when a customer was doing something the young man didn't like, he grew angry and threw the offender off the premises. Besides losing his cool, he lost his job. God expects us to demonstrate love rather than simply nod in agreement.

Love pleases the Father

No one should doubt that God is pleased with us when we learn to walk in love. If we want to be close to Him, we should follow that path before anything else. The Bible informs us that "God is love, and the one who abides in love abides in God, and God abides in him."[12] Jesus said, "Love your enemies, do good to those who hate you, bless those who curse you, pray for those who mistreat you."[13] We should love with no assurance that the object of our kindness will ever be grateful. In the end – and probably long before "the end" – God will reward us.

We have another reason to practice all aspects of love. God's measure of our love for Him is not the enthusiasm with which we sing hymns or whether we lift our hands in praise, but rather the degree to which we love the difficult ones in our lives. According to 1 John 4:20, "If someone says, 'I love God,' and hates his brother, he is a liar." This biblical principle is often ignored. When we sing hymns of love to Jesus, He consults the dictionaries of our hearts to find out what "love" means to us. He doesn't just take our words at face value. He taught: "If you are presenting your offering at the altar, and there remember that your brother has something against you, leave your offering there before the altar and go; first be reconciled to your brother, and then come and present your offering."[14]

We should all take time the night before attending church to examine our hearts. In some cases, our brother might not want reconciliation. In such situations, after seeking harmony but failing to obtain it, we should remain open to resolution while treating our adversaries with love. A key text on this topic counsels, "If possible, so far as it depends on you, be at peace with all men."[15] Jesus will know from these efforts that we mean our loving worship is "in spirit *and* in truth."[16] (Emphasis added.)

Feelings follow faith

To love someone does not necessarily mean to have warm, fuzzy feelings toward that person, but to humbly perform the actions love requires. This approach is especially important when interacting with those close to us. We are to love them for what they once were, for what they can be and for what they will be by God's grace. What they are now must not taint the picture. You will find that showing love often comes before feeling love. You may need to step forward by faith and demonstrate loving-kindness to the unlovable or to someone for whom you have no special affection. Our feelings of love usually catch up with our actions. You might call that "faith working through love."[17]

We are commanded to love others. Even though Will Rogers reportedly said, "I never met a man I didn't like," I don't think we are always expected to like everyone we are called to love. Some people in our lives are difficult to like or to keep as close friends.

Nonetheless, we should always treat them with kindness. Did Jesus like the Pharisees when He said, "You serpents, you brood of vipers, how will you escape the sentence of hell?"[18] I don't think so; they were keeping others out of the Kingdom of God. Along with the Pharisees, we are an unlikeable lot; yet according to Romans 5:8, "God demonstrates His own love toward us, in that while we were yet sinners, Christ died for us." God bypassed "not like" and went straight to "much loved." We are told to "go and do the same."[19] Don't feel guilty if you don't like someone for whatever reason and definitely don't hurt them by telling them about those feelings. Simply love all people, like 'em or not.

Love in action

I've often had fun responding with humor or mellowness to those who have tried to make me angry. In college, Pete, a football standout, resented me because I never attended the games. (I was too busy studying.) Because I looked like one of our nerdy professors, Pete used to greet me using the teacher's first name. In nasal tones, the football player would say, "Hi, Stanley!" I would simply smile back and reply, "Hi, Pete. How's it going?"

One day when walking across campus, he called out the usual nasal greeting, "Hi, Stanley!" Unfortunately for Pete, although not realizing it at the time, he was talking not to me but to the real Professor Stanley. I would love to have captured that encounter on film. I can only imagine the professor's reaction and the apology Pete must have stammered. The jock's mode of addressing me changed after that, costing no hostility at all on my part.

I know a man who was led to the Lord by the unselfish act of a Christian neighbor. Once while my friend Dean was at work,

The neighbor analyzed the problem, went back into his house, changed his clothes and spent the whole day fixing the broken car.

his wife, Dee, was unable to start their car. At that moment, the neighbor who lived across the street emerged in his best clothes, preparing to go with his family to a special church function. Dee asked him if he could take a quick peek under the hood to see what might be wrong with the car. The neighbor analyzed the problem, went back into his house, changed his clothes and spent the whole day fixing the broken car. The neighbor's family had already won Dee to the Lord, and this act of Christian love so impacted Dean that he, too, soon bowed his knee to Christ. Such love, when consistently shown, is hard to resist.

Check your ingredients

I have read about two young Chinese Christians who wanted so much to evangelize the lost in their country that they got themselves arrested just so they could go to a labor camp and witness for Christ there.[20] That's love indeed! They followed the example of Jesus. He, too, loved us so much that He got Himself arrested so He could offer the whole world the free gift of eternal life.

Where is love on the ingredients list of our lives? Is it first, or is it somewhere near the bottom, like the pork in my can of beans – a mere trace amount? In life, there are always priorities. When learning to drive, you must first learn how to stop (without the help of a tree or telephone pole). In flying, knowing how to land is more vital than knowing how to take off. Paul told Timothy that "the goal of our instruction is love from a pure heart."[21] As the Christian family in Nazi Germany demonstrated, love must always be number one.

3 Essentials of a deeper life
3.6 Faith 101

One morning, a mother heard her teenage identical twin sons arguing. Although their physical features were alike, their tastes were not. One boy focused on sports and dressed to look "cool," while the other dressed like a nerdy bookworm. Their mother stopped by their room to find out what they were fighting about this time. When she asked the sports lover why he was so upset, he answered, "Look, Mom! Look how he's dressed! His shirt is tucked in, his socks match and his cap is facing forward." Their mom replied, "Well, what's wrong with that?" The angry twin retorted, "What!? Don't you get it? What if someone at school saw him and thought he was me?"

In a way, each Christian is like a twin brother or sister of Jesus. But, because of our careless lifestyle and faithlessness, I wonder if Jesus sometimes sorrows that people may mistakenly think He is like us. In this chapter, we will consider a way of life that attracts God's favor, especially in the area of faith: "Now faith is the assurance of things hoped for, the conviction of things not seen. For by it the men of old gained approval."[1]

We all appreciate affirmation from a respected source, and the Bible assures us that we can obtain genuine approval from our Heavenly Father by demonstrating faith and trust in His loving nature. An important facet of faith is always believing that, as Paul wrote in Romans 8:28, God works everything together for our good. He arranges positive outcomes for our lives despite the darkness of any present circumstance. Missionary Jim Elliot acted on this conviction and exhorted, "Wherever you are, be all there! Live to the hilt every situation you believe to be the will of God." This perspective is the key to getting God's approval: live with optimistic faith in His will as you perceive it. The practice starts with assurance of our salvation, knowing that we are saved by faith, and leads to confidence that daily He "is at work in [us], both to will and to work for His good pleasure."[2] Thus, we can live with the certainty that God's ultimate good for us can be hindered by no one but ourselves.

Train to Kerala

The train in India was so packed that I could not place even one foot flat on the floor. For about eight hours one night, I stood on the ball of my right foot with my arm stretched out to the compartment wall to keep my balance. I was working in George Verwer's Operation Mobilization office in Bombay. He would occasionally send me south when a church requested a "free" preacher for a conference. Often, the trip was a grueling two-day journey by train and bus that ended in the hot, steamy jungles of south Kerala.

My fourth and final year with OM was like a graduate school in faith. George would arrange to purchase a round-trip train ticket – third class, of course![3] His frugality taught me a lot about living by faith in God's provision. Other than supplying train and bus tickets, George would send me on these trips with little or no money. I was expected to take books and Bibles to sell along the way so I could afford to pay for food and incidentals. Unfortunately, because India has about 13 major languages and endless dialects, I had to guess which books in which languages I should carry in my crammed book bag - (Keep in mind that if I wanted to eat, I would need to sell this literature to people who were as poor as I was.)

When I managed to make my way through the train's crowded aisles, I tried to hold three or four books in different languages in front of passengers as if to say, "Pick a book, any book," hoping they would choose one and buy it. These people, dear to God's heart, desperately needed an opportunity to read a Gospel account of the life of Christ or some other good evangelistic book. Why didn't we just give the books away? We reasoned that charging a small price would increase their perceived value and, thus, the chance that they would be read.

Riding third class in crowded India is like no trip you have ever known. God used fellow believers to help me. Sometimes, when I would get ready to leave Bombay, Indian brothers would accompany me. As the empty train backed into the station, they would run along the platform and dive through the open windows (along with other "diving" travelers) in hopes of securing a single seat for me. On the return trips, however, I didn't have help from my friends. That experience, and others like it, taught me to be deeply thankful for every good thing God affords us in our less crowded Western nations.

At the start of one trip, a young Indian brother named K. P. Yohannan accompanied me to the Bombay train station. K. P. was new to our method of working and trusting God for our needs. When he heard what little money I had for the trip, he almost cried, and he insisted that I take the small amount he had in his pockets. To refuse would have broken his heart, so I took what he offered. When I returned, I gave back all his money, reassuring him that we really can trust God to supply us. K. P. later founded and directed a large Christian mission, Gospel for Asia (www.gfa.org).

It's not likely that many of you will ever have to pay your passage by selling books and Bibles, but we all need to trust God, whatever our circumstances. Whether your challenge is a job, a family situation, an economic need or a strong temptation, commit the problem to Him in prayer and do what is right while waiting for Him to direct you. Difficult and troubling events are God's garden, where He plants us as seeds with the expectation of eventually producing a fruitful crop. Those who trust God through everyday adversities will grow to experience the reality of Christ more fully. Those who chafe under suffering will not. Many of us have memorized Proverbs 3:5-6: "Trust in the Lord with all your heart and do not lean on your own understanding. In all your ways acknowledge Him, and He will make your paths straight." However, it's time for some of us to start walking according to that principle. The preacher Charles Spurgeon observed, "A little faith will bring your soul to heaven; a great faith will bring heaven to your soul."

Another key to growing faith

If we want to expand our faith and please God, we need to do more than trust Him to create good outcomes amidst life's difficulties. While we must not put ourselves under the Law, we should practice the virtues advocated in His Word. Cultivate the fruit of the Spirit. Go the extra mile. Be forgiving. Be patient. Witness for Christ. Spend time praying. These disciplines can be genuine acts of faith when performed in the Spirit. We can be confident that God truly "is a rewarder of those who seek Him."[4] To be sure, dark times will come when it seems that God is absent. David describes this experience in Psalm 6. But we must keep doing right and waiting on God's promised blessing, which we will eventually see. A godly walk in the Spirit is an act of faith that greatly pleases the Father.

Woman at the Door?

When working in Turkey, I often traveled across country, gathering information for the tourist brochure I was writing, and compiling addresses to use for mailing invitations to participate in a Bible study correspondence course. It was not wise to carry much cash, so I would try to anticipate if I was going to run out of travel money. Then I would write to my contact person in Istanbul, telling him where to forward my mail (and money). I could pick up the mail at the main post office in the specified city under "general delivery."

On one trip, I arrived at the designated post office. My mail included a letter from my contact in Istanbul, but no money – not even a single, measly lira. He had forgotten to enclose the cash. I wrote back to inform him of the error. As my plight grew more desperate, I carefully checked the mail twice a day. My funds quickly dwindled from paper to change, and I knew that soon I would have no money to pay for food and the cheap hotel where I was staying - (I envied the Israelites who could at least pick up manna from the ground while in the wilderness.) I waited and prayed, but the day came when I would have to be out of my room by 2 pm.

Meeting with some friendly Turkish people in a very remote village, 1965

I did everything that I could

to boost my courage and trust in the Lord, Who was ultimately in charge of my life. I knew that human mistakes never compromise His power. After my last breakfast, with no money remaining to purchase lunch, I hoped for a miracle in the morning mail, but there was none. I returned to my room with nothing more to do but pray and fast, knowing that I had to check out by 2pm, or be chucked out at 2:15.

Back at the hotel, I was distracted by the tantalizing smell of a noon meal being cooked in the entryway. It was the custom for hotels to hire peasant women to prepare midday meals for the businessmen working in nearby buildings, saving them the cost of eating in a more expensive restaurant. The fragrance from just outside my door was almost more than I could bear, especially since I knew that lunchtime would come and go before I would check my mail again. By noon, the aroma wafting into my room made my hunger more intense and my prayers more fervent.

I have no doubt that the Lord uses trials to see just how confident we are in His promises and provision. He brings us to a crossroad where we must choose to trust Him and go forward on His narrow path of faith or turn aside onto the wide path of hopelessness, depression and sin. I determined that the best choice at this spiritual crossroad was to trust myself to His care, although this might mean there would be no noon meal, no place to stay and a long, hungry hitch-hike back to Istanbul. About half-past noon, I heard a knock at my door. I was surprised, as no one in the city knew me, and it was too early for the management to ask me to leave. I opened the door, and to my amazement, there stood the woman who had been cooking in the hallway (and torturing me with the irresistible aroma). She held out a large dish of the food she had prepared and said in Turkish, "I made a big mistake today. Somehow I made more food than needed. Would you like to have this plateful? It's free!"

I was so astounded that I almost fell to the floor. I wished I had some money to give her, but all I could offer were my profuse and sincere thanks as I took the dish. Later, I wondered if I might have been fed by an angel. Poor people can't afford to give food away. Whether God used an angel or a peasant woman to meet my needs, I'll never know – at least not in this world. Furthermore, that meal was one of the most delicious I ate during my four years in Turkey. And that afternoon, the money arrived at the post office. Thankfully, few of you will ever run out of food or money. But at times, we all run out of options for fixing things in our lives. We must remember with confidence and faith that God "is a rewarder of those who seek Him," and if He could give me a free meal from a poor woman or an angel in the middle of Turkey, He can do anything for you if you trust Him.

What if we fail?

Sometimes, however, the positive results we long for may fail to materialize. In those cases, we need to wait humbly and trust God to show us the reasons. As Christians, we are all learners in the school of faith. When I was a young believer, my sister was fatally wounded in a hold-up. Before she passed away, I felt it was my duty in faith to publicly declare that she would live. But when she died, I had to acknowledge I had made a mistake (I knew that God hadn't) and that someday I would learn from my error – which I eventually did.

I realized that trusting God for a good outcome was my responsibility, but dictating that outcome to Him was not. I discovered that even the death of a loved one or the death of a dream can ultimately bring about good if we entrust the situation to the caring hands of God. Paul tells us, "In everything give thanks; for this is God's will for you in Christ Jesus."[5] Although incredibly hard during the time of suffering, that path always leads to peace. I know by faith that I will see my precious sister Marj again, coming toward me with a bright smile as I approach Heaven's beautiful gates. And I picture a radiant young boy running in front of her, arms outstretched – the one who died in her womb when she was murdered. He'll be shouting, "Uncle Ken, we've been waiting for you!" Racing next to my nephew with arms reaching out to me will be another little one – the girl my dear wife, Helen, lost in a miscarriage. My daughter will be squealing with delight, crying out, "Daddy, Daddy! Jesus told me you were coming soon and you would tell me lots and lots of stories!" Will it be that wonderful? No! It'll be even better. When we live as virtuous people of faith, trusting God in all circumstances, Jesus won't mind at all if people mistake us for Him.

3 Essentials of a deeper life
3.7 Overflowing grace and peace

May grace and peace be yours in the fullest measure.
1 Peter 1:2

Grace is largely misunderstood even by Christians. Most of us appreciate that we have been enriched by it as if we had been given
millions of tax free dollars to spend. But, in fact, it's like we've
been given billions. It turns out that most of us are spiritually poor
millionaires when instead we could be basking in billions as it were of
endless wealth of God's rich grace and peace, beyond salvation alone.

Jesus told his disciples, "Peace I leave with you; My peace I
give to you; not as the world gives do I give to you."[1] To this day
in the Middle East, it is the custom to wish one another peace upon
meeting and parting. But in all the times I've been wished peace,
I've never felt it, and those I've greeted likely never felt mine.
Maybe that's what Jesus meant by "not as the world gives do I give
to you." More than simply a polite, hopeful greeting, the peace He

Grace and peace can be like a constant
overflowing waterfall for those who trust Him.

offers us is the real thing that we
can experience in our daily lives.

Grace is God's loving un-
merited action toward us and
peace is grace felt. That's why
you will find the two words,
"grace and peace," often mentioned together in Scripture.
The feeling of peace most
often follows the experience
of receiving grace. This same
combo is invoked in the opening
and closing greetings of many

New Testament letters. Peter wishes his readers grace and peace "in the fullest measure" or, as rendered in some translations, "multiplied." These divine blessings should mark our lives as we walk in the Spirit. The following stories illustrate how some believers have found their hearts overflowing with grace and peace in times of great need.

My sister, Marj

"Thief Beats Clerk," the newspaper headline announced. My sister, Marj, had been running our family store that morning. Around midday, a seventeen-year-old boy came in to rob the store. He needed cash because he wanted to take his girlfriend to a carnival that night. During the hold-up, he clubbed Marj from behind, took the money and ran, leaving her for dead.

My parents and I were at home having lunch when we got the phone call. We quickly left for the store where I let my mom and dad off in front, which was already blocked off with yellow police tape. I expected the experience was going to be rough. After parking in the next block and getting out of the car, I paused and prayed a desperate, almost demanding, prayer: All right, Lord, now please start giving all that grace You talk about in Your Word.

Marj had already been rushed to the hospital. After being questioned by the police, my parents and I headed there, too. 29 years old, Marj had recently been married and was pregnant. Although she would live another seven days after the hold-up, she never regained consciousness. At the hospital, police officers hovered around her bed, hoping she would wake up and give them some clues about the person who had committed the crime. I also hovered near her bed, wanting to give her spiritual comfort, since she had only recently trusted Christ as her Savior.

Later that evening, the police remarked that they had sprinkled sawdust over the bloody mess in the back room of the store to make the cleanup easier. Since my older brother didn't volunteer, the job fell to me, his twenty-four-year-old kid brother. That night, I was on my hands and knees scrubbing in semi-darkness because I didn't want to attract attention by turning on a lot of lights. I also cleared away my sister's unfinished lunch. It struck me that although I would normally have been squeamish and deeply depressed about such a task, I was able to work without difficulty. Yes, I was saddened for my dear sister and her husband and my grieving family, but nothing could diminish that inner grace and peace that God had given in answer to my audacious, frenzied prayer.

When my sister died a week later, my brother and I were called to the city morgue to officially identify the body. Upon arriving, we walked down the dimly lit stone steps to the basement, our footfalls eerily echoing in the hallway. Suddenly, my brother stopped and gasped, "I can't go any farther." I told him to stay on the stairs. I then continued to the room without him and identified Marj when an attendant pulled away the sheet that covered her face.

The next day, the police tracked down the young man who had killed my sister. My brother and I opened the store for the officers and watched the murderer re-enact the crime. After he was returned to the police car, I ran out and asked if I could talk to him for a minute to share the Gospel. I also wanted to tell him that I forgave him in the name of Jesus. However, the police would not let me speak with him then, and my father demanded that I stop trying to talk to the young man at all.[2]

Throughout the situation, I experienced the inner grace and peace I had requested. As the Lord told Paul, "My grace is sufficient for you, for My strength is made perfect in weakness."[3] Grace given to a Christian in serious need is like a life preserver thrown from a ship to a drowning man. The floatation device doesn't immediately get him out of the water, but it does keep him from going under. You might argue that it's probably less painful to lose a sister than a daughter, son, husband or wife, and I would agree. But God's grace is powerful and sufficient, no matter what the loss.

Barbara's story

One Christian couple I know tragically lost their twenty-nine-year-old son. The mother, Barbara, later told me how God consoled her and her husband. "What happened next is still so remarkable I wouldn't believe it if it didn't happen to me," she related. "God took over completely. His nearness, His comforting presence was always with us. We couldn't get rid of Him." Did you notice what she said? "I wouldn't believe it if it didn't happen to me."

In describing this reassurance, the Apostle Paul wrote, "The peace of God, which surpasses all comprehension, will guard your hearts and your minds in Christ Jesus."[4] This special grace and peace surprised the grieving couple and continued to bring deep comfort in the months that followed their son's death. Barbara understood that many couples who lose a son or daughter also lose their marriage. However, because of God's overflowing grace, she noted, "God drew Joe and I closer and closer. Our relationship wasn't threatened the least bit." She added, "I encourage anyone going through anything like this to turn their heart to Jesus. Let Him and the Father cover you with that amazing grace." While grace cannot be earned, we can prepare the way by taking even small steps in learning to walk in the Spirit. As the psalmist David exhorts, "Therefore, let everyone who is godly pray to You in a time when You may be found."[5]

Grace can enable you to do anything

Many Christians think God's grace is limited primarily to saving our souls. Actually, it's intended to bring us peace and joy at all times. Grace is also God's way of sustaining us through every challenge of life and enabling us to do what we would otherwise consider impossible. Paul assured the believers in Corinth, "God is able to make all grace abound to you, so that always having all sufficiency in everything, you may have an abundance for every good deed."[6]

In my younger days, as I contemplated serving Christ in a foreign field, I realized that missionaries who worked with remote tribes sometimes had to eat bugs and worms. So, resolving to do my best to get used to this unsavory fare, I went to the gourmet section of a department store where cans of such disgusting "food" were sold. While it can be prudent to prepare for specific challenges we might face, I finally concluded (coward that I was) that I would wait and ask for the grace to consume those delicacies if the time came.

One summer when I was in Spain, an opportunity of that sort did present itself. I was often in charge of buying the food for our team of twenty-four young guys. I liked the canned tuna, but it was more expensive than the sardines, which I absolutely hated. For the sake of economy, however, I bought the cheaper product and, amazingly, found grace to eat the smelly little fish all summer long. By the end of our stay in Spain, I could eat sardines as if they were tuna. Yet the day we left, I knew I could never again eat another loathsome sardine – not at least until I got a fresh supply of grace to do so.

Every day we can enjoy the abundance of His rich grace, "For of His fullness we have all received, and grace upon grace."[7] This fullness is often displayed as an increase in sustaining strength from God in the midst of serious difficulties. Grace can also give us the ability to do what we normally could not. It's also my observation that God never gives grace for imagining adversity but only for the actual trial as we face it. That's why we are not to worry about the future. God will be there even before we arrive.

Many Christians miss out

So why don't all Christians experience supernatural grace and peace in their daily routines and painful hardships? After all, sustaining grace is not just for those whom we might consider perfect Christians, or I would never have gotten any in my life. On the contrary, this provision is available to all who seek to walk in the Spirit. I suspect that Christians who claim to have been "disappointed" by God when facing serious difficulties have little idea of how to truly relate to Him. While I sincerely empathize with those who have suffered, I have observed that Christians tend to make two mistakes. First, many people think that just because they have been born again, they will automatically sense God's presence and grace continually instead of needing to grow in grace as 2 Peter 3:18 tells us. The second faulty assumption confuses participating in religious activities with cultivating a personal relationship with God. My years as a Christian have taught me that I must regularly seek the Lord before the crisis if I want to find Him in the crisis.

This conclusion is supported by Hebrews 4:16: "Let us draw near with confidence to the throne of grace, so that we may receive mercy and find grace to help in time of need." According to this verse, every believer who frequently, not just casually, comes to God in prayer before a major trial will readily find that throne of grace when the heavy trauma arrives. For example, the husband of a Christian woman I knew had a job that often kept him on the road. One day, a caller told the woman that her husband had been involved in a terrible accident. She quickly packed, but right before leaving the house, she dropped to her knees and asked for help and grace. Amazingly, as she told me later, she had perfect peace from that point on – even when she learned that her husband had died. Praying consistently, walking in the Spirit and practicing godly behavior had become her way of life even before she needed upholding grace. As Paul reminds his readers in Philippians 4:9, "The things you have learned and received and heard and seen in me, practice these things, and the God of peace will be with you."

A godly American soldier of my acquaintance had a similar encounter with God's grace. One day, the company commander called him into the office and abruptly told him his father had just died. The soldier said he was about to collapse when God's grace suddenly enveloped him. He saluted his commander, thanked him and left in peace. These stories provide living evidence of the Bible's words: "The Lord God is a sun and shield; The Lord gives grace and glory; No good thing does He withhold from those who walk uprightly."[8]

What else promotes or discourages grace?

Each time we choose to walk in the flesh and not in the Spirit, we choose not to have grace and peace pervade our lives. We simply don't realize the price we are paying when we decide to be irritable, unkind, prayerless, lustful or unloving. We know our behavior is wrong, but our response seems to be, So what? The answer to that question lies in our lack of deep tranquility, especially during times of crisis. When we constantly walk in the flesh, we forgo the many benefits of nurturing a spiritual life. Just as a bent drinking straw cannot supply us with the refreshing beverage we desire, so a life bent n careless disobedience cannot supply us with the continuous, refreshing peace we crave. The "So what?" in our behavior really matters.

Our attitudes can also promote grace. James reminds believers that they have been granted "a greater grace. Therefore it says, 'God is opposed to the proud, but gives grace to the humble.'"[9] In addition to pride, the spiritual cancer of bitterness can eat away at and destroy our inner life. Hebrews 12:15 warns against this immature way of dealing with life's disappointments: "See to it that no one comes short of the grace of God; that no root of bitterness springing up causes trouble, and by it many be defiled." Through the self-indulgence of bitterness, we aggravate the injuries of our bruised inner selves. We may have missed out on good jobs or remained single. We may be married to difficult people. Or we may have been unfairly dismissed from leadership positions. Even if we don't blame God, we might blame others. We don't realize that we're hurting ourselves the most because, by being bitter, we come "short of the grace of God." The root of our failure lies in viewing life as controlled by other people or random events, not by the sovereign hand of God. Worse yet, we might blame God Himself, as if He doesn't know what He's doing. Peter wrote, "This finds favor [grace], if for the sake of conscience toward God a person bears up under sorrows when suffering unjustly."[10] Bitterness often results when we feel we have been treated "unjustly" by people or by God. If bitterness is a major problem for you – and we are all tempted to be bitter in some areas – please reread the chapter "Out of Luck and into Grace." We want to live in grace.

"Joy inexpressible"[6]

Before leaving my job in public transit and entering a new ministry in New York, I decided to get one last physical exam while the visit would still be covered by my employer's insurance program. A few days later, our family physician called to say that my PSA test results were abnormally high. A biopsy confirmed the worst: prostate cancer. The doctor told me I had three to five years to live unless I had surgery. I checked with two other doctors, and they agreed with this prognosis. In those days, few options were available. I remember walking arm in arm with my dear wife after receiving the biopsy report. I was crying quietly – not because I feared death, but because my dream of a new ministry might die. Yet that night, upon opening my Bible to continue my nightly reading through Psalms, the next portion I read was from Psalm 118:17: "I will not die, but live, and tell of the works of the Lord." What a wonderful promise! I committed the situation to the Lord, and once again, His amazing grace and peace silently flowed into my life. I could not help but smile everywhere I went. A friend at work who I often witnessed to was a member of Jehovah's Witnesses and noticed my "joy inexpressible" in spite of my death sentence.[11] So one day, he asked in bewilderment, "How can you be so happy?!" I easily replied, "It's the grace of Jesus."[12]

Every Saturday morning, I attended a men's prayer meeting at the Plymouth Brethren assembly of Grace Bible Chapel in Fullerton, California. The previous week, we had prayed that my biopsy would come back showing no cancer. On the Saturday after receiving the test results, I got out of the car in the church parking lot, beaming from ear to ear. Someone looked out of an open chapel window and yelled, "Praise God! Kenny doesn't have cancer!" I shouted back, "No. Praise God, I've got cancer – but I've also got grace!" You, too, can have grace in the midst of your deep needs if you take time to plan ahead by learning to pray and walk in the Spirit, abiding in Chirst.

While the grace of God is free and unearned, we must prepare our hearts in advance for the subsequent peace that God desires to give us. Bitterness, hatred and other works of the flesh are roadblocks that cannot coexist with grace.[13] On the other hand, humility, forgiveness, patience and love for difficult people produce a wide highway for grace and the resulting peace of God to flow into our lives. Just as God gave me His supernatural grace when my sister lost her life and as he did to other people mentioned, He desires to multiply His peace to you in all of life's circumstances.

For it is good for the heart to be strengthened by grace.
Hebrews 13:9

3 Essentials of a deeper life
3.8 It's not counting to ten

Some time ago, I read a newspaper story about a guy who shot his lawn mower because it wouldn't start – it's a true story – and he was arrested. Face it: many of us have felt like doing that very thing, which shows how irrational we can become with impatience and anger toward objects and humans. While we all want others to be patient and kind toward us, we are not always willing to extend to them the same courtesy and can easily cite reasons for our intolerance. But Paul urges us, "As those who have been chosen of God, . . . put on a heart of . . . patience."[1] We know we should love others, and Paul reminds us that "love is patient."[2] We are about to discover that patience is not only possible but can also be satisfying and rewarding.

Who's who? Old or new?

Our ability to be patient and control our anger is based on our firm faith that God exercises sovereign control over our lives and seeks to work everything toward a positive conclusion, even when disruptive events are caused by the ineptness or evil intentions of others. Joseph, whose story is recounted in Chapter 16, "Out of Luck, into Grace," observed that God can produce good results in spite of wicked human schemes. As Christians, we are also enabled to be patient peacemakers rather than irate combatants because the new person within us bears the image of Christ. With the Spirit's power, we can be as long-suffering as God Himself. When we are tempted to become brusque and irritable, we need to remind ourselves who we really are and mentally step back into Christ.

Some readers may object, saying, "You'd be impatient, too, if you had to deal with the kind of people I have to deal with." But that remark misses the point: demonstrating patience doesn't depend on a lack of trials but on the ability to shift from the old person to the new one. This capacity does not rely on trite formulas. It's not "counting to ten." It's counting on Jesus, Who lives within us. Paul told the Ephesians he was praying that they would "walk in a manner worthy of the calling with which you have been called; . . with patience, showing tolerance for one another in love."[3]

Being patient and turning away from ungodly reactions, takes practice because our old nature is in the comfortable habit of dominating our life until we repeatedly choose by faith to deny that opportunity. We must "put on the Lord Jesus Christ, and make no provision for the flesh in regard to its lusts."[4] Recognizing that our old nature has died when we accepted Christ's sacrifice for us, we will likely respond by reflecting His patience and love. Not only have we died with Christ, but we have also risen with Him "so we too might walk in newness of life."[5] This death and resurrection is symbolized in our baptism.

However, as I have discussed in previous chapters, most of us Christians don't always function as new persons. We generally define ourselves in terms of who we've always been. We each develop a certain personality and figure, That's me. For example, a "shoot from the hip" type of person may fail to realize that the spiritual person within is gentle and not "fast on the draw." Many of us Christians manage to act more congenial on the outside, but we often remain pretty much the same inside, still living and walking in our old nature. To varying degrees, we simply become nicer impatient individuals. But God wants us to become like Christ.

The day you became a follower of Jesus, He changed who you are, and you gained the potential to become a completely new person from within. This alteration is not reformation, but transformation by the Spirit of God working in you. The image of Christ, the heavenly Father's beloved Son, is the prototype for all believers. Any other image is second-rate. To be like the archangel Gabriel would be good, but to be like Christ is perfect.

If we are going to make progress toward the goal of Christlikeness, we need to understand that some events and people that God permits in our lives may tempt us to lose our tempers.

James advises, "The trying of your faith worketh patience. But let patience have her perfect work, that ye may be perfect."[6] God permits testing so we can choose in each situation whether we want to be our old self or our new one. Our old self is frustrated by disturbances. Our new one thinks, If God wants this interruption to happen at this time, so be it. When circumstances don't go our way, God may be teaching us to stay calm and apply our faith by transferring our responses to the new control tower. Therefore, "long-suffering" is an apt description of patience. Much of our impatience is simply anger at a low boil. James warns us that "everyone must be quick to hear, slow to speak and slow to anger; for the anger of man does not achieve the righteousness of God."[7]

The typing stand

While in college, I thought I needed a stand to support my typewriter so I could write my term papers more efficiently. In an office supply store, I found a stand I thought was perfect – a nice-looking metal one with casters and two side flaps that could be raised to hold papers or folded away when not in use. Yet every time I visited the store, I felt an inner lack of peace over the purchase. Like most of us, I asked God to guide me in my life, but I didn't realize that this request meant He would seek to stop me from buying something I really wanted. I reasoned, *This is just what I need. After all, what does God – who is busy with the whole universe – care about a little typewriter stand?* I finally bought it. I was about to discover, however, that sometimes we must put off immediate gratification and wait patiently for something better.

The stand turned out to be the most frustrating device I could have brought into my life. The table often rolled away from me as I typed. I had to keep pulling it back when it tried to escape, or chase it in my caster chair. As the screws loosened, the stand tilted, forcing me to lean with it while typing. The loose screws created a noise like banging on a tin roof. I finally recognized that the contraption was designed for a petite secretary whose tiny legs could fit easily underneath and hold the stand in place. Mine couldn't.

In the end, I concluded that God really did know better and

was interested in even such minor details of my life as a typewriter stand. He did not want to control me like a robot, but to gently guide me as a son, teaching me to wait patiently for His very best. I bet the stand that He had in mind for me, which I never got, was a real beauty.

Impatience with God

As the sad saga of the substandard typewriter stand shows, we become impatient not only with others but sometimes with God. This frustration may surface because we want some object or outcome and we feel peeved that God doesn't seem to be accommodating our desire. So we argue with Him as if He needs to learn the value and reasonableness of our plan. We can ask God for just about anything that is not inherently sinful, but then we are told to wait.

It is more troubling when we act on our impatience with God regarding major, long-lasting matters, such as choosing a life partner. After I returned from four years of overseas evangelism, I became interested in a very attractive young lady, and she was interested in me. But no matter how I put it before God, I could find no peace for a decision to pursue the relationship. Remembering my experience with the typewriter stand and similar lessons, I knew better than to impatiently push ahead without His approval.

If I hadn't listened to the gentle guidance of the Spirit, I might have missed out on uniting with the fine woman I did marry.

The importance of waiting for God's leading was impressed on me by a woman who told me that she knew she hadn't submitted to His direction as she should. She said that God had clearly called her to be a missionary. She also wanted to marry, but failed to wait for God's "green light" in that

I thought I needed a stand to support my typewriter so I could write my term papers more efficiently.

matter. She got married anyway, hoping the circumstances would all work out. They didn't. She never reached the mission field, and she endured a miserable marriage.

Christ is our perfect model

How patient and calm would we have been if we had created beings who tore hair from our faces, jammed crowns of sharp thorns onto our heads and brutally beat us? Long before they got that far, we would have drawn a line in the sand, and when they crossed the boundary, we would have whistled for our legions of angels. Our tormentors would have been destroyed. But Christ did not lose His patience or become angry with His creations. Instead, as foretold centuries before He came into the world, "He was oppressed and He was afflicted, yet He did not open His mouth; like a lamb that is led to slaughter, and like a sheep that is silent before its shearers, so He did not open His mouth."[8]

We could not have a better example to follow than Jesus. His perfect patience, which truly was long-suffering, brought about great eternal good for those of us who have believed.

Patience pays off

Our own patient waiting and turning from wrath will also bring us good when we learn to persevere, even though we wonder if anyone notices our kindness or if any positive results will come from our work. For example, sometimes we need to show long-suffering and compassion toward others who may never know that we are Christians, such as aggressive drivers or people who push ahead of us in lines. Maybe no one on earth will observe your godly response. Is that effort wasted? No. By being patient and dying to our old impulses, we are developing a pattern of spiritual behaviors that will turn us into the God-pleasing people we long to be. Paul counsels, "Consider yourselves to be dead to sin, but alive to God in Christ Jesus."[9] Patient responses will cultivate a habit that allows us to increasingly act out of the new self that God gave us when we became believers.

In addition, although you think that no one appreciates your

Christ-like attitude and reactions, God is aware of them. Furthermore, the battling powers of unseen spiritual forces are aware of our conformity to Christ.[10] God, Who is glorified in the midst of the heavenly hosts just as He was through the life of long-suffering Job, will eventually reward you even for your smallest acts in the Spirit. Jesus instructed his followers, "But there is nothing covered up that will not be revealed, and hidden that will not be known . . . What you have whispered in the inner rooms will be proclaimed upon the housetops."[11]

The "Ladder" Day Saints

The conditions God allows into our lives are like rungs on a ladder that are intended to lead us spiritually higher and closer to Him. God doesn't plan for us to stay at one level for long. You can treat these daily ladder rungs as nuisances in your way or as helpers that will bring you higher and closer to God. You make the choice. When, by faith, you peacefully accept these growth-promoting events into your life, instead of resisting them, you are developing a track record that is the key to your on-going spiritual development and success. As you observe enough events that ultimately turn out well after God enables you to wait or hold your temper, you will gradually see that being patient and kind truly pays off. The author of the book of Hebrews wrote of Abraham, "And so, having patiently waited, he obtained the promise."[12]

We urge you, brethren, . . be patient with everyone.
1 Thessalonians 5:14

The furnace

It was the dirtiest job I ever had: cleaning oil furnaces during two summer breaks while attending college. The stains never came off my hands completely until weeks after I returned to classes (Working as a dishwasher in the cafeteria helped).

Each day, Elm Grove Fuel and Supply, my summer employer in Wisconsin, would assign me five oil furnaces to clean, mostly in private homes. Once, however, I saw only four locations on my list. I was delighted at the prospect of a more leisurely schedule until I discovered that the arrangement was not an oversight on the company's part. Instead, I had been allotted four units because one of the heating plants was in a large church in downtown Milwaukee, and the furnace was humongous. It was so huge that the only way I could clean it was to climb inside. After carefully turning off the master electrical switch, I shoved my brushes through the furnace door opening and tossed in my extension lamp. Then I grabbed the long hose to my vacuum cleaner and drew myself in, feet first, to what was to become my own solitary confinement cell for the next hour. Just before pulling my head into the belly of this monster, I nervously took one last glance at the master switch to make sure it was off. I had no desire to recreate the predicament confronted by three fellows in the book of Daniel, even though their outcome was a positive one.

With dust mask in place, I sat cross-legged on the burner element, swung my black furnace brush into action, followed close behind with the tip of my vacuum and proceeded to clean. My heart was full of thanksgiving for God's goodness to me, I broke into hymns of praise. Anyone in the office of the church upstairs would not have been able to hear me over the din of the vacuum.

After a few minutes of constantly reaching upward to clean, I paused to rest my arms and reflect. I had noticed that the church belonged to a denomination that years earlier had departed from a firm belief in the authority of the Bible and had instead embraced the social gospel. I grieved over this error as I realized that a rare instance of sincere worship ascending from that edifice to Heaven might now be rising from, of all places – the furnace.

To be fair, I could also have pondered the amount of genuine worship coming from many evangelical gatherings during the sacred hour on Sunday morning, especially since Jesus gave us important guidelines for worship:

But an hour is coming, and now is, when the true worshipers will worship the Father in spirit and truth; for such people the Father seeks to be His worshipers. God is spirit, and those who worship Him must worship in spirit and truth.[1]

Hindrances to true worship

Sadly, while many who attend liberal churches worship God neither in Spirit nor in truth, evangelicals – charismatics included – often fail in this calling as well. If we are born again, we do have some measure of truth and Spirit. Yet we may not be living the truth in the power of the Spirit.

If we fight with our spouses or antagonize our friends and coworkers, we are not living the power of the liberating Gospel of Christ. Thus, if we do not permit the fruit of the Spirit to flow from our lives, we are neither worshiping God in the Spirit nor in truth.

A mechanic, who was not a believer, told me he had once repaired the car of a customer who supposedly was a Christian.

The stains never came off my hands completely until weeks after I returned to classes.

He actively distributed Bibles, but failed to pay his repair bill. Although such a man might reverently or loudly sing hymns in church, even if he leaped around and raised his hands, he would not be able to worship God in the Spirit because he was not living in the truth. God does not measure our acts of adoration by the emotional energy we put into them but by the Christ-likeness we display all week long. Expressions of worship are secondary compared to our daily actions at home and in the world.

True worship

Most Christians overlook one important point about worship. It appears that we can bring the greatest glory to God while we are still on earth. We will have no trouble praising Him in Heaven, where our hearts will overflow with gratitude. But when we live for Him and die to our old selfish nature while on earth, His spiritual enemies are shamefaced because they have failed in their mission to subdue us. This victory glorifies God and makes our own praise and worship even more sincere and in truth, just as He desires.

Our lives are like a flowing stream

In the hills of Pennsylvania, Fallingwater, a home designed by architect Frank Lloyd Wright, sits atop a waterfall that flows directly under the living room. The Bear Run stream doesn't start beneath

Falling Water, a home designed by architect Frank Lloyd Wright, sits atop a waterfall that flows directly under the living room.

the building but bubbles from a spring far up the mountain. From this source, the water begins its journey, coursing down precipices and over rocks and logs before joining other tributaries and running under Wright's house. Some of the feeder streams may become polluted along the way, while others may have preserved their pristine purity. A worshiper's life reflects the same pattern.

Preparation for worship doesn't begin when we enter a church building on Sunday morning, but when we leave to return home. From that point, like a stream rippling over rocks down a mountain, the flow of our spiritual homage makes the trek toward the following week's meeting as the body of Christ. We lay the groundwork for worship when we exit the sanctuary because our behavior on the way home and for the rest of the day can set the course for subsequent services. Do we argue as we drive out of the church parking lot? Do we pick apart the sermon? Do we criticize what others are wearing? Do we remain patient with our spouses? Do we speak kindly to an irritable co-worker? Do we witness with a word or tract to those in need? As the rivers of our lives cascade through the week like a moving stream, our conduct and handling of "log jams" will affect our worship when we meet again on the next Lord's Day.

Unfortunately, many of us arrive for our corporate gathering unholy and polluted. While we may be momentarily uplifted in praise on Sunday morning, God evaluates the essence of our adoration by the truth of our life in the Spirit all week long. We may think we are swaying in a spiritual trance as we sing hymns, but how real is our devotion if we fear to sway some lost soul to the knowledge of God? What passes for a form of worship in a service is often little more than a momentary pep rally led by "cheerleaders" who, we hope, are holy and pure.

We are God's house

"Welcome to the house of God!" We've often heard that greeting from the pulpit. But can the house of God be welcomed to the house of God? The Scripture refers to believers, both singly and corporately, as the "house of God." While I let other people say what they want, yet what I teach and emphasize is that the building we meet in is not God's house – we are. Addressing individual believers, Paul asked, "Do you not know that you are a temple of God and that the Spirit of God dwells in you?"[2] Paul used a similar description for groups of believers: "I write so that you will know how one ought to conduct himself in the household of God, which is the church of the living God."[3] Paul was not referring to the building where they met. This distinction is not simply a fine point of doctrine but a truth that can change our attitudes toward our own bodies, which should be kept holy. Some of us enjoy the warm, fuzzy feelings associated with being in a building that might be called "God's house." Instead, we should get warm, fuzzy feelings from realizing that we are the dwelling place of God – both as individual believers and as His gathered body, the church and that house is to be kept holy.

When I attended services in a lovely, ornate church building as a kid, I was sternly warned never to run in the "house of God." Although I still haven't run in the house of God, since I grew up and became a Christian, my personal "house of God" has run a 5K race and has often jogged three miles to work and home again.

Consider Paul's teaching: "The temple of God is holy, and that is what you are."[4] This means we're the temple of God 24/7 so that what our eyes look at, our minds think, our ears listen to and our tongues speak – all must be done with holy reverence. Of course, we can still laugh and possess deep joy, but as Peter observed, "You also, as living stones, are being built up as a spiritual house for a holy priesthood, to offer up spiritual sacrifices acceptable to God through Jesus Christ."[5]

The Holy Spirit

As Paul reminded the Corinthians, those of us who have been born again have the Spirit of God housed within us. But many Christians do not think to apply this truth beyond salvation. They fail to recognize that the Holy Spirit not only connects us to the Godhead, restoring a relationship that had been broken by Adam's sin, but also enables us to live and worship "in spirit and truth."

As a fallen person, your spirit within you was dead to God, and your life was animated by your human flesh, which was totally cut off from God. Paul explains that:

You were dead in your trespasses and sins, in which you formerly walked according to the course of this world, according to the prince of the power of the air, of the spirit that is now working in the sons of disobedience. Among them we too all formerly lived in the lusts of our flesh, indulging the desires of the flesh and of the mind, and were by nature children of wrath, even as the rest. But God, being rich in mercy, because of His great love with which He loved us, even when we were dead in our transgressions, made us alive together with Christ.[6]

From the beginning, God intended that a person's earthly body would be governed by the spirit and not by feelings and the fleshly mind. We cannot be spiritual on our own since we have little understanding of God's spiritual world. Jesus promised to help us: "I will not leave you as orphans; I will come to you."[7] He came to make His home within us, empowering us to mature under His influence. That process should give fresh meaning to this injunction: "Walk by the Spirit, and you will not carry out the desire of the flesh."[8]

Who or what is steering your life?
Many Christians don't recognize or pay much attention to the Holy Spirit because they don't know what to expect. They move through their days, rarely experiencing God's supernatural presence or His life-changing power. By instructing the Ephesians to "be filled with the Spirit," Paul emphasized the wonderful truth that God now dwells within each believer.[9] We must demonstrate our faith by giving God complete control over our lives. Instead of allowing ourselves to be steered by the desires of the flesh as before, we should let the Spirit reproduce the mind of Jesus within us. As A. W. Tozer remarked, "It may be said without qualification that every man is as holy and as full of the Spirit as he wants to be. He may not be as full as he wishes he were, but he is most certainly as full as he wants to be."[10]

In light of this teaching, should we start praying for that additional filling of the Holy Spirit? Why not? We are commanded to be filled to the brim with His glorious presence. To prepare for this encounter, we must, by faith, "put on the Lord Jesus Christ, and make no provision for the flesh in regard to its lusts," considering ourselves dead to the old nature.[11]

Some Christians report dramatic occasions when they were flooded with the Spirit's power.[12] Tozer, an author I highly admire, supposedly remarked that he never met a man who was gradually filled with the Holy Spirit. But Tozer will someday meet that man when he sees me and others like me in Heaven. I do not deny that many wonderful spiritual experiences can be enjoyed, and I would be happy to have all the ones that God wants to give me. Although my own transformation has been gradual, I believe that the Spirit has indeed filled me. Sometimes, I feel that if God gave me a little more, my old frame would burst.

I love one phrase an African convert used with the missionary who had led him to faith in Christ. The two friends had not seen each other for some time. When they met again, the African smiled broadly and said, "I still have a sweet stomach," referring to the joy of the Holy Spirit. Jesus also described this deep satisfaction: "Whoever drinks of the water that I will give him shall never thirst; but the water that I will give him will become in him a well of water springing up to eternal life."[13] We, in turn, should respond like the Samaritan woman:, "Sir, give me this water, so I will not be thirsty."[14]

As our lives flow through the week over rocks and logs intended to impede our spiritual progress, may we nonetheless maintain holy, pristine purity. Whether as a body of believers or by ourselves, may we worship God in spirit and in truth – even from a furnace.

3 Essentials of a deeper life
3.10 Pride versus humility

In the life of earnest Christians, of those who pursue and profess holiness, humility ought to be the chief mark of their uprightness.
Andrew Murray, *Humility: The Beauty of Holiness*

When I was in my twenties, the Brethren Assembly in Wauwatosa, just outside of Milwaukee, used to let us younger guys practice public speaking at the "low turnout" Sunday evening services on the Memorial Day and Labor Day weekends. On one of the first Sunday nights I spoke, Joe Schultze and I were scheduled to preach. When our song leader Bill Erickson finished leading the music, he motioned to Joe to come up first.

Our assembly met in a former Presbyterian church with two pulpits. The Presbyterians had used the large pulpit for preaching and the small one for reading the Scriptures. Our church used only the big one – that is, until that night when Bill called Joe up to preach and pointed him toward the small pulpit. Without a word of objection, Joe humbly mounted the steps as directed and delivered his message. Meanwhile, I fumed as I sat waiting in the front row, determined to ignore the small pulpit and preach from the larger one. Of course, you know what action I needed to take as a 24 year-old college guy, but pride can blind us. Why would

The Presbyterians had used the large pulpit for preaching and the small one for reading the Scriptures.

Bill do that to us? I thought. There's no way that I'm going to preach from that dinky pulpit! (And now I'm writing a chapter on humility?!) Thankfully, when my turn came, I reluctantly realized that the small pulpit was where I belonged.

In retrospect, I believe that God, not Bill Erickson, had selected the pulpit. The Holy Spirit permits such tests to give us the choice of walking humbly or remaining in our old fallen nature. Paul urged everyone "not to think of himself more highly than he ought to think; but to think soberly."[1] That Sunday night, I had to sober up spiritually and learn the lesson Jesus taught His followers about pride:

"When you are invited, go and recline at the last place, so that when the one who has invited you comes, he may say to you, 'Friend, move up higher'; then you will have honor in the sight of all who are at the table with you. For everyone who exalts himself will be humbled, and he who humbles himself will be exalted."[2]

Thus, I should have used the small pulpit, even without Bill's prompting. As you can see, the Lord had His hands full when He called me to serve Him. It's easy to write about pride. As a fallen person, I'm an expert on the subject. However, while I will discuss the sin of pride, I want to focus particularly on the positive opposite of pride: humility.

Why seek to walk humbly?

Most Christians fail to see that God promises benefits for living humbly. For many people, the idea of humbling themselves brings thoughts only of the pain and discomfort, not of the blessings and peace promised by God.

James tried to help believers overcome this shortsighted view by reminding them that God "gives a greater grace. Therefore it says, 'God is opposed to the proud, but gives grace to the humble.'"[3] The chapter "Overflowing grace and peace" considers the practical impact that God's comfort can have in our lives, especially during trials. Often, people in the church who claim to have been disappointed by God are in need of His grace. It is possible that James understood the reason some Christians don't find this peace because he informs his readers that God's grace is not for the proud.

The last being in the universe that I want to oppose me is not the devil but God Himself. Yet if we are proud and arrogant, He probably will not be there for us when we need Him. The psalmist David cautions us that God "regards the lowly, but the haughty He knows from afar."[4] If we want to enjoy deep spirituality and nearness to the Father, we should seek to be humble in our behavior. When we are tempted to insist pompously that we are right and someone else is wrong, we need to realize we are making a decision. We are choosing at that moment whether or not we truly want to walk in the Spirit and experience the grace and peace we desperately need. When we are blamed, rightly or wrongly, and our response is to fight back and trade insults, we become like those whom God "knows from afar."

It is hard not to retaliate when we're belittled. This "fight-back" reflex is a part of the old nature that we'd rather not die to. But the deeper spiritual life we want comes not only with the privilege of abiding in the life of Christ but also at the cost of abiding in His death. As Paul advised the Christians in Rome, "Do you not know that all of us who have been baptized into Christ Jesus have been baptized into His death? . . . As Christ was raised from the dead, . . . so we too might walk in newness of life."[5] We acquire that newness of life when we see ourselves having died with Christ to the sin of pride – and all other sins – and being raised up to a life no longer dominated by the old nature. Galatians 2:20 bears repeating in this context: "I have been crucified with Christ; and it is no longer I who live, but Christ lives in me; and the life which I now live in the flesh I live by faith in the Son of God, who loved me and gave Himself up for me."

How can we learn humility?

Like all the other Christian virtues, faith in God's sovereignty enables us to walk in humility. Peter instructed, "Humble yourselves under the mighty hand of God, that He may exalt you at the proper time."[6] Problems caused by others, lack of recognition and similar slights tempt us to fight. But Peter reminds us to place ourselves under God's care, thereby removing ourselves from the control of our oppressor's hand. We must let God do the vindicating and exalting, whenever and however He chooses. In fact, we should be His instruments for exalting others. Paul counseled, "Do nothing from selfishness or empty conceit, but with humility of mind regard one another as more important than yourselves."[7]

The humble individual, who trusts God in His sovereignty to look after personal needs, is willing to suffer loss by serving and yielding to others because Someone greater will sort out and ultimately provide what is important. This submissive attitude takes practice. Normally, you might not imagine humble behavior resulting in personal blessings. But in time, you will repeatedly observe that God truly does have our best in mind.

In the 1940 Charlie Chaplin comedy The Great Dictator, Chaplin, who plays an Adolf Hitler lookalike, meets Italian dictator Benito Mussolini in a barbershop. They're seated in adjacent barber chairs. After noticing that they're on the same level, each begins ratcheting his chair up higher than the other. By the time the hilarious scene ends, both men have reached the ceiling. The episode is humorous because it accurately portrays their pompousness.

Dictators are not the only ones to harbor that kind of sinful pride. More than once, I have faced a similar temptation. While evangelizing in Spain one summer, I camped out in a field with others from our Gospel team. Since we were awakened each morning at 6:00, we had plenty of opportunity for a personal prayer time, but it wasn't very quiet after everyone started getting up. So I chose to rise at 5:45 while everyone else was still asleep. Besides appreciating 15 peaceful minutes in prayer, I felt a nudge of spiritual pride that I was up even before the team leader.

I continued this practice for several mornings until another brother, Frank, discovered what I was doing. The next morning, he got up at 5:40. We ought to assume that his motives were pure, but I have to admit that I was a bit miffed at suddenly losing my self-conferred title of "most spiritual." With shame, I confess that I was tempted to rise at 5:35. But what if Frank was equally proud and chose to get up at 5:30? Where would it end? Would we be competing by flashlight in the middle of the night? I had to put aside my jealousy and be content to start my prayer time as originally planned, when it was still quiet. I needed to remember that "love . . is not jealous; love does not brag and is not arrogant."[8]

I don't believe Frank was being competitive. I think God simply woke him up earlier to teach me Paul's principle of humility: not to think of oneself more highly than one ought to think. In your own life, watch for these battleground opportunities either to indulge or forsake pride. If you're like me, you will sometimes fail. Be more careful the next time God presents you with the opportunity to humble yourself under His mighty hand.

Learning by example

I've been blessed when others have modeled humility to me, even when they may have been unaware of the influence of their example. In the early days of Operation Mobilization, I was having a discussion with George Verwer in his office when he noticed a rip in my pants. He immediately jumped up, intending to take his off and exchange them for mine. But as he looked down, he stopped himself and said, "I'd give you these, but I see I have a hole in mine, too." George was always modeling Jesus, just as Paul taught:

Have this attitude in yourselves which was also in Christ Jesus, who, although He existed in the form of God, did not regard equality with God a thing to be grasped, but emptied Himself, taking the form of a bond-servant, and being made in the likeness of men. Being found in appearance as a man, He humbled Himself by becoming obedient to the point of death, even death on a cross. For this reason also, God highly exalted Him, and bestowed on Him the name which is above every name.[9]

Unfortunately, our pride is almost invisible to us, flying stealthily under the radar of our consciousness. When we are proud and arrogant, walking in the image of fallen Adam, we come as close as we can get to being like the enemies of God. But when we practice humility, we grow more like Christ, learning to walk in our new nature.

God often checks our progress. The leader of a Gospel team in the Middle East once asked two of us to give opinions about implementing a certain project. Although I was sure the other brother, Al, had some good ideas, I knew I had the complete answer. To appear humble, I asked Al to speak first before I imparted my supposed wisdom on the matter. As it turned out, I realized right after I had spoken that I had given dumb advice, whereas Al's observations had been very insightful. I discovered that acting humble is not the same as being humble. As Paul admonishes, "Do not be wise in your own estimation."[10]

As I have just pointed out, God frequently permits challenges to our pride so that we can die to our selfish nature and let the image of the Savior come forth as a sweet fragrance for others to enjoy. Even missionaries who have given up almost everything are not exempt from this spiritual testing. After sacrificing so much to serve the needy, one might assume that a missionary could at least lay claim to a single bar of soap. Think again. Lindy Drake, a missionary to Colombia, South America, had just spent a day with the locals, who had borrowed everything but the kitchen sink. Finally, he was able to get some downtime to go to his sauna – I mean, go to the river – and have a bath. He reported:

> I was taking a bath in the river . . . [when a] crew of workers that had been pouring a cement floor . . . came down the bank and jumped into the river near me. One of them, a complete stranger, comes up to me in the water and asks, "Can I borrow your soap?"[11]

To some people, loaning a bar of soap might not be a big deal. But for Lindy, as with most of us, this request could have been the last straw. Thankfully, at that moment, he chose to do what pleased God and humbly did what he had been teaching those under his preaching to do. We are all going to be tested from time to time to see if we really mean the statements we make to God in the hearing of others when we sing hymns such as "I Surrender All."

When I returned to the Middle East from India, a Dutch brother had been selected to lead our evangelistic team for the summer. However, because I had been the team leader before I left for India, this ranking brother insisted that I resume my position as the leader. No reasoning could convince him otherwise. The area leader was out of the country and could not be reached, so we had to resolve the issue ourselves. But how does one settle such a matter when dealing with a truly humble man? We would all meet each morning, pray, sit crossed-legged on the floor and then following, he and I would argue in a loving spirit that the other was the leader. It was the Charlie Chaplin barbershop scene in reverse. Nothing would get done unless I finally gave the order of the day. At last, after days of this repeated discussion, I yielded in desperation to my humbler brother and took the lead in order to prevent further delays in our ministry. However, when the area leader learned about my decision, he sternly rebuked me. Of course, he was right. He had chosen the other man to be the team leader but had no idea how humble the Dutchman was. You might think it was foolish for the Dutch brother to carry on that way, but I wish our churches had more disputes of this nature!

Dressed for success

Peter wisely counseled believers, "Clothe yourselves with humility toward one another."[12] We usually know that it is wrong to yield to the temptations of lust, theft or dishonesty, but we think little of succumbing to pride. Yet pride is as evil as any other sin and can often be worse. So if we want to be Christ-like, we need to recognize that pride is in the same category as other enticements to evil and then follow Peter's advice: "Be on the alert. Your adversary, the devil, prowls around like a roaring lion, seeking someone to devour. But resist him, firm in your faith."[13]

Others may sometimes belittle you at work or at home. Their assessments could be correct even though offered in the wrong spirit. Regardless of the intent or fairness of the comment, Jesus asked us to be meek peacemakers, not fighting back or trading barbs. Paul presented a godly principle for dealing with fellow believers: "Why not rather be wronged? Why not rather be defrauded?"[14] When possible, let the accuser have the last word, apart from your sincere apology. In doing so, you will begin to conform to the image of Christ.

For you have been called for this purpose, since Christ also suffered for you, leaving you an example for you to follow in His steps, who committed no sin, nor was any deceit found in His mouth; and while being reviled, He did not revile in return; while suffering, He uttered no threats, but kept entrusting Himself to Him who judges righteously.[15]

Jesus is our example, not just to admire but also to imitate. If you were teaching students a skill, you would not be happy if they merely applauded your ability without reproducing the process. Likewise, Jesus wants imitators as well as admirers. When we put on Christ, we grow spiritually rich while enriching others.

The inner workings of humility

In our struggle with the fleshly nature, pride is the last thing to go – if it ever goes before our bodies return to dust. Pride is so difficult to abandon because the more we succeed in dying to the flesh, the more the old nature wants to take credit for the spiritual victory. After fighting to prevent being nailed to the cross, your old nature is proud of the accomplishment once you have, to a degree, died to self. Imagine that! The Word of God has reason to assert that "the heart is deceitful above all things, and desperately wicked."[16] If we're proud of our humility, guess what? We're no longer humble.

Humility is most often developed and perfected through relationships with others, not by a life spent in isolation. An environment of coexistence is the sandpaper that polishes the rough edges of character. Humility often blossoms when we are confronted with hostilities or challenged to place the needs and demands of others before our own.

So, as those who have been chosen of God, holy and beloved, put on a heart of compassion, kindness, humility, gentleness and patience; bearing with one another, and forgiving each

other, whoever has a complaint against anyone; just as the Lord forgave you, so also should you.[17]

Those who practice self-abasement do not lack the courage or gumption to speak up when wronged. Instead, they demonstrate courage by not making a fuss and by trusting God with the outcome. True humility is not low self-esteem, but rather contentment with the esteem that comes from God, having faith in the power that He holds over the circumstances of our lives. No matter what people say about us, just or unjust, God will ultimately have His perfect way. The godly Christian author F. B. Meyer observed:

I used to think that God's gifts were on shelves one above the other and that the taller we grow in Christian character the more easily we could reach them. I now find that God's gifts are on shelves one beneath the other and that it is not a question of growing taller but of stooping lower.[18]

The deeper spiritual life comes when we turn our backs on pride and seek to start living in the new nature, clothing ourselves in humility by putting on Christ. About once a year, I visit my home Brethren Assembly in Wauwatosa and they kindly let me practice preaching. (I'm still trying to learn.) But now they have only the big pulpit. The next time I visit, I sure hope the small one isn't reinstalled and pointed out for me to use. I'd sure hate to have to battle that pride thing all over again.

To sum up, all of you be harmonious, sympathetic, brotherly, kindhearted, and humble in spirit.
1 Peter 3:8

On the day I called, You answered me;
You made me bold with strength in my soul.
Psalm 138:3

In the late 1800s, preacher D. L. Moody came to a city for an evangelistic event. The organizer informed the group: "Brother Jacob will do the announcements, Brother Sankey will lead the music, Brother Smith will handle the prayers - and Brother Moody will preach." Moody is said to have responded, "If I can only do one thing around here, I'd rather do the praying."

By reading these next two chapters, I hope you'll be inspired to join Moody in wishing that if you could do only one thing in the church, you would pray. However, prayer has a great deal more depth than you might think, so don't be surprised if you discover something new. Don't worry if you don't feel ready for some forms of prayer that I suggest. Just be aware that different ways of praying are available to you. "Therefore let us draw near with confidence to the throne of grace."[1]

Focused prayer

"They're testing my driving to-night," Pete, my friend at the bus wash, bleakly reported as he boarded my bus. "If I don't pass, I'll be fired," he said, slumping in the front seat. "But, Pete," I protested, "what's the big deal about driving through the bus wash? Why would they test you on that?"

"Oh, I guess I don't drive that great, so they're looking for a way to fire me." Pete was a nice guy, but he had come from a dysfunctional family and it had created problems for him. Neither of his parents seemed to love him, and his older brother had disowned him. Pete often rode my bus, and I was the one who had encouraged him to apply for the bus-washing job after the company he had previously worked for went out of business. "What time is the test?" I asked. He sighed, gazing out the window. "Nine-thirty tonight." "Okay!" I said, "I'll pray for you."

Whenever I'm asked to pray for someone with a serious need, I post the name next to my computer to remind me throughout the day. Some people require prayer immediately. Others, like Pete, may face a pressing issue that demands a less urgent, but more concentrated, time of prayer. So that night, after supper and my other responsibilities were completed, I stepped out of the house and started my prayer walk in the darkness of our backyard. I pleaded Pete's case before the Lord. I begged Him to help my friend, especially because he had come from such a difficult background in life. I humbly argued like a lawyer before a judge, mentioning my belief that Pete had become a Christian through my witness. I prayed for about 40 minutes and then went to bed.

The next day, Pete was all smiles. He told me he had driven terribly before the test, but as soon as the evaluators arrived, he suddenly drove perfectly. The examiner who had expected to fire him was amazed. Then Pete added with a laugh, "The funny thing was that after the tester left, I ended up driving as erratically as I always do." I thought, *Thank You, Lord, that You enabled Pete to pass!* But then I reflected (rather disgusted with myself), *Nuts! Maybe I should have prayed for him a lot longer so he'd be driving perfectly all the time.*[2] A. W. Tozer described this latter type of extended prayer: "There is no merit in late hour prayers, but it requires a serious mind and determined heart to pray past the ordinary into the unusual. Most Christians never do."[3] Some graces are not acquired through

. . . prayer has a great deal more depth than you might think, so don't be surprised if you discover something new.

casual moments of petition and supplication, but come only through extended prayer.

On another occasion, a good friend of mine was dying of cancer. A special event had been rescheduled so he could experience the joyous occasion before he went to Heaven. However, when I talked with him on the phone two days before the event, he said he had just finished a chemo treatment and did not expect to regain his strength in time to enjoy the ceremony. I took the matter to the Lord, pacing the master bedroom for a while, interceding and pleading my friend's cause in prayer. When I phoned him about a week later, he told me that by the day of the event, he was fine and walking around as if nothing was wrong with him.

Did my prayers make a difference in either one of these cases? I have no idea. I know only that we are instructed to pray and that God has promised to listen. Maybe, unknown to me, other people were praying, and our combined prayers made a difference. Regardless, I am sure that God's gracious answers were related to the focused prayers of His people. As David wrote, "I sought the Lord, and He answered me."[4]

Requirements for prayer

Prayer is most effective when offered by a person who also seeks to live righteously. According to James 5:16, "The effective prayer of a righteous man can accomplish much." If we pray, we should stop and consider the harmful consequences every time we are tempted to sin because a lifestyle of careless living that is lacking love will make our prayers as meaningless as "a noisy gong or a clanging cymbal."[5] After all, prayer is a labor of faith, and we shouldn't work at something so important without a "paycheck." But if our conduct is sloppy, our prayers will probably not pay off here or in the world to come. One psalmist wrote, "If I regard wickedness in my heart, the Lord will not hear."[6] Andrew Murray echoed this idea: "From a defective spiritual life nothing better can be expected than a defective prayer life."[7] We do not need to wait until we are perfect – that won't happen this side of Heaven. But those who live righteously are promised influence with God. That privilege must be taken seriously, as Peter reminds his readers by quoting a psalm: "For the eyes of the Lord are toward the righteous, and His ears attend to their prayer, but the face of the Lord is against those who do evil."[8]

Jesus said, "If two of you agree on earth about anything that they may ask, it shall be done for them by My Father who is in heaven."[9] This is a wonderful assurance, but there are unwritten rules for every prayer promise in the Bible. The Word of God is not designed as a legal document covering all conditions, such as you would find on the back of your credit card statement. That kind of technical language would make the Bible unreadable. But the principles taught or demonstrated in the Scriptures apply to each pronouncement concerning prayer. God loves to hear His children pray. He answers the prayers of Christians who are walking in the Spirit, but He may choose not to honor the petitions of those who willfully sin. Requests must be made in accordance with God's will. Some things we ask for may be denied if our heavenly Father knows they are not in our best interest. Prayer by at least two believers with great faith is far more powerful than supplication by only one person with great faith.

Prayer to know Him

Another type of prayer is the request to know God in a deeper, richer way than we presently do. If we truly want to know Him better, we must sometimes approach Him with only one focus: to enter further into the knowledge of the fullness of Christ. We may not understand all that this petition entails, but we know by faith that this closeness is available to us and that we can experience infinitely more of God than we can "ask or think."[10]

On one hand, our fallen flesh does not enjoy praying. To the old nature within us, prayer is boring. On the other hand, few Christians pray deeply because they lack faith that God really hears and will answer. We need to recognize these problems and seek God's face anyway. We must be honest with God. He knows our hearts. We should tell Him the truth that we'd rather watch television, golf or play a computer game. But we can get to the point of adding, *I know this is where I should be right now and where my new inner person wants to be. So would You please start doing a deep work within me and fix me?* In the sermon "Honesty in Prayer," A. W. Tozer observed:

Another spiritual writer of unusual penetration has advised frankness in prayer even to a degree that might appear to be downright rudeness. When you come to prayer, he says, and find that you have no taste for it, tell God so without mincing words. If God and spiritual things bore you, admit it frankly. This advice will shock some squeamish saints, but it is altogether sound nevertheless. God loves the guileless soul even when in his ignorance he is actually guilty of rashness in prayer. The Lord can soon cure his ignorance, but for insincerity no cure is known.[11]

Many Christians don't practice this type of "honest to God" prayer in which they come to God and ask for more of Him, even when they don't feel like praying at all. Despite the old nature's opposition, we must listen to that quiet voice deep within us that desperately longs for God. We must yearn for the day when we can say with the psalmist David, "O God, You are my God; I shall seek You earnestly; my soul thirsts for You, my flesh yearns for You, in a dry and weary land where there is no water."[12]

When we come to God, responding to the still, small voice within, we are taking baby steps in learning to disregard the flesh and walk in the Spirit. Remember, God is hiding in the shadows, waiting for us to seek and find Him all over again. This in part is what serious prayer is all about. It's like having the longing of David, who wrote: "As the deer pants for the water brooks, so my soul pants for You, O God. My soul thirsts for God, for the living God."[13] As Tozer, a man of prayer, noted: "Revivals (or any other spiritual gifts and graces) come only to those who want them badly enough."[14] I have found that devoting time to prayer is like tithing. You're giving, but you're not losing anything, and the cost is eventually made up to you in one way or another. God is no man's debtor.

God fixes fridges, too
We can pray for anything as long as it's in God's will. In Bangladesh,

a Christian named Zed runs a training program to help young men learn job skills to make a living, and he also seeks to witness to them.[15] One day, his former student Suon had a problem. His neighbor had brought him a refrigerator to repair, but he couldn't figure out what was causing the trouble. Suon was delighted to get some work, but he was stumped. However, he knew that in a difficult situation, all he had to do was call Zed, his teacher and close friend.

Though he spent several hours with his student trying to diagnose the malfunction, even Zed could not find the problem. Finally, he said, "Let's pray." Suon had seen refrigerators repaired in many different ways, but never with prayer! Yet they prayed and then returned to work. Suddenly, the fridge started running! Later, Suon desperately needed employment. He came to see Zed and this time was not surprised when his mentor prayed about the situation. That night, one of Zed's other students phoned to say, "I have a problem. I need help. Do you know of any of your graduates who need work?" God had answered again. The next day, Suon had a job!

Varieties of prayer

Gathering for prayer has always been an integral activity of the church, beginning with the assembly in the upper room described in Acts 1. But other prayer meetings, apart from scheduled church services, are important as well, especially when designed for specific purposes. Before I joined Operation Mobilization and went overseas, I used to meet once a month with college students in Chicago for an overnight prayer vigil that would start around 8:30 Friday night and last until about 3:30 the following morning. I also attended a weekly local meeting in a Milwaukee home where we prayed for several hours for missions. While our sessions included songs, Scripture readings and shared encouragement, the primary focus was prayer.

Some people take prayer walks in pairs through spiritually needy cities. Others join "marathons" by praying in relays around the clock. During the National Day of Prayer, I enlisted participants for as many 15-minute slots as they wanted to commit to that day. The next week, one man reported with delight that, for the first time in his life, he had discovered he was able to pray for a quarter of an hour.

Another type of prayer meeting involves two or three partners. You may find that two schedules are easier to coordinate than three. I generally meet once a week with my prayer partner, Mike, depending on his availability. We do not follow precise procedural rules. We generally talk about what's going on in our lives and then pray. I have to confess that, as important and serious as prayer is, Mike and I often enjoy some good laughs before we pray. "A merry heart does good, like medicine, but a broken spirit dries the bones."[16]

Prayer summits are events during which a larger number of people convene specifically for prayer, often at a conference center. Several years ago, I read a notice about a group of pastors that held such a gathering in Upstate New York. Prayer was the only item on the agenda. No speakers were slated to teach. The only planned activities were praise and prayer. I have to see this, I thought. I attended the summit and have never regretted going, particularly as I met fellow believers who challenged me to deepen my prayer life. One very important key to improving your walk with Christ is to always look for people who are more spiritually mature than you are. Then you can have a goal for your growth.

The debt

If we are praying according to God's "rules," nothing is impossible to ask of Him. When I felt that our family's time in Southern California might be drawing to a close, I tried more than ever to correct any shortcomings in my life before moving on to a new ministry. One matter that bothered me was that I owed money to another Christian. Several years earlier, he had given me his inventory of new Christian books to sell in a business I had been trying to establish. Unfortunately, shortly after he entrusted me with the merchandise, the business failed. With very little money and no job at the time, I couldn't repay him. We had never met in person and, after conducting our transactions on long-distance calls, he had shipped his books from the Midwest to my home in California. He eventually became a missionary, and I lost track of him. This was before the days of Google searches. Nonetheless, I felt that I needed to make a concerted attempt to find him, pay him back and ask forgiveness for my failure to uphold my part of the bargain. So I sought the Lord in prayer to help me with this seemingly impossible task.

At that time, I was also searching for the Lord's will regarding what kind of ministry in which I should become involved. At the same time, The Christian and Missionary Alliance Church of Southern California invited me to its Los Angeles office to discuss the possibility of working with them. While sitting in the waiting room before my interview, I chatted with another man who was home from the mission field and looking for a pastorate while on leave. As we talked, I realized, to my utter astonishment, that this was the very man I had been praying to find! I was stunned. God had brought him from another part of the world to connect us and answer the prayers of us both - (I'm sure he had been praying through the years that the ne'er-do-well he sent the books to would finally pay him back.)

I knew his name, but he didn't recognize mine. When I revealed who I was and what I wanted to do, he was shocked and delighted. I asked him to determine the amount I owed him, accounting for interest and inflation over the years. A few days later, he called me with the total, and I immediately sent him a check. Considering the number of Alliance Church offices nationwide, with people coming and going five days a week, God had timed our meeting perfectly. He's better than any Internet search, and He's free – unless you owe somebody money.

To be sure, I've made mistakes and have often failed. However, as a young Christian in my early twenties, I determined not to wait around until death to find out if Christianity was real. I wanted to put it to the test while I was still on earth. Guess what? It's real!

But as for me, I would seek God,
And I would place my cause before God;
Who does great and unsearchable things,
Wonders without number.
Job 5:8-9

3 Essentials of a deeper life
3.12 Prayer 102

Defeat and victory lie in this one thing. To make prayer
secondary is to . . . fetter and destroy prayer. If prayer is
put first, then God is put first and victory is assured. Prayer
must either reign in life or must abdicate. Which will it be?
E. M. Bounds, *Prayer and Praying Men*

Prayer and fasting
Earlier in my Christian life, I had no stomach for fasting – especially
not for 40 days (although some fasts can be as short as one meal).
Yet Jesus didn't say, "If you fast," but rather, "Whenever you fast . ."[1]
While attending the prayer summit mentioned in the last chapter,
I met some Christians who had completed a 40-day fast and
had not died in the process. At that time, I had some desperate
needs, so I decided that prayer and fasting might be helpful. With
encouragement from these brothers and after reading all I could
on fasting – including Dr. Bill Bright's books on the subject – I
started a 40-day, liquid-only fast, with moderate amounts of fruit
and vegetable juices, tea, coffee and bouillon.[2] While some fasts
are limited to water, I did not choose to follow that route. (In case
you're wondering, I did indeed lose weight, but that wasn't the
most significant outcome.).

When fasting, the first two days are the roughest and may result
in feelings of weakness. Although these symptoms can be tolerated
by most people who are not attempting extremely strenuous activity,
it would be prudent to consult a doctor before starting a fast. Every
day, I would pray for three extended periods of time about items on
my list, which included five major personal requests. I also made
petitions for others. Some people who begin fasts report receiving
immediate answers to certain prayers, but I did not. I simply prayed

192

in faith, trusting that God was hearing me. Thankfully, He gave me grace to complete the full 40-day fast, although at the end, I still couldn't see that I had been given any answers. But I had confidence, and I told God, It's all right that I haven't seen anything happen just yet. I know that in Your time, You will honor my requests.

However, within weeks, to my joyful astonishment, I began to notice God's hand at work, like the slow melting of an ice jam in spring. Answers started coming, and eventually, the Lord satisfied all but one of my appeals. The exception was the spiritual rebirth of an old friend for whom I'm still praying. Two of the granted petitions related to my finances and my family. I desperately required about $2,000, which was beyond anything our budget could handle. That amount of money was more than I could hope for. But I prayed. Then a few weeks after the fast had finished, a special check from my retirement system came in the mail. A court had ordered the totally unexpected payment, which was more than the sum I had told God I needed. I was so amazed that for weeks afterward, I could not help but laugh whenever I thought about it. A great load had been lifted from my mind.

My fast ended in early April, and at the beginning of June, my older brother had a stroke. However, my fasting prayer request had been for his salvation, not for his health. I had shared my faith with him often, without result. Although I had sent him all my preaching videos and everything I had published, his only responses were honest critiques. That July, as he was recovering from his stroke, I took my usual yearly trip to Wisconsin to visit, and I helped him and his wife with tasks they couldn't manage by themselves. I was also in for a big surprise.

The first Sunday morning I was there, as we sat in the living room before my leaving for church, he pleaded, "Aw, why don't you stay home today?" Well, I thought, he's my brother, and I won't have him with me forever. I reluctantly agreed. But I also thought, If I'm going to stay, I might as well do it for a good spiritual reason. So I looked my brother in the eye and asked, "Gene, if you died tonight, do you know where you'd go?" From past conversations, I knew what his reaction would be: he would say he didn't know, and then he would try to change the subject. But to my astonishment, he answered, "I'd go to Heaven." I tried not to show my skepticism when I responded, "What?! How do you know that?"

My brother, who had politely resisted all my sharing of the Gospel with him over many years, replied, "Because Jesus died for me." That was the right answer and I was momentarily speechless, but when I recovered and questioned him further, I discovered that he was sincere and that his salvation was genuine. After suffering the stroke, he had recognized that he needed to get serious about his eternal destiny and to finally surrender to Christ. *Thank You, Jesus!* I sighed. *You sure answered that prayer as well.* Three months later, my brother entered Heaven.

Nobody really wants to fast, and for some people, the practice may not even be healthy. At my age (80 at this writing), I no longer fast except for a meal or two at a time. For a short commitment, you might aim to fast for only one day or to miss just a single meal. Anyone can also take an "alternative fast." If you watch a lot of TV, you could give up those programs instead of food for a specified period of time - (Only God knows your heart, how desperate you are and what sacrifice you're willing to make!) You can also go on a short fast by skipping your favorite TV show or sports event in order to pray. God will honor any of these commitments if He sees you are determined to meet Him in prayer and have Him act on your behalf. The Apostle Paul advises us to "be on the alert with all perseverance and petition for all the saints."[3] Fasting is an outward sign of perseverance. However, it is important that you don't just fast but that you also pray. Your fasting simply shows your desperation, but your prayers put forth your requests.

Prayer changed me

For several years, I attended a weekly early-morning prayer meeting in which participants were challenged to seek revival and deeper spiritual growth. One day, our group leader John commented, almost as an aside, "We ought to do what Dan (another leader) says. We should pray an hour a day."

I was in my early seventies, and by that time, I was no stranger to prayer. Without a doubt, I spent some time in daily prayer – but generally not an hour unless there was a desperate need. Yet it was as if God had spoken the suggestion directly to me that day, and I began to invest an hour each evening in prayer. I made a prayer list. Besides praying extra for everyone in my family, I prayed for everyone in my church and for the many missionaries I knew. I also held a short session of prayer for my own needs, along with some additional thanksgiving and praise.

When I started, I usually paced in our darkened living room, although occasionally I knelt. Was the prayer regimen boring or a dreaded burden? Not at all. Did I feel as though I was being lifted up to the heavens? Not particularly, although I did look forward to that time each day. I also knew by faith that God was pleased and that my prayers made a difference in people's lives. The habit eventually became so much a part of my life that the idea of doing without it was unthinkable.

One evening about six months into my new routine, I suddenly noticed that something had happened to me. I couldn't help repeating in wonder, "I'm a changed person." Please read this carefully. I discovered that as I was praying for others, I was bathing myself in God's presence, not realizing that some of His character was rubbing off on me. My inner being began to radiate just as Moses' face glowed from his mountaintop experience with God. That glory has been with me ever since. I believe Paul referred to this closeness when he wrote, "The grace of the Lord Jesus Christ, and the love of God, and the fellowship of the Holy Spirit, be with you all."[4] We often use this verse as a sweet, "feel-good" benediction when, in fact, that sense of God's presence – that "fellowship of the Holy Spirit" – is meant to be a constant privilege. I often find that all I need to do to encounter Him is stop anything I'm doing, turn to Him and talk, and He's there. If you take time to seek God's face by faith and "bathe" in His presence, I believe He will immerse you in His glory as well. As the psalmist David confirmed, "The Lord is near to all who call upon Him, to all who call upon Him in truth."[5]

Now that I'm older, however, I find that I don't always have the stamina to pray for 60 consecutive minutes on my own, so I have divided my prayer list into eight sections and spread them over the day. I try to stop at different times to pray through a section. I also pray when I'm eating alone. How long you spend on each topic is up to you. For some requests, you might briefly mention the name or need, or you might elaborate. Prayer is flexible – you can spend an hour praying for 100 people or 40 minutes praying for one. There is nothing inherently spiritual about praying for an hour. One person's 10 minutes may be more faith-filled than another's two hours. Martin Luther once said, "God doesn't measure prayers, he weighs them."

I save and update my prayer list as a file on my computer. I also write new items on my card. For major changes, I print a new card and cut it down to a small size that fits in my pocket. Sometimes, I pray the list backward just to avoid getting into a rut. Remember that whether you labor in prayer and fasting or simply pray, you are under grace and not under the Law. We should seek God's face as an act of faith and love. At times, I have drifted away from this hour-a-day commitment because of busyness, but I have always come back to the practice. If you're sick or have an impossible day, the Lord is gracious. Occasionally, I've gotten so busy that at the end of the day, I've had to go through the requests quickly. Still, I try to be faithful to those on my list, for my benefit as well as for theirs. Young moms and dads may find it hard to make much time for prayer. Perhaps you could start by carving out 10 or 15 minutes a day. The time and place is between you and God, but you will be richer for the effort. As King David attested when in great need: "This poor man cried, and the Lord heard him and saved him out of all his troubles."[6]

Spiritual interference

Paul wrote, "For our struggle is not against flesh and blood, but against the rulers, against the powers, against the world forces of this darkness, against the spiritual forces of wickedness in the heavenly places."[7] He implies that our prayers bring us into an unseen, cosmic conflict between the forces of light and darkness. When the prophet Daniel had been praying over an issue for many days, an angel came to him and said:

Do not be afraid, Daniel, for from the first day that you set your heart on understanding this and on humbling yourself before your God, your words were heard, and I have come in response to your words. But the prince of the kingdom of Persia was withstanding me for twenty-one days . . . Now I have come to give you an understanding of what will happen.[8]

Keep this ongoing struggle in mind as you pray, and know that your petition can affect the outcome. The answers to our prayers may be delayed, and it is our responsibility to persevere.

Pray without ceasing

The Bible also challenges us to "pray without ceasing."[9] No one completely succeeds in obeying this command, but just as we continue to seek to be holy, so we need to continue to work at nonstop prayer. According to the Apostle Paul, a widowed woman should persist "in entreaties and prayers night and day."[10] No spiritual slouch himself, Paul wrote to Timothy: "I constantly remember you in my prayers night and day."[11] So in addition to praying for whatever length of time you have decided for each day, you might also seek to pray whenever your mind is not occupied. This practice takes discipline, but as with any prayer, you will benefit from turning your thoughts toward God.

I find that I don't need to write a list for my "without ceasing" prayers, which focus on missionaries and churches throughout the world. I just picture them in my mind as I prayerfully travel around the globe. The advantage of this kind of prayer is that you can offer it when you're doing something that does not require much concentration, and you can start and stop any time you want. You can pray while you walk to the mailbox, fry an egg, empty the dishwasher or wait in a line. Is "praying without ceasing" easy for me? No. Am I succeeding? Only in the sense that I'm getting better at cultivating the habit. You will realize that you do many mindless tasks each day that are well-suited for going into prayer mode. This practice keeps us from straying too far from the attitude of prayer and "the fellowship of the Holy Spirit." If there were a spiritual contest in life, I would love to win this one, so I keep trying. The key is to never let your mind wander or go blank, but to be ready to pray for any immediate need or the next item on your heart. When I was growing up, my friends teased each other by saying, "If brains were dynamite, you couldn't tilt your hat!" Similarly, you might think your little spur-of-the-moment prayer lacks enough spiritual dynamite to "tilt" a missionary's situation, but the combined prayers of many believers can have explosive power.

We are not prayer wheels

Prayer is simply speaking with God. Thus, our prayers must not be thoughtless or rote recitation, but should instead resemble a conversation with a close friend. My own prayers include certain words and phrases that I am likely to repeat every day. For example, I pray that God will bless the suffering church with "warming or cooling, with food and drink." However, if I catch myself saying these familiar words mechanically, I will back up and repeat them with more focused attention. We are not grinding out senseless sounds like prayer wheels, but sincerely speaking to God from our hearts. Remember that Jesus instructed His disciples, "When you are praying, do not use meaningless repetition as the Gentiles do, for they suppose that they will be heard for their many words."[12]

The "PS" prayer

Jesus also told his followers "a parable to show that at all times they ought to pray and not to lose heart."[13] We may think that some things we ask for seem frivolous and that we shouldn't waste our time badgering the Lord about them. In my life, one item that might fall into that category was a request tacked on to a much more important prayer, like a little "PS" or an insurance rider. I wanted God to grant the main prayer, of course, but would He also answer the "pretty please" petition that might seem silly to others but would mean a lot to me? Sometime in the late 1980s, the Orange County, California, newspaper reported that Billy Graham was coming to the area for a series of evangelistic meetings. The most famous evangelist of the century, he had preached throughout the world and had served as the unofficial pastor to every American president since the 1950s. So from the time I read the announcement, as the year of preparations progressed, I prayed daily that the coming event would save souls and change lives. I also added, And grant that I may meet Billy Graham. Of course, this plea had nothing to do with the advancement of Christ's kingdom. If everyone had been granted this prayer, Dr. Graham would have had no time to preach. However, God could do as He pleased with my daily "PS."

About three months before the start of the crusade at Anaheim Stadium, all the Christians who had volunteered to help were called to a large gathering at the Garden Grove Crystal Cathedral. Billy Graham and other speakers would encourage us to give an all-out effort for the event. I was able to change my work hours, and I headed to the rally wondering if this was the day God would answer my "PS" prayer. However, when I arrived at the Crystal Cathedral, the enormous parking lot was so full that I had to park on the street. There goes that prayer, I thought. I won't meet Dr. Graham today. Inside, I found a seat high in the balcony and listened as Dr. Graham rose to give his moving challenge. When he finished, he stepped down, waved at the applauding crowd and walked back-stage. Before introducing the next of several speakers remaining in the lineup, the announcer apologized that Dr. Graham's busy schedule would prevent him from meeting anyone that day. *Of course not!* I thought. *There's no way he could shake hands with everyone in this place and still get to bed by midnight.*

Since I had to get back to work, I headed down toward the main door, but as I did, an idea came to me: *Just for a lark, why don't I jog over to the automobile ramp where the celebrity guests go in and out? Maybe I could at least see Dr. Graham close up as he rides by.* So as soon as I got out the front door, I jogged around the building to the Chapman Avenue side, reached

Billy and Ruth Graham

the ramp and looked down over the retaining wall. Sure enough, there was a car at the bottom waiting for Dr. Graham. But just then, I saw Dr. Graham step out of the church door at the bottom of the ramp. To my astonishment, he smiled, waved at the driver who was offering him a ride and proceeded up the ramp by himself. Billy Graham – alone – walked toward me.

I thought, *How can this be?* God must have been smiling and saying, *Isn't this what you've been asking for over the last nine months?* I thought, *Sure, but . . !* As Dr. Graham got closer to the top, I stepped around the low wall and greeted him. We shook hands, and I told him I had heard his wife, Ruth, was sick and that I was praying for her. Brightening, he looked me in the eye as he shook my hand and said, "Thank you! God bless you!" Then I let him continue on to meet his friends waiting in the parking lot. When I got back to my car, I pressed my face on the steering wheel, sobbing like a baby – not because I had met Billy Graham (although that was a privilege) but because the God of the universe had kindly answered my persistent "PS" prayer. In my mind, the encounter was an absolute miracle. It seemed as if God was saying to me, again with a smile, *See, my son, I can do anything – even when others announce that it's impossible. Don't you ever believe them. And don't stop asking.*[14]

God does not answer every one of our prayers the way we would like because He is all-wise. Nonetheless, if you're not practicing prayer, you're missing out on a lot of blessings. As David advises: "Delight yourself in the Lord; and He will give you the desires of your heart."[15] Upon reflection, I feel a bit bad about the whole thing. If I had known that God would answer my prayer so easily, why didn't I have the faith to tack on, *And grant that I may have lunch with Billy Graham!* Nuts! I could just kick myself!

Now to Him who is able to do far more abundantly beyond all that we ask or think, according to the power that works within us, to Him be the glory in the church and in Christ Jesus to all generations forever and ever. Amen.
Ephesians 3:20-21

3 Essentials of a deeper life
3.13 Practicing mercy and grace

Say it again, Sam

While I was evangelizing in India for six months in the mid-1960s, Operation Mobilization Director George Verwer occasionally sent me to south Kerala to preach at rural church conventions. During one of these events, people from the steamy surrounding jungles gathered each evening to listen to a light-skinned preacher – me – followed by a darker-skinned Indian evangelist. He was more culturally relevant than I was, but because I came from the other side of the planet, my participation helped draw curious crowds.

Standing on an outdoor platform illuminated by torches and kerosene lamps, I spoke in English while a local pastor translated into Malayalam. To better fit in with the culture, I was dressed in the white *dhoti* often worn by Indian men. The *dhoti*, which hung down to the ankles and felt cooler than trousers, was made from a cloth about half the size of a bed sheet that was wrapped around the waist and tied at the front. No belt was needed - (Once when preaching, I happened to look down just in time to see the knot about to loosen and drop my *dhoti* to the ground. While that exposure would have felt cooler yet, the sight definitely would have affected the crowd size the next night – although I'm not sure in which direction.).

At this convention, after I finished my turn preaching each evening, I retired to a nearby hut where I was served a meal of rice, plantains and coconut milk. For my personal enter-tainment while I dined by the light of a flickering candle, I watched a parade of tiny lizards climbing up and down a wall of dried-mud bricks in front of my table.

As I ate, however, something stranger than the playful reptiles soon caught my attention. When the native evangelist got up to preach, he spoke in short sentences and paused after each one as I had done, even though his words needed no translation. During those brief lulls, the pastor who had translated for me and now stood next to the evangelist would repeat the identical words just spoken, still in the same language. At first, I thought I was hearing an echo. Or maybe, due to the oppressive evening heat, I was losing my senses. I even wondered if the high temperatures had fermented my coconut milk. But, uncanny as it seemed, I realized that the pastor was repeating the same words spoken by the evangelist, phrase by phrase. That process made the message twice as long, but, as I had discovered, a lengthy service was never considered a problem in rural India. Nobody looks at the clock – even if one can be found.

Perspectives on Biblical mercy and grace

Upon further reflection, repetition might not be a bad idea, especially for neglected biblical teachings such as mercy and grace. Shakespeare wrote a famous description of mercy:

The quality of mercy is not strain'd.
It droppeth as the gentle rain from heaven
Upon the place beneath. It is twice blest:
It blesseth him that gives, and him that takes.
'Tis mightiest in the mightiest; it becomes
The throned monarch better than his crown.
His scepter shows the force of temporal power,
The attribute to awe and majesty,
Wherein doth sit the dread and fear of kings;
But mercy is above this sceptered sway;
It is enthroned in the heart of kings;
It is an attribute to God himself;
And earthly power doth then show likest God's
When mercy seasons justice.[1]

Mercy – extreme kindness – is undeserved, loving grace in action. Paul declared in Ephesians 2:4 that God is "rich in mercy." Jesus told His disciples to apply this truth in their lives: "Be merciful, just as your Father is merciful."[2] Showing mercy allows the essence of God's love to flow through us. However, those who offer mercy must usually pay a price. Jesus Christ exemplified this principle when, as God incarnate, He gave Himself for our sins. But mercy also comes with rich rewards, and Christ by His sacrifice obtained a bride, His church.

Similarly, a generous return awaits us when we consistently practice unearned kindness and forgiveness toward others. Jesus said, "Blessed are the merciful, for they shall receive mercy."[3] Obviously, our heavenly Father is greatly pleased when we extend benevolence to others and is displeased when we blatantly disregard opportunities for grace. Jesus illustrated this truth with a parable (Matthew 18:23-35). A man begged to have his debt forgiven, and the king mercifully granted this request. But when the man did not render the same kindness to those who were indebted to him, his callousness angered the king.

God expects all of us who are forgiven spiritual debtors to demonstrate mercy and grace. Not only that but it is rewarding as Paul asserts, "whatever good thing each one does, this he will receive back from the Lord." No one can lose by showing undeserved thoughtfulness. Shakespeare rightly observed that mercy "blesseth him that gives, and him that takes."[4]

Out of options

During the United State's second major gasoline crisis, I attempted to produce and market Volkswagen Beetles retrofitted as electric cars.[5] Unfortunately, just when I had finished creating the prototype, the 1979 oil shortage ended. Interest in electric vehicles nosedived, and I suffered a business failure. As a family we were in danger of losing everything to our creditors, so my wife and I sold whatever we could in an attempt to make the back payments on our mortgage. We even rented out a room in our home. One of our assets was a promissory note for $500. However, repeated attempts to collect the money failed. The

Ken with his electric Volkswagen Beetle in 1979. Nowadays, there are more electric cars in Los Angeles than anywhere else in the world.

debtor claimed that she was nearing a nervous breakdown because she and her husband were in more dire straits than we were. It was evident to me that the woman needed mercy, just as we did. Thus, I returned the promissory note to her marked with these words: "Forgiven in the name of Jesus."

It is important to understand that, although we do not earn mercy from God, the Scriptures indicate that He is more inclined to render grace when we ourselves have been gracious. God never overlooks acts of mercy. The Bible does not say when we will receive mercy, only that we will receive it. In the case of my family's financial crisis, within two weeks of forgiving the woman's debt, our situation was suddenly and completely turned around by an unrequested, unexpected monetary legacy that restored our fiscal stability. While this example does not necessarily indicate the way God might work in your life, the principle is the same. As Jesus taught, mercy begets mercy.

Finding mercy and grace

God extends mercy to us in addition to the grace we have already gained through salvation. The book of Hebrews gives Christians a road map for navigating life's difficulties: "Let us draw near with confidence to the throne of grace, so that we may receive mercy and find grace to help in time of need."[6] If we have made prayer part of our lives, as discussed in previous chapters, we are more likely to benefit from God's attention. Remember that we don't merit God's grace, but as our heavenly Father, He loves it when we seek His face and do acts of mercy as He does.

So if we sincerely want to be like Christ, we should follow His example by extending kindness and forgiveness to everyone, including those who may not be deserving. According to Proverbs 11:17, "The merciful man does himself good." (Shakespeare was right about mercy, but then I'm sure he got it from the Bible.) Like the message of that preacher in India, the themes of mercy and grace can bear repeating.

3 Essentials of a deeper life
3.14 Forgiven in Jesus' name

The day following my sister's death, the phone rang. My mom wiped her hands on her apron and picked up the receiver. "Hello."

"This is the Milwaukee Police Department," said a gravelly voice on the other end. "We've caught the kid who killed your daughter. He's 17 years old."

"What?!" my mom gasped. "Yes, ma'am. Now we need to take him to your store to re-enact the crime. Could someone open up?" Moments later, my mom explained the call to our family gathered in the living room. My dad drew long on his cigarette. After exhaling, he grimly looked over at my older brother. "Gene, would you and the boy go down and open up?"

Gene glanced over at me – "the boy," his 24-year-old younger brother – and asked, "Okay with you, Ken?" "Yeah . . sure." I swallowed hard. "Let's go." When we arrived, the police car was already there with the kid sitting in the back seat next to a cop. My brother and I unlocked the store. Then we stood aside and watched how, step by step, the young man had carried out his holdup and bludgeoned my sister. She and her unborn child had died a week after the assault, just before the arrest.

When the kid finished his demonstration, he returned to the squad car with the police. I realized that this was my chance to speak with him. I bolted out the door and dashed to the police car. Peering through the rolled-down window at the young man and the cops, I said, "I want to talk to the kid about Jesus. Could I do that now?" The officer behind the wheel, who had just lit a cigarette, blew a cloud of smoke out the window. After a pause, he replied, "No, I'm sorry. Not now. We're recording his every move." He reached over and started the engine. "Give us a call, and we'll see what we can do."

I looked for a moment at the forlorn figure in the back seat. I wanted so much to tell him that I had forgiven him and that Jesus would forgive him, too, if the kid would trust Jesus as his Savior. But taking a deep breath, I stepped back as the car pulled away. From that point on, my dad and the police hindered me from reaching my sister's killer.

On a Sunday evening just after I had completed the manuscript for this book, I dialed a number and waited. A cheerless voice answered the phone. "Hello." It was the person I had longed to speak to for over 50 years. I had finally located the man who had killed my sister.

"Hi! I'm Ken Cetton. We met a long time ago, and this is a friendly call. I want to sincerely forgive you for what you did to my sister in our store so many years ago."

"I'm sorry," he meekly apologized.

"I forgive you in Jesus' name."

"Thank you," he responded sadly.

I went on to share the Gospel, telling him that Christ had died on the cross for all our sins and that through faith in Him, we will be forgiven. When I finished, the offender claimed that he now had assurance of spending eternity in Heaven. The next morning, I wrote a letter summarizing the Gospel message and concluding, "If you have truly believed the Good News, then you and I are brothers in Christ." I signed, "Sincerely, your friend because of Christ."

Some people would say they could never forgive as I had the privilege of doing. Yet they feel that way only because they fail to realize the depth of their own depravity, which has been forgiven if they are Christians. I know enough of my sinfulness to be more than happy to render forgiveness to others. What about you? Can you speak these words of mercy and peace to your adversaries: "I forgive you in Jesus' name"?

Be kind to one another, tender-hearted,
forgiving each other,
just as God in Christ also has forgiven you.
Ephesians 4:32

3 Essentials of a deeper life
3.15 Don't let anyone give you a haircut

When hippie fashions were in vogue in the 1960s, many guys began to wear their hair super long. Even when I was a teen in the 1950s, I sported a ducktail with longer hair on the sides and a crew cut on top. The common cry from the "respectable" community (including my big brother) was "Get a haircut!" In fact, during the hippie era, a couple of dockworkers were arrested in my hometown because they grabbed a long-haired man and shaved his head while laughing with derision. In the late 1960s, when I led a group of college students doing door-to-door evangelism, one of my team members knocked on a door and greeted the answering resident by saying, "Good morning, ma'am. We're visiting your neighborhoo – Oh, excuse me, I meant to say, 'Good morning, sir.'"

Mind you, I'm not against barbers, but I'm telling you not to let anyone give you a haircut – at least not a spiritual one. We can learn some lessons from a certain famous man who failed to pay attention to this principle, even though he had been blessed by God with incredible physical strength. Samson's girlfriend, Delilah, tried using her best seductive charms to get her "Sammy boy" to reveal the secret of his power.

Then she said to him, "How can you say, 'I love you,' when your heart is not with me? [My, can't you just feel her pain?] You have deceived me these three times and have not told me where your great strength is." It came about when she pressed him daily with her words and urged him, that his soul was annoyed to death. So he told her all that was in his heart and said to her, "A razor has never come on my head, for I have been a Nazirite to God from my mother's womb.[1] If I am shaved, then my strength will leave me and I will become weak and be like any *other* man."[2]

Following that revelation, the deceptive temptress collected 1,100 pieces of silver from the Philistines, Samson's enemies, and:

> She made him sleep on her knees, and called for a man [here comes the barber!] and had him shave off the seven locks of his hair. Then she began to afflict him, and his strength left him. She said, "The Philistines are upon you, Samson!" And he awoke from his sleep and said, "I will go out as at other times and shake myself free." But he did not know that the Lord had departed from him. Then the Philistines seized him and gouged out his eyes; and they brought him down to Gaza and bound him with bronze chains, and he was a grinder in the prison.[3]

Picture it. The Philistines overpower Samson, and he's screaming, "Delilah, Delilah! Help me!" But she doesn't even look up from counting her silver coins. "Twenty one, twenty . . . Get that creep out of here!! Twenty . . . where was I, anyway? Oh, phooey! Now I hafta start all over again. One, two, three, four . . . "

We often see Sunday school pictures of Samson looking like a wrestling celebrity – Gorgeous George or Hulk Hogan – someone with long hair and bulging muscles who could crack open walnuts placed in the bend of his elbow. Wait a minute – Stop the presses! Change the artwork! Instead, use me as a model for Samson; the depiction should possibly be of a short, unimpressive 150-pound weakling who couldn't crack walnuts even with a nutcracker. After all, Scripture tells us that his strength was hidden not in any muscle mass but in his hair. Who would have guessed that? Of course I might be wrong but because I'm 150 pounds and unimpressive I was hoping maybe I could qualify to model for him.

The source of our strength

Similarly, we Christians have a secret source of power that can develop us into spiritually deep, strong children of God. The problem is that most of us don't have a clue where to look for that source.

And when and if we do find it, we may be tempted to run in the opposite direction. If I were to ask where you think your potential spiritual strength lies, you might say it's in being more holy or in knowing and memorizing the Word of God. These are vital aims, but I know people who act holy and know Scripture but are in no way spiritual. I'm all for learning the Word, but it's possible to earn a degree in Biblical Studies and still not understand how to draw upon God's power for a holy life.

Could it be that our potential hidden strength lies buried and unrealized (sit down for this one!) in the worst things we face in our lives? Consider the story of Naaman the leper in 2 Kings. He was told by the prophet Elisha that he would be cleansed of his leprosy if he dunked himself seven times in the (probably muddy) Jordan River.[4] Like Naaman, we would prefer something more comfortable for our spiritual muscle-building. We would rather attend a Deeper Life conference or a plush weekend "spiritual" retreat. We'd even be willing to go to an all-night prayer meeting rather than acknowledge that gold can be mined in our trials. But that's what James tells us:

Dear brothers, is your life full of difficulties and temptations? Then be happy, for when the way is rough, your patience has a chance to grow. So let it grow, and don't try to squirm out of your problems. For when your patience is finally in full bloom, then you will be ready for anything, strong in character, full and complete.[5]

You might have a horrible job or a difficult mate. You might be single and yearning for marriage or be sick or handicapped and chafing under your affliction. You think that if you could just rid yourself of your problems, you would be free to live a "normal" life. Be careful what you wish for. Many have fled terrible marriages and ended up grinding in prisons of guilt and regret.[6] They didn't realize that God was developing their spirituality through a process of suffering and that His results might take a while. I knew a young Christian couple whose marriage abruptly changed when the husband developed multiple sclerosis and was confined to a wheelchair. Instead of having children, the wife had to adjust and settle for being a lifelong caregiver. Her dream was seemingly going down the drain. Yet increasingly as the years went by, she radiated so it seemed you could have read a book in the dark by the glow on her face. Sadly, many others have not borne up under adversity, but have let their heads be shaved. We know that in order to have a bountiful crop, we need both sunshine and rain. We may hate getting caught in a downpour, but we rejoice when we finally feast on the harvest.

Examples

I know many people who have let the world give them haircuts - (I've also had a few of my own "close cuts" that could have left me hairless but for the grace of God.). One woman, who claimed to be a Christian, felt that her husband was a wimp and an absolute bore. She would "accidentally" bump into me at the supermarket and would press her body next to mine, waiting for an invitation. (Each time I would have to step away.). She finally got her invitation from some ne'er-do-well; she lost everything and became a "grinder" in her self-made prison, having to live with him in cheap motels without her children. How often we've heard of a pastor who's run off with the church secretary, only to end up with his spiritual eyes gouged out.

How about us? In what areas of our lives do we suffer, areas where God wants to grow our strength? If we look for the places of greatest pain, we will probably find our spiritual mother lodes. Don't misunderstand. We may seek relief by any appropriate, God-given means. We may legitimately pray that the trial be removed, just as the Apostle Paul prayed concerning his affliction.

Because of the surpassing greatness of the revelations, for this reason, to keep me from exalting myself, there was given me a thorn in the flesh, a messenger of Satan to torment me – to keep me from exalting myself! Concerning this I implored the Lord three times that it might leave me. And He has said to me, "My grace is sufficient for you, for power is perfected in weakness." Most gladly, therefore,

I will rather boast about my weaknesses, so that the power of Christ may dwell in me. Therefore I am well content with weaknesses, with insults, with distresses, with persecutions, with difficulties, for Christ's sake; for when I am weak, then I am strong.[7]

Yet if God chooses to keep your situation unchanged at present, refuse to go to sleep on the knees of a temptation which promises sweet dreams but ends with a rude awakering. Instead of trying to flee from your trials and heartaches, embrace them – and thank God for showing you what can be done with them. Of course, it's hard. I've been there, and in some areas, I'm still there. But if you rebel and submit yourself to the enemy barber, like Samson, "[You] will become [spiritually] weak and be like any *other* man."[8] On the other hand, through careful obedience and surrender to God you will eventually find that you have become spiritually rich and have deepened your relationship with Him. I have read that when John Wayne was dying of cancer, his nurse commended him, saying "You are such a fine example to others, Mr. Wayne." The aging actor answered in his he-man drawl, "I'm tired of being a fine example. I just want to get well!" But let's not get tired, for there is great reward in perseverance. Let's not allow anyone to give us haircuts and remove the difficulties that will give birth to greater spiritual reality and strength for our lives, as well as rewards for eternity. Remember what Paul said: "when I am weak, then I am strong."

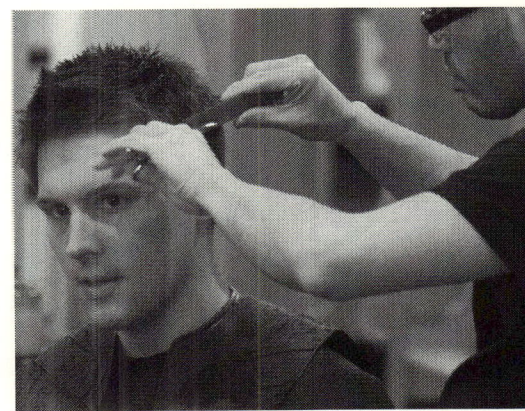

I know many people who have let the world give them haircuts.

We have all heard that suffering facilitates spiritual growth, but that assertion is only partially true. To illustrate - if you want to make bread and all you have is wheat flour, you are going to have to add something else, or you won't have anything to put your peanut butter and jam on.

Flour needs to be combined with yeast, water and other ingredients before baking. Similarly, spiritual growth from suffering requires certain essential mixing on our part. If we don't have an attitude of optimistic faith and a willingness to persevere, our lives will end up being neither "sweet smelling" offerings to God nor spiritually nourishing portions for others.

I have found that my darkest hour of chastening, when it seemed as if God had hidden His face from me, was the time to grab the shovel and dig deeper. That's why I treasure the Psalms. When David had to go through terrible trials, not only did he benefit, but he also left an example for those who were to follow. He might have been tempted to think that God was needlessly tormenting him, not knowing that he would be forever loved for his writings. What Christian would deny having been blessed by David's psalms?

While you may never write anything, others will "read" your life as they see you growing through your faithfulness in difficult circumstances. Sunlight shines at the other end of the tunnel, and so we are not to give up. We are to walk in the steps of the saints who preceded us to victory through faith in our great God and Savior. Until the Son breaks through the heavenly clouds, we are to continue in patience: loving the unlovable, witnessing to the lost, spending time in prayer and living for God. Peter wrote, "Therefore, those also who suffer according to the will of God shall entrust their souls to a faithful Creator in doing what is right."[9]

If you have failed, there is still hope

Still, some people reading this may have been shaved bald by a spiritual failure. But take heart. The Word of God tells us that when Samson was in the grinding mill, "the hair of his head began to grow again."[10] We may have suffered spiritual shipwreck by wandering outside of the will of God. But when we repent and wait for the experience of His intimacy to return to our souls, we will know we are suffering in the will of God.

Most of us remember how Samson's life ended. At a celebration of the Philistines, he was brought out of prison for his enemies to ridicule. Through the providence of God, Samson found himself standing between the supporting columns of the large temple in which a great multitude of Philistines had gathered.

Samson grasped the two middle pillars on which the house rested, and braced himself against them, the one with his right hand and the other with his left. And Samson said, "Let me die with the Philistines!" And he bent with all his might so that the house fell on the lords and all the people who were in it. So the dead whom he killed at his death were more than those whom he killed in his life.[11]

If you have failed – and all of us have failed to varying degrees along the way – let your hair grow back again in the midst of your heartache and trial. Neither be bitter nor chafe under your sufferings, but see those burdens as equipment for building spiritual muscle. Remember David's admonition: "Wait for the Lord; be strong and let your heart take courage; yes, wait for the Lord."[12] The Word of God promises, "After you have suffered for a little while, the God of all grace, who called you to His eternal glory in Christ, will Himself perfect, confirm, strengthen and establish you."[13] So remember, don't let anyone give you a spiritual haircut in the first place. Yet also remember that no matter how badly you've done in the past, God can still do for you what He did for Samson – bring down the house. I've seen it happen, to me and to others, because *God is the God of all grace.*

3 Essentials of a deeper life
3.16 To, from and around the altar

The couple's big day had finally arrived. Shortly before the service, Jim told me he planned to surprise his bride, Lynn, by singing a Christian love song to her during the ceremony.[1] Because the groom had a great voice, I gladly added his musical interlude to the program. I was not familiar with the piece, but I thought Jim's idea was touching. However, knowing from experience how women sometimes respond to amorous songs, I pocketed a few tissues in case the bride's eyes became teary.

Just before the vows, the background music started on cue. With a broad grin, Jim looked into Lynn's glowing face and began to sing. Through the words of the song, he told his beloved that, no matter what their life together would bring, he would stick by her. I smiled. *What a beautiful assurance for your bride.* Then, Jim sang that even if she faltered in her love, she could still count on him. I was so struck by that commitment that I wanted to stop and ask him, "Are you sure of that? Are you – " But he continued singing, promising that even if she was silent at times, he would understand, and everything would be okay. Again, I wanted to turn to him and say, "Wait a minute, young man! Do you have any idea what it's like when a woman suddenly stops talking, you ask her what's wrong and her only response is, 'Nothing'? 'Nothing'?"

Oblivious to my thoughts, Jim added melodiously that he would be sympathetic even if his wife were sad or depressed. I wanted to touch the groom's arm and inquire, "Hey! Do you have any clue what it's like to console someone who is sad or feels down?" I thought, *Maybe we should stop everything and do some more premarital counselling.* But Jim kept singing, elaborating promises upon golden promises while looking into Lynn's eyes as she gazed approvingly back at him.

I stared into space and recalled the many hills and valleys my dear wife and I, like most couples, had passed through. I hoped I had not failed her too badly in the promises I once made, and I wanted to question Jim, "Are you sure you can uphold all those beautiful pledges – even if the future seems as black as night?" But he kept singing, still looking into Lynn's eyes with sincerity, repeating that she could always count on him.

When the song was over, I felt proud that I had thought to bring the tissues. That was so smart, I congratulated myself. You know how women are. But when I looked up, the bride was still beaming at her lover. Nonetheless, I drew the tissues from my pocket because they were very much needed – by me. I wiped away my tears and blew my nose so we could conclude the happy service. Of course, in hindsight, I can laugh at my unexpected teary response to that song. Yet marriage is a serious step and should not be taken lightly. (And thus, this chapter is very serious.) The couple makes a vow before God to keep a lifelong commitment. For some readers, the standard of Christian conduct in relationships presented here may seem a bit high. But remember that this book is a call to a deeper spiritual life, requiring us to "humble [ourselves] under the mighty hand of God."[2]

Dating and courtship

Several decades ago when I was young, a few home sellers might put a house on the market for a very low price – but not permit prospective buyers to enter and inspect the building. They could only walk around the outside and peer through the windows. The scene inside might have been inviting, or it might have been a mess. Regardless, those who were attracted by the low price and willing to take the risk would buy the property – for better or for worse.

The couple makes a vow before God to keep a lifelong commitment . . . the standard of Christian conduct in relationships presented here may seem a bit high.

Courtship is a bit like that old real-estate practice. Usually, you only get a glimpse into the windows of the other person's soul. You might even think you could fix him or her up. However, you don't really know what you have until you're married and the two of you have become "one flesh," to use the biblical expression. Therefore, you have a strong incentive to get to know your betrothed as well as possible before marriage. One of my acquaintances exemplifies the miserable experience of countless other spouses. This woman "fell in love" much too quickly and soon discovered she had married an abusive alcoholic. Returns and exchanges are much more problematic with marriage partners than with bum toaster ovens from your local superstore. However, that difficulty doesn't give you the right to live together or have premarital sex in order to try each other out. God does not permit such behavior. The Scriptures clearly affirm that "marriage is to be held in honor among all, and the marriage bed is to be undefiled; for fornicators and adulterers God will judge."[3]

Premarital advice

When considering the person you think might be your life partner, never believe you can change him or her after marriage. You will probably fail. My wife and I knew a woman who fell in love with her psychiatrist. She divorced her second husband to marry the therapist. If he had been as familiar with her problems as we were, that doctor needed to have his head examined. I'm sure he failed to change this woman who, he should have realized, was developing a history of fleeing past marriages and abandoning the children of those unions.

Age differences usually play a more important role as couples get older. Anecdotal evidence suggests that differences of 10 or 15 years have little effect on younger couples and may even help the relationship. But, with time, the senior partner's advancing age is more likely to be a problem for the younger spouse. While one of the pair is "dying to live," the other is "living to die." Differences in cultural background may also pose the challenge of reconciling divergent concepts of spousal and parental responsibilities.

Observe the way your intended talks about and treats others.

Some women are impressed by tough, macho guys who stand their ground. But I assure you, ladies, that if you marry a man like that, someday he'll be standing his ground against you – that's his character. Notice whether the person you're interested in speaks graciously of others, even when he or she may not care for them. That attitude predicts how your prospective spouse will behave toward you when the two of you are at odds.

Don't engage in premarital sex. This behavior is not part of God's plan. The union of marriage between a man and a woman is sacred in the eyes of God. Don't compromise what He deems holy. When I was in college, I refused to date. I recognized that if I had started a relationship, I would have had to marry in order to stay pure. Otherwise, the temptation would have been too great. I passed up several opportunities for courtship, mostly because I knew it would be more difficult to enter the mission field if I had a brood of children. I would probably even have had to drop out of college in order to support my family.

We live in a highly promiscuous culture, and because sex can create such gratifying feelings, it's used to sell almost everything. As a result, many men are constantly "charged up."[4] That situation might be fine for married men, but not for unmarried ones. So whether you're a guy or a girl, if you want to stay pure, it may be a good idea to "kiss dating goodbye" for a period of time.[5] On the other hand, take heart if you have violated God's rules concerning sex and marriage. Jesus freed one woman from her adulterous past with these words: "Go. From now on sin no more."[6]

Marriage

Paul's words from 1 Corinthians 13 have become the gold standard of love and are often read at weddings.

Love is patient, love is kind and is not jealous; love does not brag and is not arrogant, does not act unbecomingly; it does not seek its own, is not provoked, does not take into account a wrong suffered; . . bears all things, believes all things, hopes all things, endures all things.[7]

The Word of God admonished men in particular concerning marital affection: "Husbands, love your wives, just as Christ also loved the church and gave Himself up for her."[8] Thus, a man's love for his wife reflects the tenderhearted love Christ has for His own bride, the church. Furthermore, Paul continued: "Husbands ought also to love their own wives as their own bodies. He who loves his own wife loves himself."[9] In addition, Paul instructed older women to "encourage the young women to love their husbands."[10]

Unfortunately, some men and women can be classified to varying degrees as "difficult" marriage partners. It seems their marriage vows read, "In health and wealth, for better but not for worse, until death of love do us part." As a pastor who has done some counseling, I know that church members are not immune to such attitudes.

Dysfunctional spouses (which might include any one of us) can be unreasonable, hostile and demanding (In some instances, irrational behaviors may be triggered by psychological conditions for which the individuals should not be blamed). While some people appear to function surprisingly well outside of a marriage relationship, they have difficulty treating their spouses kindly. These "problem partners" can be like black holes in space; they continually take in, but seldom give back.

If you are married to a challenging mate (or if you are one yourself), get counseling – preferably as a couple, but on your own if necessary. In any case, develop Christ-likeness. Consider that you have been blessed with the opportunity to cultivate the treasure of deeper spiritual growth. Peter advises those who confront adversity: "If you are suffering according to God's will, keep on doing what is right and trust yourself to the God who made you, for he will never fail you."[11]

God often uses people in our lives to humble us and bring us to the cross. You can't buy that kind of spiritual transformation anywhere, so try to embrace it - (Start practicing the message of the "What Would Jesus Do?" jewelry and T-shirts). Those who have had to walk this path confirm that the journey is not easy at first. But they also testify that ultimately, they experience God's rewarding grace. There is, of course, a great temptation for people with a dysfunctional spouse to be unfaithful. I've known men who have given in to that sin, and they suffered more afterward than they had before. It was evident that they acutely felt God's displeasure, which is far worse than enduring the displeasure of a human spouse.

If you want to restore a broken relationship, it's important to do all you can to maintain an atmosphere of love and peace. Don't be cold and distant, putting up barriers that the other person must overcome to reconnect with you. Always leave the door of reconciliation wide open so your mate can resume the relationship in good standing. It is crucial that you seek God's forgiveness for your part in the discord and forgive your partner for contributing to the disharmony, even if he or she has not asked for your forgiveness. As Paul suggests, "If it is possible, as far as it depends on you, live at peace with everyone."[12]

Husbands and wives occasionally find it hard to understand or reason with each other not only because of their individual personalities, but also because of gender distinctions. We need to patiently navigate these clouds in our relationships by the instruments of grace and love. Men can follow Peter's admonition: "You husbands in the same way, live with your wives in an understanding way."[13] I have no doubt that the Lord wants wives to do likewise.

Couples entering marriage expect to be treated fairly. But when one member of the pair feels hurt by a lack of consideration and the two cannot resolve the situation between them or through counseling, it's time for the spiritually stronger mate to be humble. In every relationship, one person is at least slightly more emotionally needy than the other. As a result, like it or not, one mate will tend to give while the other will tend to take. It is up to the more mature one to remain intensely loving and to seek the best for his or her partner. God will satisfy and reward the giver. After all, a major aim of the Holy Spirit is to make us like Christ while we are still on earth and to bless us both here and in Heaven. As John observed, "The one who says he abides in [Christ] ought himself to walk in the same manner as He walked."[14] Even if you fight for your rights and demand to be treated fairly on earth, you still probably won't always get what you want. But many spiritually mature Christians maintain that, if you are willing to accept less than your due for now, then the peace and presence of Christ will bring a bit of Heaven to soften your suffering on earth.

Paul taught us, "See that no one repays another with evil for evil, but always seek after that which is good for one another and for all people."[15] Consequently, we should never use sarcasm with our mates. Proverbs 10:19 reminds us that "he who restrains his lips is wise."

Other relationships

In a college art class, I learned the maxim "Form follows function." If you're designing a spaceship, its appearance should not be based on current styles or your personal tastes but rather on what best enables the craft to perform its function. Long before humans discovered that concept, God had the same principle in mind when he created the first man and woman. He designed humans to be sexual – as well as spiritual – beings, capable of reproducing after their own kind. A casual glance at the bodies of men and women as depicted in a medical textbook reveals that their parts were designed to function together. This simple observation shows that homosexual relationships are not the intent of the Designer.

Moreover, the Bible clearly states that homosexual behavior is not acceptable:

Do you not know that the unrighteous will not inherit the kingdom of God? Do not be deceived; neither fornicators, nor idolaters, nor adulterers, nor effeminate, nor homosexuals, nor thieves, nor the covetous, nor drunkards, nor revilers, nor swindlers, will inherit the kingdom of God.[16]

Homosexuality cannot be justified merely on the basis of personal inclination. Christ did not call us to live by the old hippie saying, "If it feels good, do it!" Yet because the popular philosophy of secular humanism theorizes that we evolved by chance, many people think there is no God and, thus, no absolute standard by which to govern behavior. In contrast, those of us who accept the Genesis account of God's creation of human beings understand that He designed men and women for heterosexual relationships. People who embrace other sexual mores should not denounce us for respecting what we perceive as God's Word on the matter. As Christians, we believe the "I'm okay, you're okay" attitude is not okay with God because He gave us solid principles to follow.

When considering whether a Christian should befriend people who hold other beliefs and practices, such as homosexuality, remember that Jesus sometimes befriended and dined with those whose behaviors did not meet with His approval. Following our Lord's example, I have always attempted to be genuinely friendly toward most non-Christians, regardless of their lifestyles, in hopes that they would be drawn to Christ. Of course, if you're tempted to adopt their lifestyle, it is best to stay distant.

I once had a gruff, arrogant neighbor whom I didn't like, but I loved him anyway and won him to Christ - (After that, I ended up liking the fellow, too!). We may not like what some people do, but we are to love them for Christ's sake. In any case, as Christians, we must practice the moral purity that the Scriptures require. As for those of us who are married, we should faithfully live up to the sacred promises of the wedding vows which we, like Jim and Lynn, made in the presence of God.

Beloved, I urge you as aliens and strangers to abstain from fleshly lusts which wage war against the soul. Keep your behavior excellent among the Gentiles.
1 Peter 2:11-12

This has been serious stuff but in this next chapter, we're going to have some fun.

3 Essentials of a deeper life
3.17 This for that

Ted: Good afternoon, ladies and gentlemen! This is your announcer, Ted Haphazinsky. Welcome to the verbal tennis game *This for That*. We're here at the crowded Wimpy Stadium for this year's championship playoff match. The challenge is between husband and wife for the best put-downs, retorts and insults. And sitting beside me is my co-host and dar-rr-ling wife, Cindy Haphazinsky.

Cindy: Thank you, Ted. However, you forgot – again – that I always go by my maiden name, Cindy Smith.

Ted: So sorry, dear. It's funny, folks, but my wife never could pronounce our last name.

Cindy: That's not true, Ted, deary. It's just that your last name sounds too much like "haphazard," which pretty much describes someone I know too well. Anyway, ladies and gentlemen, it's a miserable, overcast day today, perfect for this back-and-forth zinger competition determining who can get off the worst digs against their mate and win the title match in this put-down competition.

Ted: Right, Cindy. On each serve, one player throws out a clever sarcasm, called "this," which is returned, we hope, with an equally excellent retort, called "that."

Cindy: According to the information given to me about our first players, Ms. Brenda Jones has been married three times before. This is also the fourth marriage for her present husband, Willard Jones, so they're fairly evenly matched.

Ted: That's right, Cindy. Wait a minute, folks. I've just been handed this very important note from our program director. Wow! Are you ready for this, Cindy? It says that God is sitting among the other judges in the judges' booth today, notepad in hand. But He's in disguise, so we can't tell which One He is.

Cindy: That's scary! I'm looking over there right now, folks, trying to figure out which One He could be.

Ted: I wonder if He's the One with the big cigar. That would be a perfect disguise!

Cindy: Oh, look, Ted! Here comes the unhappy couple now, stepping out onto the turf of the *This for That* court.

Ted: Yes, Cindy, and did you notice that they're not even shaking hands?

Cindy: That's a good sign, listeners, that this is going to be a very heated back-and-forth insult match. And may the best woman win.

Ted: Cindy, didn't you mean, "May the best – "

Cindy: I meant what I said, Ted, and – Oh, I have to tell you, ladies, that Brenda Jones looks absolutely stunning. She has a short-waisted top with adorable white lace trim. But look, Ted, at the short shorts that Willard guy is wearing. It's ridiculous! [Laughing] He looks like a schoolboy.

Ted: Dear, of course they're short. This is a tennis-like match, you know. But I'd say your description is half right. Brenda Jones definitely looks short and very wasted. She can hardly walk.

Cindy: I won't waste my time on that one, Ted. And there goes the first serve, everyone, by Brenda. She's angry. She says, "You always leave your clothes lying all over the bedroom floor. Do you think I'm a hotel cleaning lady?" Ha! Tell me about it, Brenda!

Ted: Ah, but we see Willard running back to return her "this" with his own "that," swinging hard and retorting, "Well, most mornings you actually look like a frazzled hotel cleaning lady!" Beautiful, beautiful return! I wish I'd thought of it.

Cindy: Bro-ther! Now Brenda glides in and swoops down for that low remark. Hitting it hard, she says, "So now we're talking about your mother again!" She's right, you know, Ted. Your mother always looks like a frazzled old

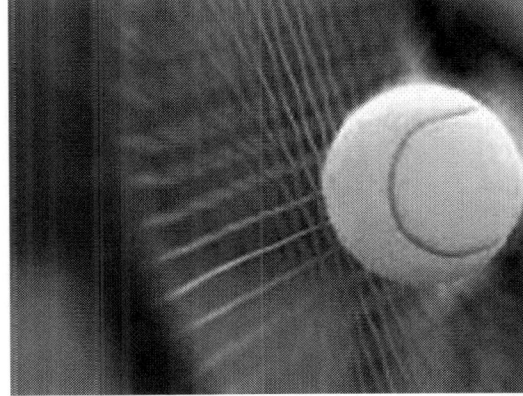

. . . this is going to be a very heated back-and-forth insult match. And may the best woman win.

cleaning lady even though she never cleans a thing.

Ted: Let me tell you – but wait! Here comes Willard with what will likely be a brilliant return. Listen to his response: "Did you notice I left you a note on top of the baby grand piano?"

Cindy: Well, that sounds like he's finally trying to communicate, which is more than you do. And I see Brenda running over to the side to return his "that," snapping, "I didn't know you had learned to write yet. What did your scrawl on the paper say?" Fancy that, Ted! There's someone else whose writing is as bad as yours. You both should have been doctors.

Ted: Oh, how I would love to write a prescription that would send you – but now Willard is in the middle of the court. He easily reaches up for the return: "It wasn't on note paper. I simply wrote in the dust on top of the piano!" Good one, Will, good one! I should try that sometime.

Cindy: Yeah, you should try dusting the piano, you big lazy galoot!

Ted: Now you listen to me –

Cindy: Ted, I've got to interrupt you. I just wonder which One up there in the judges' booth might be God? Do you have any idea?

Ted: No. But I've been watching One in particular Who seems to be taking copious notes.

Cindy: You don't think He's keeping a record of all this silly banter, do you? Oh, there goes another good retort, folks, as Brenda races back for an excellent return of "this" for her husband's "that": "Well, Willard, you do remind me of our piano. While you're not grand, you sure are a big baby – and out of tune." Bingo, sister!

Ted: On that sour note, Willard runs to the side of the court and makes a beautiful spike: "You and the baby grand also have some-thing in common – you both have piano legs." Hah! Right on, Willard, but now you're talking about *my* wife.

Cindy: Very funny, Mr. Comedian.

Ted: And she misses! She misses returning the put-down, folks, and the crowd is going wild! Well, at least the men in the stands are. And Willard, our brilliant This for That player, now holds the lead with a score of fifteen-love.

Cindy: What kind of love is that, you big jerk? Of course the men are going wild! All of you guys are wild men anyway.

Ted: Uh oh! That one Judge in the booth Who's been taking all those notes – Cindy, He's turned, and He's staring right at us!

Cindy: Oh, He is . . . God![1]

Hopefully, you didn't get winged by this tongue-in-cheek story of back-and-forth put-downs. The real-life *This for That* matches played by many couples, even Christian ones, are not so funny. God, Who instituted marriage, frowns on such destructive behavior. Far too many couples have made bickering a way of life. If not corrected, this habit can become a way of death for marriages that are already terminally ill. Peter reminds us that we are to be "humble in spirit; not returning evil for evil or insult for insult, but giving a blessing instead."[2] Because of pride, tit for tat will never bring about an "aha" moment when the sudden awareness of personal flaws floods the mind with light.

On the other hand, if we are truly seeking to honor God and to love our spouses before ourselves, we should be willing to humbly admit our failings and not try to even the score by finding fault with our mates. Instead, if the accusations are true, we need to apologize, admit that the other person is right and ask for forgiveness. Even if one spouse continues to harp on the other's shortcomings, the repentant partner can take comfort in having at least pleased God. While we have the right to deny charges that are untrue, our responses should be meek rather than combative. We must take our cue from Jesus: "For you have been called for this purpose, since Christ also suffered for you, leaving you an example for you to follow in His steps; . . . while being reviled, He did not revile in return; while suffering, He uttered no threats, but kept entrusting Himself to Him who judges righteously."[3] If we sincerely desire a deeper spiritual life, not simply a religious one, we need to adopt this model in our love relationships.

The best way to get in the last word is to apologize.
Unknown

And the one on whom seed was sown on
the good soil, this is the man who hears
the word and understands it; who indeed
bears fruit and brings forth,
some a hundredfold,
some sixty,
some thirty.
Matthew 13:23

4 Essentials of usefulness
4.1 The Orient Express – expressing your gifts

But to each one of us grace was given according to the measure of Christ's gift. Therefore it says, "When He ascended on high, . . . He gave gifts to men."
Ephesians 4:7-8

Hitchhike 1,900 miles from Istanbul to catch a plane out of London?! Oh, no! I thought, *Please, not again!* The last time I "thumbed" my way across Europe, I ended up sleeping under bridges and trudging through a swamp when the German police kicked me off the Autobahn. In August 1967, after working overseas for four years, I felt it was time to return home. But how could I get to London for my scheduled flight? No vehicles from our group were going west to England, and no funds were available for me to take the train. I had only one option – hitchhike. While mulling over this terrible prospect, I was informed that if I was willing to smuggle Bibles into communist Bulgaria by train, an outside party would pay for my third-class ticket. *How much better could it get?* I thought. *I've smuggled Bibles in by car. What's the big deal about doing it by train?* So I happily agreed – happily, that is, until I was told I would be taking a large suitcase full of Bibles. *Whoa!* I pondered. *How in the world am I going to hide that many?*

The train I would ride was called the Orient Express. For those of you who were just born, that's not a fast-food Chinese

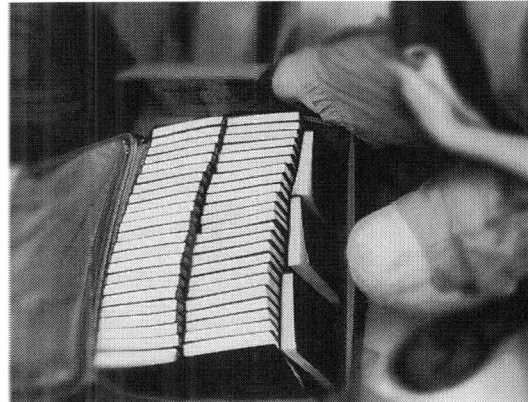

I was informed that if I was willing to smuggle some Bibles into Communist Bulgaria by train, an outside party would pay for my third-class ticket.

restaurant. It's the famous train that traveled from Istanbul on the Black Sea to Calais, France, on the English Channel. Move over, Agatha Christie! We've got a new mystery to solve.[1] I prayed, *Lord, help! What am I supposed to do? How are You going to pull off this one?* Then His plan started forming in my mind.

I learned that a third-class ticket covered the full length of the trip; I could get off and back on the train at any point. Furthermore, I would travel in the train car designated for the country of my ultimate destination. I could ride in the carriage marked for London and not go through customs until the end of the line. The passengers in the car that was designated for Sofia, Bulgaria – the drop-off point for the Bibles – would face customs inspection there, but I wouldn't be on board. Theoretically, I would be able to go undetected. Never mind, Agatha Christie. Move over, James Bond![2]

To the rhythmic clacking of wheels and rocking of cars, the steam train puffed and slowed to a stop at the Bulgarian capital. The passengers in the Sofia car disembarked and went through customs. While waiting for the right moment to leave the train, I imagined the intrigue that must have taken place through the years along this route connecting Calais and Istanbul. Because Turkey was neutral during World War II, Istanbul had become a hub for spy activity, and Sofia was under the watchful eye of the Nazis. Now, I was caught up in a new era of conflict, with Bulgaria gripped in the iron rule of Communism under the watchful eye of Russia.

As the train sat, still hissing small clouds of steam, the platform gradually emptied of passengers and customs agents. I carefully approached my car's exit. Looking both ways, I checked to see that the coast was clear. Then I stepped down and confidently walked away from the train, lugging my oversized Bible suitcase and a smaller bag of personal items. *That was easy!* I thought. Suddenly from out of the shadows stepped a large, grim-faced man in an official uniform who abruptly confronted me. He barked a question in Bulgarian, probably demanding, "Where do you think you're going?" "Um . . . " I stammered, thinking, *Oh boy! Now what, Lord?* The man glared at me and pointed to a building that was likely the customs office, motioning me to go there.

Maybe trudging through swamps and sleeping under bridges isn't so bad, after all, I considered. But then after breathing another quick prayer, I did the next thing that came to my mind. I said loudly, "Zab jingo thub de-ringa puttin da . . . " It was simply all gibberish. Even I didn't know what I was talking about (which, I've been told, is nothing new). I put down my smaller case and used my hand to motion wildly – pointing at the train, pointing at my watch, pointing at the town – while carrying on with this nonsense talk. I looked either like an Italian fish merchant trying to sell the day's catch or like the conductor of the Sofia symphony orchestra. The uniformed man and I chattered alternately for close to a minute. He spoke in a recognizable tongue while waving at the customs house, and I jabbered in a tongue unknown even to angels, gesturing frantically anywhere and everywhere. Finally, the man threw up his hands in disgust and probably said something like, "I give up!" and stomped off. After wiping the perspiration from my free hand onto my shirt, I reached down and picked up my smaller case. Letting out a deep sigh and sending a prayer of thanksgiving, I walked off to deliver my precious baggage of Bibles, humbly amazed by God's protection.

All believers are assigned tasks with appropriate gifts

When we have jobs to do for the Lord, He will equip and enable us to carry them to completion, whether it's Bible smuggling or preaching from a pulpit. Peter reminds us, "As each one has received a special gift, employ it in serving one another as good stewards of the manifold grace of God."[3] My smuggling trip was a test of trusting God to work within and alongside me by supplying wisdom as needed, and He rewarded my faith by helping me accomplish His mission. Like my Orient Express assignment, the process of applying your gifts will probably pose a few challenges. Yet the Bible teaches us that, as members of the body of Christ, God has tasks for each of us, and He wants to enable us to perform our duties. Using the human body as an illustration, the Apostle Paul teaches that one believer might be compared to an eye, another to a hand and still another to a foot. All parts are important. If you neglect your gift and responsibility, the body becomes lame.[4] All our abilities are gifts from

God, yet not all are "spiritual" gifts. You may have the natural gift of teaching or public speaking, but you could develop those talents even if you were an unbeliever. However, as we grow spiritually, these "natural" aptitudes will be enhanced and our additional spiritual gifts will gradually become evident. Paul encourages believers to employ their gifts to benefit the church:

Since we have gifts that differ according to the grace given to us, each of us is to exercise them accordingly: if prophecy, according to the proportion of his faith; if service, in his serving; or he who teaches, in his teaching; or he who exhorts, in his exhortation; he who gives, with liberality; he who leads, with diligence; he who shows mercy, with cheerfulness.[5]

While the lists of gifts in the Bible include contributions such as instruction and exhortation, I don't believe all gifts are enumerated.[6] You may have the gift of prayer, the ability to inspire people through your public prayers or to provide an example of faithful private prayer. All of us should be people of prayer, yet believers such as my neighbor Barbara will pray instantly for anyone anywhere – even in a grocery store. In my mind, this ministry is a great gift. Likewise, while we should all encourage others, you might have the gift of encouragement if you have made a natural habit of pointing out and commending the positive qualities in those you meet. My friend Buddy has the gift of "helps" referred to in 1 Corinthians 12:28. He helps others far more extensively and consistently than anyone I have ever seen.[7] We should all help others, but I think Buddy's grace in providing assistance is one of his spiritual gifts, because "every good thing given and every perfect gift is from above, coming down from the Father of lights."[8]

Remember, we will all be rewarded for developing our spiritual gifts, and the other blessings God has given us, as part of the body of Christ. Whatever your gift is, you will find that it feels easier to implement with practice. Also, it is important to understand that none of the spiritual gifts are obtained through formal biblical instruction. Education is excellent for equipping us for God's work, but spiritual gifts will only come as we learn to put on the image of Christ.

What are your spiritual gifts? When you start dying to the

flesh, walking in the Spirit and plunging into service for the Lord in whatever way you can, then your gifts will begin to shine. Thankfully, we don't have to reach spiritual perfection in order to manifest our gifts, but we do need to have a measure of Christ-likeness. Consequently, many in the church don't ever discover their spiritual gifts because "the natural man [one who walks in the old nature] receiveth not the things of the Spirit of God . . because they are spiritually discerned."[9] As you seek to identify your gifts (each person can have several), anticipate being challenged to do something for the Lord you've never done before. Be careful not to shrink from the task. God, Who helped me get past the suspicious official in Bulgaria, can see you through any difficulty that arises as you honor Him with the gifts He has given you.

The Easter event

When you are prompted by God to do something different, ask Him for the plan and the gift of ability to follow through. Once I had to trust Him for a skill I felt I didn't yet possess, only to discover that He was developing that same gift within me. In the days when colleges still held Easter Convocations (an event before Easter that celebrated the coming holiday), I was on the committee whose job it was to choose the speaker. Each campus religious group had one member on the panel. However, by the time we had our second meeting, we were still stumped. While the event was billed as an Easter Convocation, as far as I can recall, only secular motivational speeches were given on such occasions. I insisted that the group invite someone who would talk about the true meaning of Easter, but none of us could think of a member of the campus community who would deliver that message to the student body and faculty. As a shy person, I certainly felt that I didn't have the natural gift of public speaking even though I desired it, so I did not volunteer.[10]

Finally, the Catholic representative turned to me and said, "Since you think the theme should be religious, why don't you do it?" The idea of addressing a large audience of faculty and fellow students staggered and frightened me. I dared not give an answer just then. Instead, I returned to my dorm room. However, after praying about the opportunity for several days, to my surprise, I sensed an inner peace that the Lord was saying, *Do it!* Despite my outward fears, I sent my acceptance to the committee.

Convocation Day of the assembly arrived, and while attendance was not mandatory, a relatively large group of students and faculty gathered in the campus auditorium. When I stood up to speak, I stated that because this was an Easter Convocation, I was going to give the reasons why we can believe in the resurrection of Christ. Although I was scared silly, I had no choice but to go through with the presentation. Fleeing like Jonah would not have been wise because I knew God's plan was for me to be there at the microphone. Thus, I delivered my speech. When I finished, the auditorium emptied. But backstage, the dean of the school walked over as I was leaving, looked me in the eye and firmly shaking my hand, thanked me for the message. Hopefully, he conveyed the same feeling of others in the audience that day.

Later, my roommate, Jim, told me, "You know that wasn't you up there today, right?" Then, to make sure I understood him clearly, he looked at me and repeated, "You know that, don't you?" Thank the Lord! I surely did know it wasn't me, but God's power working through me. The same might be said of you as you dare to walk spiritually and answer the challenges placed in your path.

According to Ephesians 2:10, we all have "good works" to accomplish in our lifetimes (besides helping older people cross the street). Paul teaches that "God prepared [these works and tasks] beforehand so that we would walk in them." God will furnish us with whatever gifts we need to allow us to carry out His plan and calling. When you obey God and resist the enemy, Satan – like the uniformed man on the train platform – will throw up his hands, at least temporarily, and stomp off, exclaiming, "I give up!" Like me, you will be humbly amazed by what God has just done.

I can do everything God asks me to with the help of Christ who gives me the strength and power.
Philippians 4:13 TLB

4 **Essentials** of usefulness

4.2 Literature evangelism – its easier than you think

Stop! Don't let the title scare you. At least enjoy the fun and encouraging stories in evangelism.

I paid for a meal at the local McDonald's, thanked the teenaged employee, handed him a Gospel tract and turned away with my purchase. Suddenly I became aware of a struggle behind me and whirled around to witness an incredible sight.

Two young workers were jostling behind the counter. One tightly clutched the cartoon-style Gospel tract I had just given him, while the other was trying to wrestle it away for himself. Within moments, other workers moved in, all vying for a look at the same tract, "Heaven's Gate." Amazed, I sprinted to my car, tossed my burger on the seat and brought back similar pamphlets for the rest of the spiritually hungry staff.[1] While it's unusual to see people fight over Gospel literature, it's not uncommon for tracts to be eagerly received. As surprising as it seems, I have found people consistently open to these small "messengers" everywhere I go.

One day I rented roller skates for our family at a surfing shop in Newport Beach, California,. When I returned the skates, I thought, *This might be tough, offering a tract to this cool long-haired surfer dude.* But when I did hand him one, he said sincerely, "Hey, man, thanks!" Another time I gave the popular Gospel booklet *"This Was Your Life"* to a young carwash attendant just before I rolled up my window. He looked

Generally non-confrontational and always rewarding. Gospel-tract evangelism offers a place for everyone regardless of experience.

at the paper leaflet, smiled and exclaimed, "I'll read it! I'll read it!"
Once our church in California had a Saturday picnic in a state park.
I came late because I had to work until early afternoon. When I
paid my entrance fee, I felt sheepish offering the attendant a tract.
After all, the whole congregation had passed through this same
gate, and by now he must have had a stack bigger than a collection
of baseball trading cards. But he thanked me and looked at the tract
as if he had never seen one in his life.

People need to hear and believe

We read in the Word of God, "How then will they call on Him in
whom they have not believed? How will they believe in Him whom
they have not heard? And how will they hear without a preacher?"[2]
Many reading this may not be preachers, but the small pamphlet
you offer can do the preaching for you. That's the beauty of this
technique. You don't have to be a gifted evangelist to obey the
Great Commission. Generally non-confrontational and always rewarding, Gospel-tract evangelism offers a place for everyone regardless of experience. But to be motivated for tract evangelism,
you must believe that people are lost without Christ and that they
can find Him through believing the Gospel, whether by hearing or
reading it.

Determine to start

Developing a habit of distribution is essential, or you'll simply fizzle
out. An old proverb says, "Habits are at first cobwebs, later cables."
To start, include tracts every time you pay bills or conduct business
by mail. I send a tract with every bank deposit. After one such
mailing, I received a reply on my return receipt saying, "Thanks
for your little message." Although we may never meet many of
the people to whom we mail tracts, we do have an opportunity to
dramatically touch their lives.

Send tracts with birthday and Christmas cards. While we want
to be sensitive to those who are grieving, the death of a loved
one can sometimes open opportunities for evangelism. I had been
getting nowhere in telling my neighbor Ed about Christ. So when

Ed's father died, I sent a condolence card and a carefully selected Gospel tract, which instructed those who received Christ to sign a commitment and send it to a listed address to receive a free Gospel of John. The address I used was my parents' residence halfway across the country. Two weeks later, when I received a letter from my mother, she included the Gospel tract that Ed had signed. I jubilantly grabbed a Gospel of John and hurried three doors down the block. That started a friendship that lasted for years until Ed went home to heaven.

Leave tracts anywhere they can be found and read – on bus seats, in waiting rooms, on lunch tables where you work, in restaurants with a decent tip and in motel rooms when you travel. I have a friend from Romania whose father became a Christian after finding a tract on the street in the mud. I know a man who placed Gospel tracts on various seats of the city buses I drove. He especially liked to put them at the back of the bus, where young teens often sat. On several occasions while I was driving, I actually heard a teen reading the complete tract he had discovered loudly enough for all of the bus passengers to hear. In one case, the tract listed four steps to find peace with God. As clearly as if the teenager were a famous stadium evangelist, he read it point by point, including the closing prayer of dedication. At the next red light, I had to lay my head on the steering wheel to muffle my joyous laughter. The Apostle Paul wrote, "Some, to be sure, are preaching Christ even from envy and strife, but some also from good will. . . What then? Only that . . whether in pretense or in truth, Christ is proclaimed; and in this I rejoice.[3]

If I had stood up in the bus and preached the Gospel and given an invitation to repent and be born again, I would have been fired. But because someone had left tracts on the seats, others, like this teenager, unwittingly did the work for me. Now can you see how you may be missing out on having the time of your life?

Approaching people

In addition to leaving tracts where people will find them, you will eventually want to try the direct approach of actually handing someone a tract. This task is not as difficult as it seems. I find the best method is to give tracts to people with whom I do business and whom I naturally contact every day. This practice has become second nature to me. It is easy because I already have a rapport with the recipients. Generally, people will not be rude if you have just done business with them. When I left my dentist's office one day, I gave a tract to the receptionist. Not only did she receive it gladly, but later that evening she phoned our home and said that her marriage was breaking up and the tract had just the right message for her. Frequently people smile and thank me when I hand them a tract. One friend in another state wrote me,

The last time you were here, we talked about handing out gospel tracts, not just leaving them somewhere. We were in Hawaii last winter, and I decided to do just that. We were in Waikiki, staying at a hotel just off Kalakaua Ave., the busiest street in the city. It was Spring Break and I mean it was wall-to-wall people. I handed out tracts, and it was amazing. The people I didn't think would be interested were the ones that took them. Looks don't mean a thing![4]

Mass distribution

Similarly, you also might want to hand out tracts at large gatherings. At such events, I've seldom had problems. A friend and I gave tracts at a cinema after the movie "*The Passion of the Christ*." Sports games are also easy venues. But circumstances got a bit more challenging once when a team of us gathered on the concluding day of the national Jehovah's Witnesses convention at the Milwaukee Baseball Stadium. We were roughed up and dragged around by some people who opposed us, but nonetheless we rejoiced that the Gospel truth got into more hands than if we had played it safe and not done anything. Do we truly believe that we hold the life-saving message of the only way to get to heaven? If we do, then we should want to get the Good News out to people and not leave it to chance that they will hear. However, you might want to avoid mass distribution involving potentially hostile confrontations like the incident I just mentioned until you've tried all of the other methods described.

Once I was with a Dutch brother in Christ moving Christian literature across downtown Ankara, Turkey, to a new hiding place so that the police wouldn't find and illegally confiscate the materials. We hired the Turkish equivalent of Two Guys and a Truck Moving Company. In this case, the service consisted of a guy, his horse and an open cart. My partner and I rode along, sitting on top of the boxes in the back of the wagon. Suddenly a strong wind started blowing some of the Turkish Gospel tracts all over the busy street. As I was frantically trying to close the lids on the boxes for fear of discovery and arrest, my Dutch friend calmly looked up and exclaimed, "Luk it dat! Mass distribution!"

Suggestions for getting started

- Buy good-quality tracts. Don't be cheap. Choose the kind of literature you'd be comfortable with and excited about sharing. Visit your local Christian bookstore or read samples of tracts online from reputable companies. (See the list of publishers at the end of the chapter.) If you want, you can also go to my website to download a number of free tracts I have written and print your own copies. However, please do not edit or change the tract content.

- Don't give out dog-eared tracts. Purchase protective tract holder for your pocket, purse and car to keep the pamphlets looking fresh. Also, don't look "dog-eared" yourself. Generally, I don't give out tracts if I'm dirty and sweaty from yard work. I believe that if our looks or appearance distract people from appreciating the Gospel message, it's best not to evangelize at that time in this manner. I've been in Christian homes where there was trash everywhere including newspapers piled up giving only a narrow walkway to the next room. As sincere as these homeowners may be, they should not be giving out tracts to visitors or neighbors. The same goes for the way you maintain the outside of your home. If you don't cut the lawn, control the weeds or repair your house, people might link that disheveled appearance to the flawless message of Christ.

- Content is as important as how the tract appears. While the leaflet should have an attractive cover, if the Gospel is absent, you need to find a different tract. You will recall from an earlier chapter the essentials of the Gospel: Jesus Christ died for our sins and, three days later, rose from the grave. Through faith in Him we can have the assurance of forgiveness and eternal life.

- Keep tracts where you pay your bills and write letters and by the entrance doors of your house. The appliance repairman and the plumber deserve a chance to choose where they will spend eternity. I always have some tracts in my car in case I go on an errand and forget to take some with me. However, we should not be driven by guilt nor be prideful in trying to make points with God. Nor do we need to feel that we should be a Gospel-tract-dispensing machine (unless that's your calling), thinking that we have to give a tract to everyone we meet. We are under grace, not under the Law. Rather, be relaxed and sensitive to the Spirit's guidance, prayerfully seeking to give out the Word more often than not.

- If you own a business, place a tract rack where customers will see it. If you work in an office, place an eye-catching tract on your desk. A friend of mine did that, and while he made a phone call, his secretary picked up the tract and read it.

- Carry a variety of tracts for the different types of people you will meet. You may also want to obtain tracts in other languages commonly spoken in your area. In a store where I recently shopped, a Vietnamese woman was thrilled to receive a tract in her native tongue.

- You may also want to give someone a specialty tract such as one that features sports. You might say, "Here's something I think you'll enjoy, because you like sports."

- If you have relatives or close friends who need to learn about the Lord, there are several ways you can approach them with literature. You may want to speak to them alone at the close of a visit. Make eye contact with a suggestion such as, "Uncle John and Aunt Sue, there is something that I'd like to share with you that means a great deal to me. I wish that I could say it as well as this little pamphlet does, but because I can't, I hope that this will not seem too impersonal. This message changed my life, and I would like to know what you think of it." Leave the tract and then say goodbye. You have planted the seed. The next time you visit, ask for their thoughts about the tract. You can do the same thing by mail and enclose the tract in a letter or an appropriate greeting card.

- Don't become discouraged by rejection. While it does not often happen to me, there are some times when a tract is turned down. At one of our garage sales, I offered a tract to a man who shrugged it off without saying a word. I try never to take negative response personally or feel that they are affronts to God. People are not rejecting the giver; they are most likely dismissing the piece of paper and what they think it represents. They may have unpleasant feelings associated with negative experiences in the past. In any case, while refusals are rare, if you are turned down the first time you try to give out a tract, don't send up the white flag of surrender. The enemy of men's souls would be pleased with that. Instead, realize that the rejection rate is so low that you will succeed more often than not.

- If someone doesn't want to take the tract, simply smile and say something like, "That's OK," or, "Thanks anyway." Since that person is not going to read the tract, you still have an opportunity to reach him or her by your friendly tone and body language. You may prove to be more convincing than the tract, causing them to take one the next time that they are offered the Good News.

- Use tracts as an adjunct to your personal witnessing. After you have shared the message of Christ with people verbally, always give them tracts (and possibly a Gospel of Luke or John) that they can use to review the Good News when they are alone.

- Can a person receive too many tracts? Once in a busy K-Mart garden shop, I handed the young clerk a tract. She quickly brightened and said, "Oh, yeah, last time you gave me one called 'Head-on Encounter.'" Then she looked very serious for a moment and said of the new tract, "This is just what I need right now." I also gave her a Gospel of John and our home phone number if she wanted to talk.

- What words can you use when you give someone a tract? I usually say, "Here is something about the Lord (or about Jesus,)" or, "Here is something you will enjoy reading. It's very interesting." I might also add, "This message changed my life." Like the choice of tract, your choice of words should be comfortable for you. Relax, be yourself, look directly at the person and smile sincerely. Imagine if you yourself were still lost. Wouldn't you want someone to bring you the Good News of Christ so that you could be forgiven and enjoy eternity with the Living God? We should do this for others just as we are glad it was done for us.

A key to the deeper life, and its easy

Hopefully you have been reading this book because you want a more abundant spiritual life than you now possess. Being an unashamed witness for Christ can help you to learn to walk in the Spirit and go deeper in the faith. Furthermore, if you're a concerned Christian, or a pastor or part of a group praying for a spiritual awakening in your area, that's great. On the other hand, if while crying out for God to move, you're not witnessing and giving out tracts to people who come to your door or when you shop, that's not great. Be honest with yourself. What you're really saying in your prayer is at first just like Isaiah, "Here I am!" But unlike the prophet – "Send someone else."

Just before Christmas a few years ago, I met a dejected-looking woman leaving the courthouse. My heart went out to her, and because I had a special tract for the Christmas season, I smiled and said, "Hi! This is about the Christmas story." She looked up at me, suddenly brightened and exclaimed, "Thanks, I need that!" So do a lot of other people, and as has been demonstrated, *it's easier than you think*.

Literature and Gospel tract sources

If you're looking for Gospel literature, first try your local Christian bookstore. The following is a list of several publishers that offer a variety of Gospel tracts:

American Tract Society

P.O. Box 462008, Garland, TX 75046-2008. www.atstracts.org

Good News Publishers

1300 Crescent St., Wheaton, IL 60187-9962.
www.crossway.org/tractsBible

Tracts, Inc

P.O. Box 188, Bloomington, IL 61702-0188
www.bibletractsinc.org/available-tracts

Chick Publications

www.chick.com (The name "Chick" refers to Jack Chick, the originator of these unique cartoon-style tracts. I like using their "This Was Your Life" booklet.)

www.kencetton.com

Check for any tracts we might have for you to download for free. They will only cost you the price of ink and printing paper.

This chapter may also be downloaded at my website, and can be copied and shared with others as long as no changes are made and the copyright line is retained, along with the information on my book. (Tract publishers who wish to use this article to promote the distribution of their tracts may remove this last paragraph and the above sources for Gospel literature.)

4.3 Whatever happened to Smokey?

You are the light of the world. A city set on a hill cannot be hidden . . . Let your light shine before men in such a way that they may see your good works, and glorify your Father who is in heaven.
Matthew 5:14, 16

In the early 1960s, I spent my nights amidst the clatter of the noisy cafeteria dishwashing room at the University of Wisconsin working with Smokey. In spite of his uncontrollable habit of using profanity, he was a likable fellow. A good-looking, 18 year-old farm boy and college freshman with a sincere, disarming smile, he would listen with interest while I shared what Christ had done in my life.

Another guy we worked with also swore like a sailor – probably because he had been one. Because I was not hesitant to talk about my faith, he would often greet me by saying sarcastically, "Well, here comes Reverend Cetton." I would respond good-humoredly and with feigned pomp, "Please, I'm the Most Holy Reverend." This co-worker had told us that while serving as a ventilation technician aboard a navy ship, he had once fixed a cabin air conditioner for President Eisenhower, who was on board to observe naval maneuvers. When the repair was completed, the President smiled, reached out his hand and said, "Thanks, son." But as far as I know, during the

In the early 1960s, I spent my nights amidst the clatter of the noisy cafeteria dishwashing room at the University of Wisconsin.

period we worked together, the former sailor never reached out his hand to meet the ultimate Commander-in-Chief.

In contrast, Smokey would sometimes sit with me in the cafeteria over a Coke after work and further discuss the subject of his eternal destiny. On one such occasion, he pulled out a picture of his attractive 17 year-old girlfriend. Later, I heard that she attended a small Baptist church in the farming community where they both lived. I wondered how she could be dating Smokey. He was a nice guy, but he didn't really know God. On the other hand, even though she had been brought up as a Baptist, maybe she didn't know God yet, either.

During the spring semester, Smokey started to come to the weekly InterVarsity Christian Fellowship Bible study. While I was glad to see him there, he never gave any indication that he had made a commitment to Christ. Summer came, sending us back to our homes to earn some additional money for college. When fall arrived, Smokey didn't, and I busied myself with my studies and renewed campus evangelism. Meanwhile, my normally easy-going roommate, Jim, a Norwegian from a dairy farm in Central Wisconsin, was seriously concerned about Smokey. "Why don't you write him and find out how he's doing?" Jim would prod me, running his fingers through his thick, blond hair. But I couldn't be bothered, and his badgering annoyed me. Our entire campus needed to hear about Christ, I would protest and in my enthusiasm to reach new people, I suppose I figured Smokey was old business.

Maybe Jim's gift for shepherding shone through because he was planning to be a pastor. Although Smokey had been my friend and only an acquaintance to Jim, he considered this lost sheep to be part of his flock. In the end, my roommate wrote to Smokey, asking about his spiritual condition. Like a stone taken out of a shoe, the "Smokey" issue had been dealt with, and things returned to normal for Jim and me. About a week later, however, my roommate greeted me with an increased burst of enthusiasm, beaming like a kid who had just gotten a "smile" sticker on his homework.

"Guess who wrote me?" he asked, as I returned to the room that we shared. "President Kennedy!" I responded like a smart aleck because I hated that kind of trick question. "No. Smokey!" Jim glowed even brighter. "And guess what happened at our very last campus Bible study in May?"

As I began to sense what was coming, my guilt about dismissing Smokey hit me, and I sat down. Knowing the news was likely good made my own failure even more apparent to me. I was only able to stammer one word, "He . . " Jim filled in the rest, ". . . became a Christian." My roommate added a joyful chuckle. For a few moments, I sat in deep embarrassment and reflected, *What a fool I have been to think that God only works when I see Him working!* "You were right, Jim." I sighed and slowly looked up at him. "I'm sorry for the way I acted. I should never have written Smokey off. Praise God!" Then I added thoughtfully, "So Smokey found the Lord."

After learning a lesson from Jim about having a more caring attitude, I corresponded with Smokey and did my best to encourage him in his new faith. Later that year, he joined the Army and was stationed in Florida. One day after not hearing from him for a longer-than-usual period, I received a letter from his hometown girlfriend. With grief, she explained that, following a weekend spent with a Christian family, Smokey had been returning to his base and was killed in a head-on collision. Obviously, we were all saddened by the loss. But I was grateful to have learned that he had become a Christian, and I knew I would see his handsome, smiling face again. Jim had taught me that because God does not give up on people, neither should we. I also realized that while I had been privileged to disciple Smokey after hearing of his new faith, sometimes we may not see the fruit of our work until this life is over. On that great eternal day in Heaven when we realize the outcome of our Bible studies, witnessing, loving, giving and praying, we will understand that our "toil [was] not in vain in the Lord."[1]

First things first

Imagine if Jesus came to your church today and said, "And you shall be My witnesses both in [this town], and in [your state and region], and even to the remotest part of the earth."[2] How would you react?

244

What would you say? "No thanks, Lord, it's not for me." Or, "I'll get right to it, Lord. Just show me how." When Jesus gave the Great Commission to evangelize the entire world, He gave it to all of us. Therefore, we need to do our part in fulfilling His command.

First, you want to be sure that you yourself are saved and on your way to Heaven before trying to tell others the Good News. If you're not confident about that issue, then reread Section II and be sure you understand the Gospel as explained in the chapter "Accept No Substitutes." Second, write out your testimony of how you became a Christian. For some of you, the moment of salvation might have taken place when you were a child, and you may think your story lacks appeal to the average listener. In that case, learn someone else's interesting testimony to tell as an example; then add that while your story is not nearly as dramatic, the resulting salvation is the same.

A testimony can be broken down into four points. First, tell what your life was like before Christ entered your heart. Second, tell how you became a believer. During this part, you should mention that we have all sinned against God and do not deserve Heaven, so Christ died on the cross and suffered for all the sins of the world. Third, tell how you came to faith and how your life changed. Describe the assurance of forgiveness and eternal life that you have gained. Fourth, ask if the person would also like to know that he or she is forgiven and going to Heaven, and offer to lead in prayer. Use Bible verses you've memorized, and consult a Bible if one is available.

You may be a shy person. I am. I knew of a woman who could start a Gospel conversation in a checkout line at the grocery store. That's not me. I can almost guarantee you, though, that the first couple of times she witnessed, she was scared to death. It just takes time and practice to find your niche. As you already know from the previous chapter, I often use Gospel tracts. Recently when I spoke with a young man behind the counter at McDonald's, I gave him a cartoon tract that he was overjoyed to receive. Later that day, I gave a woman at a repair shop an article I had written about someone else's conversion. Because of her interest, I followed up by telling her my testimony. Evangelizing is like learning to swim. You do it best by doing it, and doing it often.

Those who had been scattered went about preaching the word.
Acts 8:4

What you don't know may hurt you

For several years, my family had next-door neighbors with whom we had never had a natural opportunity to share the Gospel. When we were told that the wife was dying of cancer, I knew I could no longer wait for "just the right moment." Shortly after, I dropped by one day to talk with her but found her pastor visiting and having a glass of wine with them. I excused myself and said I would come over another day.

When I stopped in a few days later, the woman and her husband were alone. I could see her rocking in pain, so after a short exchange of pleasantries, I quickly shared the Good News along with my testimony. Amazingly, almost miraculously, as soon as I started to explain how she could know she was forgiven and going to Heaven, she stopped rocking and listened intently. (I believe those years of observing my family's Christ-like example had won me a hearing.) After making the Gospel clear, I asked her to follow me in a word of prayer and personally trust Christ. When I left, I had no idea what had taken place in her heart, and I thought I wouldn't know until eternity. She died about a week later.

Her husband took her body to another state for burial and shortly after returning, he stopped me on our front lawn. He was happy that I had visited his wife, although he was a bit mystified over what had happened to her after our conversation. He said, "You know what, Kenny? My wife had such peace after you talked with her that day." Thank You, Lord, I whispered in my heart. Now I know I'll see her in Heaven. Although I wasn't able to reach the husband at that time, I was grateful to have been an agent of salvation to his wife. We can all be channels of the same wonderful peace as we faithfully share Christ with others.

And so . . .

Why are we discussing evangelism in a book on the deeper spiritual life? Just as prayer and mercy and other virtues are essential for a closer walk with God, so is bold proclamation of the Gospel of Jesus Christ. In fact, I've known Christians who forever remained spiritual babes and did not share their faith because they wanted to look "respectable" among their peers.

Don't be fearful. There are many ways to make Christ known besides wearing a sandwich board on Main Street or holding up a sign announcing that the end is near. We are not all meant to evangelize in the same way. Some of us are shy, others more out-going. But if we are children of God, we all have a message, and "those who lead the many to righteousness [will shine] like the stars forever and ever."[3] In the following chapter we'll seek to encourage you more in the ways we can enter into the joy of becoming proclaimers of His Glad Tidings.

4.4 People are dying to meet Jesus

But sanctify Christ as Lord in your hearts, always being ready to make a defense to everyone who asks you to give an account for the hope that is in you, yet with gentleness and reverence.
1 Peter 3:15

D. L. Moody, founder of the Moody Bible Institute in Chicago, was a famous evangelist in the late 1800s. Someone once told him, "Moody, I don't like the way you evangelize." Moody replied, "Well, how do you do it?" The man hesitated for a moment and finally admitted, "Ah . . . well, I don't really do it at all." Moody responded, "I like my method better." One time when Moody got on a train leaving Chicago, he sat down next to a man and asked, "How far are you traveling today?" The other passenger responded, "Oh, not too far, just about 10 minutes down the line." At that, Moody opened his Bible and said, "In that case, we better get started right now." He proceeded to tell his seat-mate about Christ.

While few people are as bold as Moody, each of us should share the Gospel in our own way if we are convinced it is the most important information in the entire universe. Whenever I fly, I know that I need to make an effort to reach the person God has placed next to me. Most of the time, but not always, my conversation leads into a

D. L. Moody, founder of the Moody Bible Institute in Chicago, was a famous evangelist in the late 1800s. © Yale University Divinity School Library.

discussion of the Gospel. Regardless, I always try to leave my fellow flier with a Gospel tract. For many travelers, that pamphlet may be the start of a journey that will someday lead to Heaven.

Years ago, I met an old, godly preacher who had been a performer on the stage in vaudeville earlier in his life. He told me that one day when he got on the train to go to his next booking, he met someone who led him to the Lord. As the performer humorously put it, "I got saved, but my trunks got lost." Of course, that was the end of his old show business and the start of his new show business – showing people how to find Christ.

A variety of methods

It has been my privilege to engage in many types of evangelism, from street-corner preaching with an amplifier and mass tract distribution to door-to-door witnessing. You may be surprised to learn that this last method is a favorite of a shy guy like me. When I was a young pastor, I went from house to house, and God blessed my efforts by allowing me to see people being saved and joining the congregation. After I had a nice first-time visit with one couple at their home, the wife said to me, "If you had come sooner, we would have been to your church all the sooner." I discovered that, if I visited enough homes, I would always find someone open to the Gospel. Only on rare occasions did I meet hostile people.[1]

Another good way to reach people is to invite your neighbors and your friends from work for a barbecue or a special event at church. Don't take too long to bring up the subject of the Gospel. From early in their relationships with you, your acquaintances should know that you are a serious Christian. You might even want to start a Bible study in your home. If you lack confidence in sharing the Gospel, don't be afraid to take a course in evangelism offered at a church, Bible college or reliable online Christian institution.[2] In the meantime, you might ask a more experienced soul-winner to join your gathering and share the Gospel. That way, the Word goes forth, and you can learn techniques by seeing and following a helpful example. Would you like to be a missionary to people from other cultures right in your own backyard? Then invite foreign students into your home for dinners. They will absolutely love the attention, and you may be able to reach some young people whose countries don't permit missionaries. "Behold, I have put before you an open door which no one can shut."[3]

Sometimes you wonder

You may never be a gifted evangelist (I don't feel that's my foremost gift), but don't ever be ashamed of Jesus. He is so wonderful that you will want everyone to know and enjoy Him. Nonetheless, there may be times when you wonder whether you are accomplishing anything.

A number of years ago when I was going through a time of discouragement, I was driving a city bus in Southern California. For several months, one of my routes had a convenient 30-minute break at the end of the line that enabled me to sit quietly in the bus, read my Bible and have breakfast. Perhaps I should say, it would have been a quiet time if it were not for a young career woman (we'll call her Debbie) who would show up each morning at my closed bus doors well before the next scheduled run. Normally, it wouldn't bother me to see someone waiting on a bus bench while I ate my leisurely breakfast, but it happened to be a cooler time of year near the beach, so I let her get on the bus each morning. Instead of going to the back and leaving me to finish my breakfast

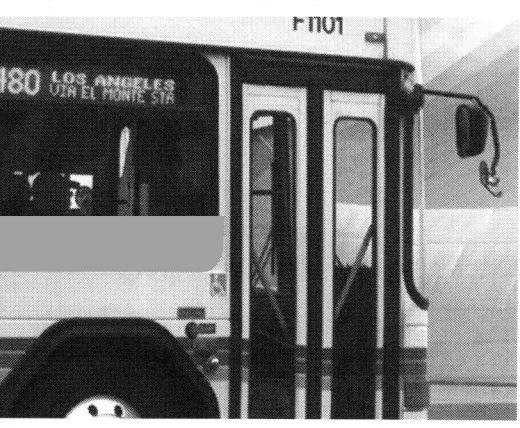

Instead of going to the back and leaving me to finish my breakfast in peace, Debbie would sit down in the front seat so that she could talk with me.

in peace, Debbie would sit down in the front seat so that she could talk with me. I believed that God had arranged these circumstances so that I could share the joy of Jesus with her. As a result, in the weeks that followed, I gradually introduced Him into our conversations. I talked to her about receiving Christ, but at that time, she didn't respond. When I changed bus routes after a few months, I never expected to see Debbie again.

Not leading Debbie to Christ after all the time I had sacrificed to give her the message just added to my discouragement. *Lord, why is it that for all the Gospel fires I try to light, I generate so little heat?* My depression continued for a few days until one morning when I pulled into a bus transfer point early and had to wait several minutes before I could leave. In my misery over seeing so little spiritual fruit, I draped my arms over the steering wheel and leaned my head on them. Suddenly, I heard someone call my name. It was Debbie! She had spotted me while waiting for another bus. Her eyes sparkling and her face full of joy, she leaped on my bus and threw her arms around me in a big hug. She cried out, "Kenny! After not seeing you at breakfast anymore, I went to a Bible study and became a Christian. I'm saved!"

I was numb with excitement. After she got off and I drove away, I had to fight back tears. I bit my lips and thanked the Lord who had mercy on me. It was as if He had said, "All right, my son. I'll part the curtain a bit so you can see a sample of what you will enjoy in eternity – like I did with Smokey, remember?" I never saw Debbie again, yet I am confident that I will meet her someday in Glory, just as you'll reconnect with many of those to whom you have faithfully witnessed during this brief life. The Scripture says, "Let us not lose heart in doing good, for in due time we will reap if we do not grow weary."[4] I learned that not seeing the results of our labor is not the same as not having results. As Paul wrote, "Now I know in part, but then I will know fully."[5] The outcomes with Debbie and Smokey are only two of the wonders I'll happily behold someday. Such joys can be yours as well.

How then will they call on Him in whom they have not believed? How will they believe in Him whom they have not heard? And how will they hear without a preacher?
Romans 10:14

The blizzard
There will be times when you want to share Christ with a person and

something gets in the way. But don't give up! We need to persevere because Satan will constantly attempt to steal the seed from where it was intended to be planted and take root.[6] Don't let him trick you into giving up. You don't know how much time either you or the other person has left. Peter tells us, "Be of sober spirit, be on the alert. Your adversary, the devil, prowls around like a roaring lion, seeking someone to devour. But resist him, firm in your faith."[7]

That point was emphasized for me by another incident. One family in my congregation had a brother-in-law who didn't attend church. I heard he was slowly dying of cancer. Although he lived about an hour away, I asked his relatives to inquire whether he would mind having a visit from me. A week later, I received word that he'd be happy for me to come. Armed with his phone number and address as well as my Bible, I waited for an opening in the fickle Upstate New York winter weather to make the trip.

It seemed, however, that each time I planned to go, a blizzard blew in.[8] The Lord impressed on me that this was a man who needed to hear the Gospel sooner rather than later, so one Sunday afternoon, in the midst of yet another blizzard, I called the family and said that I was coming, bad weather or not. The man's soul was far too important for me to worry about a storm. To my amazement, as soon as I got out of town, the blizzard stopped and the rest of the trip was easy. When I got to the home, I was warmly welcomed.

After a short conversation, the dying man, who had resisted becoming a Christian all his life, willingly trusted Jesus as Lord and Savior. Over the next two weeks, I spoke to this new believer on the phone and was able to confirm that his faith was genuine. Before he died, he arranged for me to handle his funeral in the church I was pastoring.

This man had been an

No wonder I encountered so much opposition in the form of the weather!

252

4 Essentials of usefulness

engineer and was highly respected by other engineers who had worked with him. Many colleagues from all over New York State traveled to our little country church to memorialize him. Some of them may have been surprised to hear the Gospel that their esteemed friend had come to greatly appreciate. No wonder I encountered so much opposition in the form of the weather! I often contemplate the other fruit we'll see in Heaven just because of reaching this one man.

Christ has left us to be His arms, legs and lips here on this earth. If people don't hear the Gospel from us, they may never hear the message of grace at all. How sad that some have the remedy to save others from eternal disaster and do nothing! But thank God that's not you who is being neglectful – because you're going to go forth and tell them.

How beautiful are the feet of those
who bring good news of good things!
Romans 10:15

Grace be with all those who
love our Lord Jesus Christ with
incorruptible love.
Ephesians 6:24

5 Epilogue
5.1 A thumb on your scale

Therefore I am well content with weaknesses . .
difficulties, for Christ's sake;
for when I am weak, then I am strong.
2 Corinthians 12:10

Hi, my name is Raindrop – at least that's what neighborhood kids
used to call me when I was in grade school. Raindrop! I suppose
they gave me that name because they couldn't come up with a
more insignificant tag. Snowflake would have suggested endless
variety – no two flakes are alike – but Raindrop? A single raindrop
is useless and often an irritant. Yet that became my label. Actually,
this story is not so much about me as it is about you – well, some of
you. Through Scripture and my personal testimony, I want to show
what God can do with the insignificant. While I haven't achieved any
great heights in this world, I've made a long journey from being just
plain Raindrop, a failure, to . . . well, since you have read this far
in the book, you be the judge. But you can make that same journey
and, with God's help, do even better.

God's thumb
When I was a kid, I was often sent to the butcher shop to buy
meat as supermarkets with their prepackaged cuts were not that
common. The butcher would weigh the meat on his scale in front of
you and determine how much he was owed. But you had to watch
certain butchers' thumbs very carefully because they could sneakily
press them on the corner of the scale. In so doing, they increased
the weight of the meat you were buying and also the price. God, of
course, doesn't cheat people like some of those butchers did. None-
the-less, if you trust Him with your life when facing the impossible

– even if you feel that you're a featherweight – He can put His thumb on your scale, and up goes your weight, along with your worth and abilities. When I think back over my experiences, I can see the power His thumb added to my life.

Poor grades

I didn't do very well in grade school. My allergies prevented me from keeping up with the other kids. My eyes would water, so I couldn't read the blackboard or even the book in front of me. I often carried torn-up bed sheets for hankies because I sniffled and sneezed so much. One day, a girl in my class walked up to me during recess and asked sympathetically, "Why're ya cryin', Kenny? Who beatcha up? I'll get 'em fer ya!"

Because of constant allergy problems and poor academic performance, I was kept back in grades and placed in "Special B." As a result, unfortunately, my dear old dad called me dumb and stupid, and about that same time I got my Raindrop name. I fulfilled those labels, and I did even worse in school. When I reached high-school, my family gathered in a huddle, trying to figure out what to do with me. Because they felt I was not much good at using my mind, they decided I should attend a boys-only trade school to learn auto mechanics (as if an auto mechanic doesn't need a brain!). But if you think you're dumb to start with, you won't learn much no matter what you're studying. I spent a lot of shop time sleeping under cars.

.. even if you feel that you're a featherweight – He can put His thumb on your scale, and up goes your weight ..

Early signs of hope

However, there was a bright spot in my miserable academic career. I loved to write stories, and I made profitable (if a bit shady) use of this talent by completing written assignments for my fellow English-class students at 25 cents a pop. That was good pay in 1951 for such easy work. You might say I had become a professional writer at age 16 - (I hope the IRS isn't reading this!). When I returned the ghostwritten compositions to my customers, they would copy them in their own handwriting and turn them in. I did a brisk business; not many rough-and-tumble Boys' Technical High Schooler's enjoyed writing as much as I did.

Then one day after class, our English teacher called me aside and asked me to accompany him. Uh-oh! I thought. I've been discovered! He must've done some fine detective work. I knew we were headed for the principal's office. He silently led me down the old, well-worn wooden stairs and, to my astonishment, right past Principal Hagan's dread chamber and into the student newspaper office. Once there, my wise teacher simply told the faculty adviser, "Put this guy on your staff. He can write!" Bless him! I thought. As a result, my English teacher was the first person to confirm that I had an ability to create things for print. The second confirmation came years later, in college, after I had become a Christian. My freshman English professor looked me in the eye and paid me the highest compliment a writer can receive: "You have something to say!" Nonetheless, it would be many years before I had an opportunity to say it. When I had finally graduated from high school, my adviser had told me I ranked eleventh out of a class of about 200. Not bad! I thought, but then he added, ". . from the bottom."

As a GI in Korea, I didn't do badly, despite my lack of self-confidence. Our commander ordered me to run the PX (the company store), brushing aside my strong insistence that I lacked the proper skills. After discharge, I wanted to be with my new girlfriend, and I applied for admission to Milwaukee State Teachers College, where she was a student. But my high-school grades were so low that the school wouldn't accept me unless I first attended a junior college. That experience would have been a sad joke except for one thing. During the first semester at the junior college, Jesus met me. That's when God put his thumb on the scale of my life to increase my impact for Him in the world.

God often chooses those on the bottom

One of the important things that I've learned in life is that the people

God chooses to work with are frequently at the bottom of the human scale of prestige, skills and accomplishments. That's where I was, and that's why I take joy in my life verse:

For consider your calling, brethren, that there were not many wise according to the flesh, not many mighty, not many noble; but God has chosen the foolish things of the world to shame the wise, and God has chosen the weak things of the world to shame the things which are strong, and the base things of the world and the despised God has chosen, the things that are not, so that He may nullify the things that are.[1]

While I thank God that He usually glorifies Himself by "dealing from the bottom of the deck," so to speak, He occasionally shows His sovereign grace by working off the top as well. I have a remarkably intelligent friend, Judith, who attended one of the churches I pastored. A brilliant graduate of Radcliffe, she barely had to study to achieve that status. Much later in life, this beautiful, accomplished Jewish radical was brought to the feet of Christ. But more often, it seems that God deals from lower in the deck. Enter stage left, Raindrop.

He often uses others in our lives

This is not to say that God simply waves His hand over us to fulfill His purposes. He often uses challenging circumstances and positive help from others to bring about those changes. One of the key players in my life whom He used was a young woman named Jane Fabian. She was a former neighbor and friend of my sister. After Jane found the Lord, I would often give her rides home from our InterVarsity Christian Fellowship campus Bible studies. Jane enjoyed classical music and had an urban, sophisticated way of speaking. She struck me as quite intelligent. On our trips, I would often lament, "Oh, Janie, I'm so dumb," to which she would sharply retort, "No, Kenny! You're *not dumb!*"

God was at work. Jane's frequent reassurances ultimately

erased the recording my father had burned into my mind, and I was forever changed. Thankfully, I was able to return the favor a few years later. I helped bring to faith in Christ the man who later became Jane's husband, Robert Woolly.

Electric "Lightning Bug" and writing

God put His thumb on my scale in other ways as well. Skipping ahead a number of years, after graduating from the University of Wisconsin, I became obsessed with the idea of building an electric car. I daydreamed about it the way many guys fantasize about quarterbacking for the Packers or pitching for the Yankees. But only a few tell themselves, I'm going to do it! It was the late 1970s, during the second global gasoline crisis. While at the university, I had learned how to conduct research, so I tackled the challenge of building an electric car based on an existing gas-fueled model. I'm no engineer, and I wasn't the first person to make an electric Volkswagen, but as far as I know, I was the first to design a prototype suitable for mass production. I recruited experts who supplied the technical knowledge I lacked, and together we built a car that looked like it had just rolled off the assembly line. It made such an otherworldly whine that someone once chased me through a mall parking lot to see if I was driving a Volkswagen or landing a small jet plane. Raindrop couldn't have developed that car, but because God had His giant thumb on my scale, He could do it through me.

Unfortunately, the electric "Lightning Bug" was never put into production because the gas crisis passed, ending public interest in alternative power sources. (I was born 30 years too soon!) Nonetheless, God used the project spiritually in my life, and in amazing ways, He is still using the results in the lives of others. (You can see and hear a video of the car for free on my website, www.kencetton.com.)

God has also been at work in my writing ministry, turning the talent I demonstrated as a teenage ghostwriter into something that glorifies Him. I'm not a great writer, and I'm still a small player in the world of writing, where many authors have been read by countless millions. But my work has reached a potential audience of up to five million people through publication in several major Christian periodicals and some smaller magazines both in America and in Europe. One of my pieces has also been read over the radio. Raindrop could not have accomplished any of this, either. But God, working through Raindrop, did. And none of it would have happened if God had not entered my hopeless life at age 22. Are you getting the idea that you might be underplaying the role in life God wants you to have? I'm just an ordinary person. Yet God by His grace has brought me a long way, and He wants to do the same for you.

David faced the impossible

We can take a similar lesson from David's life. God demonstrated His ability to remove formidable obstacles when King David decided to conquer Jerusalem. It was a city that, while being in the land that God had promised to the Jews, was still not under Israel's control but remained in the hands of the Jebusites.[2] After David had replaced his longtime enemy, Saul, as Israel's king, he decided it was time to rid the land of other ungodly enemies. (At this point in the story, some readers may object that David should have been more tolerant of other beliefs. But the Jebusites were pagan idol worshipers, some of whom sacrificed their children to false gods.) From the very start, God had told this new nation to cleanse the land of sin. As a result, David led his troops to Jerusalem to fight against the Jebusites, undefeated enemies who were so cocky that they said, "'You'll never come in here . . . Even the blind and lame could keep you out!' For they thought they were safe."[3]

David was intent on taking a fortified city whose inhabitants were confident that his seemingly ragamuffin band of warriors would fail. No one had succeeded in conquering and holding Jerusalem before that time, so why would David be any different? But this reasoning had a huge flaw: it omitted the God of Israel, the Creator of the universe, with whom David had a personal relationship. In time and by God's grace, our old, seemingly impregnable fortresses of personality shortcomings and flaws will also fall if we persevere in the light of Who our God is and our relationship with Him.

Determination

We likely all still have some negative things in our lives that we have not yet driven out. They might be addictions or other cripplers: smoking, overeating, excessive drinking, drug dependence, pornography, marital discord, poor health, low self-esteem or lack of skills to get ahead in life. We might be successful in our work, but we face unwanted problems that checkmate us, keeping us from getting around them and moving on. I know this description once fit me and that it now fits many reading this book.

People need to understand that the things we think stand in the way of our success and spiritual growth in life are bully fortresses just like the one David faced when he eyed Jerusalem. They mock and belittle us, saying we cannot go forward and accomplish our dreams or potential, and they will defeat us if we're gullible enough to believe their lies. That's why David is our example. When he saw the fortified walls of Jerusalem, he didn't say, "You know what, guys? I think that smaller town of Hebron will do just fine for a capital. Let's just go and fix it up." He probably said, "I know God wants me to take this pagan pit and clean it up. And by His grace and power, we're going to do it!" David believed in a big God, and so must we. The Jebusites did not think the Israelite king looked like he could take the well-fortified city of Jerusalem, but they could not see that God had His thumb on the scale of David's life. The same can be true for your life and mine in whatever we face. Do you have any dreams you'd like to fulfill, any mountain fortresses of negative thinking or bad habits you want to conquer? Take them in faith to Jesus.

The ingredients for success

So how, exactly, do we attract God's thumb to the scales of our lives? Do we puff out our chests and chant, like the popular self-help guru in the 1920s, "Every day, in every way, I am getting better and better"?[4] No, just the opposite. We fall on our knees and seek the face of God. That's what David did: "I sought the Lord, and He answered me, and delivered me from all my fears."[5] As David adds in another psalm, "When You said, 'Seek My face,' my heart said to You, 'Your face, O Lord, I shall seek.'"[6]

Unlike David, we have no earthly army. His first strength, however, was in knowing and having faith in the Creator of the universe. We must do likewise. But knowledge and faith alone are not enough. As Scripture makes abundantly clear, even the devil and his angels believe in God. The catalyst is obedience. Jesus said, "If anyone loves Me, he will keep My word; and My Father will love him, and We will come to him and make Our abode in him."[7]

It is only when we unite "knowing" and "doing" that we will grow spiritually. When we turn away from gossip and replace it with good words about the person under discussion; when we turn away from hatred and go out of our way to be kind and like Christ to those who despise us; when we turn away from fear and dare to speak up and share Christ, or when we turn away from pride and show forgiveness and mercy to those who seemingly deserve neither, then we will become strong. As we obey His commandments, we will start to see inner progress. Instead of actual troops as David had, this obedience and perseverance in trials will be our strength.

Someone loaned my family the film "*Ever After*". I thought it was a good movie of the story of Cinderella, but I was disappointed by the conclusion when the heroine, now the queen, showed little mercy toward her stepmother and stepsisters (although I'm sure the theater audience loved that kind of ending). Everyone will eventually get a comeuppance, but if we want to succeed as Christians and overcome the mocking fortresses that we are up against, we are going to have to aim at Christlikeness and let God even the score. Just as David's strengths were his walk with God and the warriors God had given him, so our close walk with Christ and our godly behavior will give us the strength to take on the seemingly impossible citadels blocking our lives. As the Word of God tells us, "For though we walk in the flesh, we do not war according to the flesh, for the weapons of our warfare are not of the flesh, but divinely powerful for the destruction of fortresses."[8] And 2 Corinthians 6:7 adds that we have been given "the weapons of righteousness for the right hand and the left."

The Roman fortress

Years ago, while working door-to-door in Spain with an Operation Mobilization team, I came across an old Roman fortress. I was in awe of such a historic place. As I mounted an outside stairway, I pictured the legionnaires fiercely battling waves of attackers while trumpets blared and banners waved in the wind. But when I reached the top of the wall and looked inside the ancient ruin, all I saw was a large herd of grunting pigs. How inglorious!

That's exactly what will happen to the fortresses standing against us if we dare to trust God. Does this mean that all the negative things in our lives will disappear? Probably not. I still can't spell - I read slower than slow - and I don't know an adverbial clause from Santa Claus. But I thank God for the tremendous changes He has brought about in me and for the fun I'm having in the process.

This is all about you

As I noted earlier, this message is not so much about me as it is about you and what God can do in your life against those seemingly unconquerable personal strongholds. It's not "positive thinking" but positive believing, praying and obeying that will enable you to live in the power of God. I've traveled far in my spiritual walk, and you who face daunting obstacles can do the same and even better if you believe He is at work within you. As recorded in 1 Chronicles: "David and all the Israelites marched to Jerusalem (that is, Jebus). The Jebusites who lived there said to David, 'You will not get in here.' Nevertheless, David captured the fortress of Zion – which is the City of David."[9]

Hi, my name used to be Raindrop, but by the grace of God, it's not that anymore. And even if anyone wants to call me by my old tag, Raindrop can now represent a tiny drop from heaven to encourage you to do better things for God's glory. Hey! It really is true that "I can do all things through Him who strengthens me."[10]

Now, I don't know what they call you, but remember that if you trust God and bend your knees to Jesus and seek to be like Him, He'll lay His heavy thumb on the scale of your life.

5.2 Finishing well

When we do something important, we try to finish well. Whether we're working on a weekend house project or a 40-year career, we want to feel we have given our best. Especially at the conclusion of our lives, we want to be able to say with Paul, "I have fought the good fight."[1]

The "Gospel Train"

The old steam train slowly chugged out of Istanbul's Sirkeci railway station and headed toward the Bulgarian border. This time, the Turkish police were not only sending me out of the country but were also accompanying me. Fortunately, the officer who was on the train with me was friendly and simply riding along to ensure that I made my exit. While I hoped to be able to turn around and re-enter through another border crossing, I could not be certain about getting back in. So I prayed that, if this were my last departure from Turkey, I might have the chance to go out in style, sharing the Gospel.[2]

Ken working as a writer and evangelist in the Middle East.

The Turkish cop who traveled with me let me sit by myself while he walked the train and chatted with the conductor. That arrangement literally opened up a window of opportunity I had not counted on, but for which I was fully prepared. In those days when Turkish trains had no air conditioning, the windows of the cars could be opened during the ride and closed to keep out the smoke when the steam engine passed through tunnels. Hence, I opened my window, and every time we chugged over a road, I would toss out Turkish Gospel tracts in hopes that they would be found by someone riding their donkey and or carting produce to market. This task proved to be fun, and I challenged myself to improve my aiming abilities.

However, when we pulled into one of the stations, I learned that my Gospel "bombing" had not always been accurate. As the conductor disembarked, he found one of my tracts lodged in the train steps. After picking up the pamphlet and seeing what it was, he turned to the policeman and exclaimed with surprise in Turkish, "Look, Ihan! Christian propaganda!" I laughed and cringed. But fortunately, they never put tract and "det-act" together, and my bombing practice continued all the way to the border. Even if they had suspected me, they couldn't have done much more than lock me up in the baggage car where I could slip Gospel tracts into the luggage. If this was to be my final time in Turkey, I was not going to leave as a "meek and mild" captive.[3]

We should all adopt this attitude while passing through our short lives on earth: the desire to finish well. As John admonishes, "Watch yourselves, that you do not lose what we have accomplished, but that you may receive a full reward."[4]

I once ran a 5K race with my younger son, Brian, who patiently waited for me at the finish line. When I finally arrived, I even received a bit of applause from others who, like my son, had run much faster than I had. Similarly in the Christian life, we will all cross the finish line someday. Peter encourages his readers, "As long as you practice these things, . . the entrance into the eternal kingdom of our Lord and Savior Jesus Christ will be abundantly supplied to you."[5] But will there be any applause and anyone anxious to welcome us?

When I returned from military service in Korea in 1955, an Army Band was waiting on the dock to welcome us GIs back home. I imagine that entering Heaven will be like that, only with an angelic Salvation Army band playing to greet each of us as we arrive at our Eternal Home. However, as I picture the scene, the size of the celebratory band may depend on the depth of our spiritual development. In that case, I sure hope I'm met by more than just a lone flute player.

Impediments

As you know by now, various earthly challenges create bumps in our Heaven-bound road. I'm sure you have noticed that the disruptive events we encounter are not marked with signs stating, "Win with patience over this adversity, and your experience with God will be enhanced." Nonetheless, God sends that message with each commonplace difficulty.

Paul informs us that we are engaged in warfare not against flesh and blood but against spiritual forces of darkness.[6] These foes do not want us to obtain any laurels or accolades. Peter reminds us, "Do not be surprised at the fiery ordeal among you, which comes upon you for your testing, as though some strange thing were happening to you."[7] Don't be startled by pitched battles with darkness. Hell wants to destroy our faith; Heaven wants to deepen it.

"Your adversary, the devil, prowls around like a roaring lion, seeking someone to devour. But resist him, firm in your faith."[8] While Peter's words may sound ominous, a wonderful promise from God follows the exhortation not to give in: "After you have suffered for a little while, the God of all grace . . . will Himself perfect, confirm, strengthen and establish you."[9] As an older man with considerable experience in this earthly journey, I can confirm that when, by faith, you reject sin and shun the enemy of your soul, you will become spiritually stronger and richer.

Don't be fooled by the devil's enticements. The tug from the flesh does not come from God, but the inner tug to follow Christ does. If you have even a small gold nugget of desire to know God and live for Him, don't set it aside thinking that you can pick it up later, since you may have difficulty retrieving it when you no longer feel that heavenly yearning. "Today if you hear His voice, do not harden your hearts."[10]

We all fail at times. But just as Peter was restored after he had foundered, so we are reinstated by Jesus when we return to Him.

Even when we fail, the Holy Spirit does not give up on us because God's chief desire is like that of the father in the parable who wanted his prodigal son to come back home.[11]

William Donovan, coordinator of the Office of Strategic Services, America's World War II spy agency, promoted a useful motto: "If you fall, fall forward."[12] With that mind-set, we should keep moving forward even after we trip. When we do, we will be able to claim Paul's triumph as our own: "I have finished the course, I have kept the faith; in the future there is laid up for me the crown of righteousness, which the Lord, the righteous Judge, will award to me on that day; and not only to me, but also to all who have loved His appearing."[13]

Yes .. but no!

I have learned that it is important to make a commitment to Christ and to follow through with it. During my first summer in Spain, the heat sometimes got to me as I went from house to house with Bibles and books. In fact, in one area, it was so hot that when a door opened, the first phrase out of my parched lips was, "¡Hola! ¡Agua, por favor!" (Hello! Water, please!)

After the residents rushed to bring me a drink, I would reel off my Spanish phrases about the great need for them to have Christian books. My presentation went something like this: "Good day! I'm a student in Spanish, and I'm here to distribute very good literature especially for you." I added that the literature was available for any small donation, and I held out the books for them to examine. The response was often: "Sí .." (Yes ..) *Wow!* I would think. *They want one of these books. It was worth it for me to travel a quarter of the way around the world and give up my summer to bring them the Word of God.* But I would hardly complete that thought before the person at the door ended the sentence with, ". . para no" (but no). "But no"? I would feel shocked. You just said, "Yes," and now you're saying, "No"? *Maybe if I try another phrase ..* "I have much literature for the whole family," I would stammer in my best Spanish. "Sí .. "

Yes! Hurray! They mean it now! I would brighten. Sure, it's hot here – maybe 110 in the shade – but who cares as long as I can get a good book and a Bible into their hands? Again they would interrupt my thoughts and add, ". . para no." "But no"? I would scream in my mind. I thought you just said, "Yes!" So I would try another line from my small repertoire of phrases, often to receive the same disappointing response. I discovered later that within the culture of this impoverished region of rural Spain, people did not speak bluntly, but declined gently. They would first answer, "Yes," and then add, "No." So I would go on to the next house, and the house after that, until I found someone who would say, "Yes," two times in a row.

In retrospect, of course, I find those memories amusing. But it is not funny at all when we respond that way to God. How often have you heard a moving message from the pulpit or through other media and (at least inwardly) shouted, "Yes, Lord, I'll do it"? You might even be having that thought as you finish this book. Hopefully, you have been instructed and inspired by each chapter, and you have said in your heart, *by faith, I'm going to put off the old self, put on Christ and practice walking lovingly in the new person.*

Yet if we do not follow through on our commitment, we are like the Spanish villagers who, after their positive answer, "Si," added, "paro no." Only this time, we are speaking to God. When Jesus stirs our hearts, we don't want to say, "No." But if we do, He will keep looking until He has found someone else who will sincerely and enthusiastically reply, "Yes!" Will you be that person who responds to the challenges of this book and His Word, "Si, Lord Jesus, si"?

"Run in such a way that you may win," and finish well.[14]

5 Epilogue
5.3 Forever young

> The amount of time given us for our earthly lives is like the sand gathered in an hourglass. God pre-measures for each the portion of granules placed in the top half; some are given more, others much less. To save anxiety, our Father has kindly hidden from our view the amount of sand remaining in the top half of the glass. As a result, what is gathered at the bottom is often not an accurate assessment of how much is left in the top.

So beware, you who think you are young. As for me, while I can't see the top half of my glass either, I sure do have an awful lot piled up at the bottom.

As for the days of our life, they contain seventy years,
Or if due to strength, eighty years . .
For soon it is gone and we fly away.
Psalm 90:10

Faded glory

I didn't wear a chauffeur's uniform as my father did when he drove in the 1920s for "old lady Richter," as he used to call her. He chauffeured until the 1929 stock market crash, at which time she lost much of her fortune and my dad lost his plush job. I chauffeured three decades later, three afternoons a week, right after finishing my last college class of the day. Like Dad, I chauffeured a wealthy, elderly widow. However, my charge was accompanied by her aging private nurse.

Before each drive, I would stop by the front door of the duplex that Mrs. Ashworth[1] shared with her son and his family, and picked up the car keys. After backing her low-mileage, unpretentious 1948 Pontiac out of the garage, I would tell her nurse I was ready to take them on whatever meanderings Mrs. Ashworth desired. After they had readied themselves, they descended the front steps, the aged dowager leaning shakily on a cane with one hand while her cheerless nurse firmly gripped her other arm and hand. Meanwhile, I would hold open, the back door of the car for them to enter and be seated.

Mrs. Ashworth was a somber woman whose face was etched by the deep marks of time that makeup had long ago ceased to erase. She had reached the age when sleep was preferable to waking, and nightly dreams of things past were far more satisfying than the grim, ever-present realities of having grown old. Although she was a woman of means, she never felt the need to possess a fancier automobile such as the luxurious limo my father had driven. After Dr. Ashworth died, she had become quite frugal with her money. Her spending above normal needs consisted only of what she felt were necessary luxuries, which, for her, were a full-time live-in nurse and a college kid to drive them around town.

On some days, we would stop by a store, pick up a few items, after which we might cruise Milwaukee's Lake Shore Drive. At other times Mrs. Ashworth would tell me to drive to her elegant former home in the wealthy community of Whitefish Bay. After being instructed where to park for the best, yet most inconspicuous, view, I would cut the engine, and we would sit in silence as she gazed at the beautiful home. I imagined she was reliving the past and seeing what we could not see – a radiant young woman, impeccably groomed and fashionably dressed, strolling the grounds while her children skip gleefully by her side. A hired nana followed, pushing the baby buggy. Like pictures in a faded album, she likely turned the pages of recollection in her mind. This time she saw herself, arm-in-arm with her doctor husband, his pipe in hand, welcoming guests to a garden party. Again on another page she saw cheerful Christmas decorations and a glittering tree glowing warmly in the bay window. Yet another leaf in her book of memories recalled their old St. Bernard playfully pulling laughing children on a sled through the snow-covered grounds.

One day after such reverie, she broke the silence and bitterly exclaimed, "And I thought . . I would never grow old!" Sometimes we would drive to nearby Graceland Cemetery and stop next to her beloved husband's final resting place. Again I cut the engine, and we would silently gaze as more precious memories flipped through pages in the old woman's mind. Now and then she would break the hush by telling us to remove some fading flowers from the grave. Next to his place, another space lay waiting for one more to be added at the toll of the cemetery's bell – but it would have to wait a little while longer.

Reminiscences of a friend

My recollections of Mrs. Ashworth remind me of a Christian friend who has since gone to heaven. At the time I knew him, Bert Gordon was older than me, although that has now been reversed since his arrival at the Eternal City. There Bert has taken on the likeness of Jesus who, although He is the "Ancient of Days,"[2] He Himself is forever young. Bert had undergone many hardships, including war and eventual personal loss. Reared in a Christian home in Scotland, he strayed from that faith and, for adventure, joined the British army. Regrettably, he got much more than he bargained for and was caught up in the harrowing 1940 Allied retreat from the "impregnable" fortifications of the Maginot Line in France to the seacoast at Dunkirk. Despite constant shelling of the beach by the Germans, he and many other British and French troops were able to escape. Their deliverance came about by what appeared to have been divine intervention in response to earthly petitions. So serious was their plight in that dark hour that King George VI called for a week of prayer during what seemed to be a totally hopeless situation. Summoning help from all over the British Isles, nearly a thousand ships and smaller boats were sent to rescue the stranded, battered soldiers. Thankfully, well over a quarter million of them were transported to the safety of England. Miraculously, the mighty German war machine was mysteriously held back until it was too late, to perform what would have been a final, killing blow.[3]

Later, under the leadership of General Montgomery, Bert fought his way through North Africa, Sicily, and into Italy. One day he found himself in a bomb crater with several other British soldiers. Fire from surrounding Germans reduced their number down to him and one other Brit. In that desperate situation, Bert finally surrendered to Jesus. Amazingly, he was once again rescued but this time, he was a new person. When I met him years later in Southern California, he was a sincere dedicated believer and became a treasured older friend.

Late one afternoon, Bert came to our home for dinner. Unlike previous times, he came alone, for he had recently lost his wife of many years to cancer. As I was about to seat him in our living room, while my wife Helen prepared dinner, something caught his attention on our outside patio. Gazing for a moment, he quickly asked in his light Scottish brogue, "Da yee mind if I sit out there fer a few minutes, Ken?" Because he did not ask if "we" could sit out there under the awning, I guessed what he was thinking, and I opened the sliding glass door for him. Eight months earlier, Bert and his wife, Beth, had been at our home for a summer pool party, and this was his first return visit. Now, as in a vision, he saw his beloved wife sitting there, as if she were alive again and waiting for him.

Watching from the shadows of our living room, I saw him draw two lawn chairs together. He sat down and placed his arm on the chair next to him as if he were once more touching his beloved. He looked over and likely pictured Beth in her flowered sundress, her body turned toward him, smiling at him as she so often did. His lips were moving and I guessed he was whispering tender words to her. In his memory, her eyes must have shone as she reached out to touch him, straightening his collar and brushing back his hair in her usual gentle manner. He savored every moment of this flight of fantasy with his bride. But like the morning dew under the rising sun, the imagined image soon had to dissipate. Nonetheless, he knew in his aching heart that he would be seeing her soon, and that their reunion would not be played out on the temporary silver screen of his imagination only to again fade away. Although he was not prepared to lose her – none of us are ever prepared to lose our loved ones – she had been well prepared to depart. And Bert knew they would once again lovingly embrace and tenderly hold hands.

No need to fear death

We all seem to think – especially in our younger years, as did Mrs. Ashworth that we will be the exceptions and will never actually age. Even when we do daydream about our retirement, we do not visualize a face full of wrinkles or a body bent and smarting with arthritis. Nor do many of us make realistic spiritual preparations. But as I write this, I myself am nearing – albeit peacefully – the end of earth's brief trip. My train of life has slowed, having some time ago left behind a blooming countryside of rolling meadows and budding woods and saplings. Now it's passing by the backs of aging, rusting factories, with shattered windows, surrounded by withered grass and toxic smells, nearing the central terminal. With train coupler joints squeaking, the engine slows further and the clanging of its bell, like the one at Graceland, will soon be tolling as it enters that final stop.

I used to fear death before my faith came to a rest in Jesus. Now I look forward to its arrival and to meeting my old, yet – now youthful – family members and friends who await my appearance on that high arrival platform. They will be young again because their celestial bodies will no longer be marked by the ravages of time from having lived in a fallen world. Even better, I will be met by the very King of that boundless eternal habitation of love. This same Jesus said in the Gospel of John, "I am the resurrection and the life; he who believes in Me will live even if he dies, and everyone who lives and believes in Me will never die." To these words, Jesus added the question, "Do you believe this?"[4]

The return visit

After graduating from college and working for four years overseas sharing the message of Christ, I returned to my parents' home in the United States. One day, I visited our family plot in the same Graceland Cemetery to which I had formerly driven Mrs. Ashworth. Having tarried at our burial site, I drove over to the Ashworth resting place. At long last she too had made her final trip – this time to her husband's side. As I had done so many times before, I cut the engine – now alone – and stared in silence at the headstone while recalling images of the past.

Not only did I see the three of us – she, her nurse and myself – but I also pictured her in her in enchanting former home. I visualized a happy, trim young woman picking flowers in her colorful gardens. I saw Dr. Ashworth arriving home from the office and embracing her, and the children running happily to meet him. Life seemed so very much alive and she thought it would never end—but it did. And I hoped for the times I shared the Good News of Jesus with Mrs. Ashworth and her nurse, that they had become prepared. I hope that I might see them again, this time looking young and at long last, carefree. For we shall all grow old – at least if we live long enough – but we can be forever youthful if we are wise and believe the Gospel. The Good News proclaims that Jesus suffered on the cross to take the punishment for our sins, and that three days later He rose from the dead in triumph over death. If we believe this and embrace not only the message but Jesus Christ Himself, we are now completely forgiven, and aging and death will have no lasting power over us.[5] In the Bible Book of Revelation, John wrote, "And He [Jesus] placed His right hand on me saying, 'Do not be afraid; I am the first and the last, and the living One; and I was dead, and behold, I am alive forevermore, and I have the keys of death and of Hades."[6]

Bert and Beth were prepared. I can picture them now, him holding his beloved and laughing as she beams back, bursting with joy, while lovingly brushing back his hair – now no longer as husband and wife, but as very deeply loving friends who are forever young. Some may ask, "What about my cantankerous mate? Will I be bound to him or her forever?" The answer is no. Heaven is not hell, but a place of unimaginable, overflowing love, and Jesus taught that there will be no marriages in heaven.[7] Instead, each of us will be changed into the likeness of the Savior. Our past, fallen natures, which hindered us in being Christ-like, will be firmly replaced with the very nature of God Himself. And because God is love, we too will be filled with deep affection for a numberless fraternity of other redeemed whom we had never even known. Heaven will be absolutely permeated by God's exhilarating, rapturous love, like the inescapable wafting of an intoxicating perfume.

Heaven is real

In "*Heaven Is for Real*", author Todd Burpo tells an amazing true story about his four-year-old son, Colton. During an emergency operation, the boy made an astonishing but brief trip to heaven and back. In this New York Times best-seller, the child's unanticipated, offhand remarks gives his story the ring of truth. The boy nonchalantly speaks of his trip assuming this sort of thing happens to everybody during surgery. He also often talks about meeting Pop, his father's own beloved grandfather whom the boy had never previously seen.

One day, Todd showed his son a picture of Pop taken shortly before the old man's death and asked him if this is whom he had seen in heaven. "Colton took the frame, held it in both hands, and gazed at the photo . . . Then a frown crinkled the space between his eyes and he shook his head. 'Dad, nobody's old in heaven,' Colton said."[7] Undaunted, Todd phoned his mother and asked her to mail him a picture taken when her father was in his twenties. A few days later, after the picture had arrived, Todd showed it to his young son.

Todd writes that the boy "took the picture from my hand, looked down, and then looked back at me, eyes full of surprise. 'Hey!' he said happily. 'How did you get a picture of Pop?'"[8] And if you believe in the Savior and the Good News, you, too, shall be forever young.

Old age is a terminal illness for which there is no cure, but the beautiful event that follows, for the Christian, is out of this world.

Postscript

The following incident demonstrates how all the events of our lives are in His hands if we but trust Him and rest in His sovereign grace and power.

After arriving in India on a flight from Afghanistan in 1966, our small evangelistic group visited the Golden Temple of Amritsar. We had been urged to see the famous building, and because we had a long wait before our train would leave for New Delhi, we decided to take advantage of the free side trip. Just before entering the temple, someone sternly warned us that taking pictures inside was punishable by instant death. That was no problem, of course, as none of us had cameras. I did have a tape recorder, however, and because audio devices were not forbidden, I thought it would be interesting to have a tape of the music that accompanied the Sikh cere-mony. So after we found a spot, I pulled the recorder out of my bag, inserted a tape and started recording.

When we left, one member of our group who had been sitting farther back told me that as I was setting up my recorder, a man nearby had stood up, walked over and stopped behind me. My friend was terrified when he saw the man suddenly reach into the upper part of his cloak to grasp something as he leaned over to see what I was doing. After a moment, he withdrew his hand from the con-cealed object and walked away. We surmised that he had thought I was taking pictures. Thankfully, he was not a man who – as people might say in that part of the world – "stabbed first and asked questions later." Had he been, I would have finished life long

The Harmandir Sahib in Amritsar, in the Punjab, India, is also known as The Golden Temple. It is a prominent Sikh place of worship built in the 16th Century.

before writing this book. But God in his merciful care and wisdom has provid-ed me with many more years on earth, perhaps so that others might learn from my adventures of growing in His grace and sharing the Gospel.

Now I am finished, at least with this book, and I pray that you have been enriched by your reading. We need to be like the man who found a treasure in a field and sold all he had to buy that field (Matthew 13:44). Hopefully, in addition to accepting the precious assurance of Heaven, you have been awakened to the availability of the spiritual treasure of knowing God more intimately while on earth. The riches of salvation are freely given to us through faith in Christ's atonement. The prize of spiritual growth is offered when, by faith, we diligently seek to walk with God while on this side of Glory. As the man in the biblical parable paid a high price to purchase the field where he had found the buried cache, so uncovering the mother lode of the fathomless knowledge of God will likely come at great personal cost. But this sacrifice is simply a wise eternal investment.

As I say, I am finished, and it's your turn to start, if you haven't already, on this quest for the deeper spiritual life. While your exper-iences may not be published in the pages of a book such as this here on earth, may they be recorded in the glorious pages of the history of Christ's Church in heaven.

I have enjoyed this journey of discovery with you. Thank you so much for reading. May we meet and laugh together for joy in that great eternal city in Heaven.

Ken Cetton July 2013

The grace of the Lord Jesus be with you.
1 Corinthians 16:23

Postscript

Further reading

The following is a relatively limited list of mostly older books by great authors, or stories of believers we would do well to imitate. In time I will seek to expand this list on my website: www.kencetton.com.

Andrew Murray is a much read author who I greatly enjoyed in my younger days. He has written many books on the Christian life, so take your pick.

A Passion for the Impossible by **Miriam Huffman Rockness** is a very inspirational book about the life of Lilias Trotter.

A.W.Tozer always seem to challenge one's soul. His most popular book is *The Pursuit of God* but his other writings are also excellent and generally challenging. Books such as *Born After Midnight* are a serious collection of articles that he wrote which are true soul food.

China's Christian Millions by **Tony Lambert**.

C.S.Lewis was a very skilled apologetic writer besides his excellence in fiction. For those who want to be challenged intellectually, *Mere Christianity* is a classic.

Hudson Taylor's *Spiritual Secret* Is a excellent book on a man who desired to live by faith and go against all odds and become a missionary in China in the 1800s.

Isobel Kuhn wrote *By Searching* and in fact was a prolific author who is bound to be good because of her obvious spiritual walk with the Lord. *In the Arena* is to be read after *By Searching*, but there are many more. It is not that she is teaching spiritual principles but she lives them.

John and Betty Stam – there are a number of books about these two martyrs so take your pick.

Pilgrim's Progress by **John Bunyan** is a classic you don't want to miss. However, unless you are a user of the *King James Bible*, get an edition of **Pilgrim's Progress** in modern English.

Shadow of the Almighty by **Elisabeth Elliot** who wrote of the life of her martyred husband Jim Elliot, a zealous and deeply spiritually young man.

Watchman Nee was a man of God and wrote such books as *The Normal Christian Life* as well as others relevant to my theme.

50 People every Christian should know by **Warren W. Wiersbe**. You will certainly find any number of these fifty people who it would be good to imitate in their spiritual quest.

Understanding this book

1. Two of the many books on this important subject include L. E. Maxwell, Born Crucified (Chicago: Moody Press, [1945]) and Watchman Nee, The Normal Christian Life (Carol Stream, Ill.: Tyndale House Publishers, 1977).
2. "I have been crucified with Christ; and it is no longer I who live, but Christ lives in me; and the life which I now live in the flesh I live by faith in the Son of God, who loved me and gave Himself up for me." Galatians 2:20.
3. "Therefore we have been buried with Him through baptism into death, so that as Christ was raised from the dead through the glory of the Father, so we too might walk in newness of life." Romans 6:4.

Hide 'n' seek

1. Acts 17:26-27.
2. Scripture verses such as Psalm 14:2-3 and Romans 3:12 declare that none of us instinctively seeks God because of our fallen nature. However, through the convicting work of the Holy Spirit, we are awakened to our need for God.
3. The subject of evolution is addressed in Ch 6 –

Evolution: the sacred cow.
4. Matthew 18:3.
5. Luke 19:10.
6. Acts 17:27.

1.1 Is there not a God?

1. I heard this story many years ago related as a true account.
2. A living cell contains more than 60,000 proteins in at least 100 specific configurations. Chance assemblage of a functional combination is one in nearly 105 million. Those are high odds, and you wouldn't want to bet your life on them; but people make that very bet when they dismiss a Creator. Information taken from Joseph Mastropaolo, "Evolution Is Biologically Impossible," Acts & Facts 28, no. 11 (1999).
3. Robert B. Jackson, "Why Don't Tree Branches Point Straight Up?" EarthSky (EarthSky, 21 Jan. 2010), Web, 12 Feb. 2013.
4. Romans 1:19-20 TLB

1.2 It's a fallen world

1. For a deeper look at Creationism, please see the following resources: www.creation.com and www.answersingenesis.org
2. Genesis 2:16-17.
3. The test was a success and a three-minute video of that electric car can be seen at: www.kencetton.

com.
4. The reader may wonder if one's conscience operates as a governor, but it doesn't. The conscience is more like a tachometer, which serves to warn of excessive engine speed but does not itself restrict it.
5. While we know that Satan was the cause of man's fall, we don't really know how Satan became evil. We can only speculate as to how he fell. In 2 Thessalonians 2:7 Paul calls it ". . the mystery of lawlessness . . "
6. Genesis 3:1-7.
7. Genesis 1:26-27, "Then God said, "Let Us make man in Our image, according to Our likeness".
8. John 14:30 ". . the ruler of the world . . "; 1 John 5:19 "We know that we are of God, and that the whole world lies in the power of the evil one."; 2 Corinthians 4:4 "The god of this world has blinded the minds of the unbelieving . . "
9. Jesus described the nature of Satan in John 8:44 where He said, ". . there is no truth in him . . . for he is a liar and the father of lies."
10. Luke 4:5-7.
11. Romans 5:6-8.
12. Isaiah 53:5.
13. John 3:5-7.
14. Galatians 5:16, "But I say, walk by the Spirit, and you will not carry out the desire of the flesh."
15. A female Salvation

Army worker, especially during World War I.

1.3 What is God like?

1. Romans 1:20.
2. Genesis 1:26.
3. William P. Young, The Shack (Newbury Park, Calif.: Windblown Media, 2007).
4. Matthew 23:37.
5. Psalm 56:8.
6. Job 4:17.
7. Romans 6:23.
8. John 3:16.
9. 1 Timothy 6:15-16.
10. Colossians 1:15-17.
11. Romans 14:11.
12. Psalm 139:1-2, 4.
13. Hebrews 4:13.
14. Psalm 139:7-8.
15. Psalm 33:9.
16. Job 9:10.
17. Revelation 4:8.
18. Psalm 8:1.
19. Psalm 76:4

1.4 The Son also rises

1. I can't remember the older gentleman's exact name.
2. John 1:1-4.
3. 1 John 1:1-3.
4. John 14:9.
5. John 1:14, 18
6. Revelation 19:11-13.
7. Isaiah 9:6.
8. Isaiah 7:14.
9. Matthew 1:23.
10. Isaiah 53:2.
11. Luke 19:10.
12. 1 Peter 2:24.
13. Philippians 2:10-11.

1.5 You've got mail – from God

1. Psalm 119:160.
2. Colossians 1:26.
3. Matthew 1:23.
4. Good resources on the validity of the Bible include Erwin W. Lutzer, Seven Reasons Why You Can Trust the Bible (Chicago: Moody Press, 2008); J. I. Packer, God Has Spoken (Downers Grove, Ill.: InterVarsity Press, 1979); F. F. Bruce, The Canon of Scripture (Downers Grove, Ill.: InterVarsity Press, 1996); and the full-length movie The Jesus Accounts Film (www.youtube.com/ watch?v=-2HFs2cVKNU).
5. Acts 2:22-24.
6. Acts 4:19-20.
7. Luke 1:1-4.
8. This sort of "word drop" has happened only twice in my life. Such phenomena are sometimes explained as the supernaturally given "word of knowledge" spoken of in 1 Corinthians 12:8: "To one is given the word of wisdom through the Spirit, and to another the word of knowledge according to the same Spirit." I mention my second such experience in the chapter "Where is God when bad happens?"
9. The story is from OM International, www.om.org
10. Carol Terry Talbot and Virginia J. Muir, Escape at Dawn (Wheaton, Ill.: Tyndale House, 1988), pages 320-323.
11. Romans 8:28.
12. My chapters on prayer will provide additional examples of times when God stepped in and granted the requests of His children.

1.6 Evolution: the sacred cow

1. For a deeper look at Creationism, please see the following resources: www.creation.com and www.answersingenesis. org. I believe in the Genesis account of creation and that we live on a Young Earth. These positions are bolstered by good evidence, which also substantiates the worldwide flood described in the Bible. A great flood is reported in the folklore of many unconnected non-Christian cultures around the world, but of course, you will not encounter these narratives in most scientific circles.
2. Some Christians believe in Theistic Evolution, which contends that if Evolution occurred, God guided the process. However, because Evolution is an attempt to completely remove God from the picture and the Biblical account in Genesis does not make room for Theistic Evolution it is not a reasonable position for a Christian to embrace.

2.1 Something missing

A version of this chapter first appeared in Moody Monthly Magazine in the May/June 1996 issue.
1. Peter and I were always friendly through the years whenever we met. As for Doris, we are still friends to this day. Once she asked me, "Ken, how can we be friends when I did such a terrible thing to you?" I answered, "Because what you did ultimately made me so spiritually rich, I can't help but be your friend."
2. Luke 15:7.

2.2 Accept no substitutes

1. 2 Corinthians 11:4 TLB.
2. Galatians 1:6-9.
3. Titus 3:5.
4. Some who think that baptism is necessary for salvation cite Mark 16:16: "He who has believed and has been baptized shall be saved; but he who has disbelieved shall be condemned." Notice, however, that a person is condemned simply by disbelief. Also look up Acts 10 and read the account of the first Gentiles who were saved in the early church. You will discover that as Peter was preaching to them, "the Holy Spirit fell upon all those who were listening" (v. 44). After seeing that they had received the Holy Spirit,

Peter recognized them as believers who had now been born again. He thus had them baptized (vv. 47-48). Later, Peter defended his contact with Gentiles and subsequent baptism of them as believers by telling the Jewish Christians in Jerusalem, "Therefore if God gave to them the same gift as He gave to us also after believing in the Lord Jesus Christ, who was I that I could stand in God's way?" (Acts 11:17). So clearly, a person is saved apart from baptism, although baptism should follow as soon as possible to affirm of a believer's commitment.
5. Acts 16:31 NKJV.
6. John 10:9.

2.3 Forgiven

1. 1 John 4:9.
2. Isaiah 64:6.
3. Isaiah 6:3.
4. Romans 3:23 TLB.
5. Isaiah 53.6.
6. 1 John 1: 7, 9.

2.4 Heaven is out of this world

1. 2 Timothy 1:10.
2. Colossians 1:26.
3. Deuteronomy 28:9, 11.
4. Ecclesiastes 9:10.
5. Isaiah 38:18.
6. Ecclesiastes 9:5.
7. Job 19:25-27.
8. Psalm 23:6.
9. Psalm 6:5.

10. Daniel 12:2.
11. Luke. 20:27-40.
12. John 6:68.
13. John 11:25-26.
14. John 8:51.
15. Philippians 1:21.
16. Philippians 1:23.
17. There are some who teach that we are not going to have a completely new earth, but a renewed one. While there will likely be a renewal of the earth in preparation for the thousand year reign of Christ when "the wolf will dwell with the lamb" (Isaiah 11:6), the earth and all the heavenly cosmos will subsequently be entirely destroyed. According to 2 Peter 3:10-13, But the day of the Lord will come like a thief, in which the heavens will pass away with a roar and the elements will be destroyed with intense heat, and the earth and its works will be burned up. Since all these things are to be destroyed in this way, what sort of people ought you to be in holy conduct and godliness, looking for and hastening the coming of the day of God, because of which the heavens will be destroyed by burning, and the elements will melt with intense heat! But according to His promise we are looking for new heavens and a new earth, in which righteousness dwells. In Revelation 20:11, John also describes the time that follows the thousand

year reign of Christ and the rebellion of Satan: "Then I saw a great white throne and Him who sat upon it, from whose presence earth and heaven fled away, and no place was found for them." The heaven spoken of by John and Peter is not the heaven of God's throne, but the star-studded cosmos. While the Scripture seems to imply that there will always be an earth, that does not mean that it won't be replaced with something better.

2.5 The other place

1. In some translations of the Bible you will not find the Old Testament Hebrew word Sheol or the New Testament Greek word Hades. Both words refer to the nether world which is the place for the dead. In the Bible translations that do not use those words, (usually older ones) the term Hell is used throughout those Bibles for either word including the term Gehenna. It is important then to be clear on what the words being used mean. According to Strong's Greek and Hebrew Dictionary Gehenna, which was an actual place of burning, is in New Testament times "a name for the place (or state) of everlasting punishment." In all translations that I know of, the word Gehenna

is always translated, Hell. As for Hades, according to Strong's Greek Dictionary, Hades is "the place (state) of departed souls." And according to Strong's Hebrew Dictionary Sheol means: "hades or the world of the dead (as if a subterranean retreat), including its accessories and inmates." As for the Lake of fire in Rev 20, I believe that represents Hell and we are told that both Hades and death are thrown into it. As is noted in this chapter, Sheol/ Hades is a waiting place for the dead. For the Old Testament believers, Sheol was apparently a place of unconsciousness. It is only when we get to the New Testament that we discover that Sheol/Hades had two compartments, suffering and non-suffering. At the resurrection of Christ, the non-suffering part emptied of its occupants and the place itself, now called Paradise was relocated to heaven.

2. MacDonald, Believer's Bible Commentary, 1433.
3. 1 Samuel 28:11-15.
4. 1 Samuel 28:19.
5. Luke 16:22.
6. Luke 16:23-26.
7. MacDonald, Believer's Bible Commentary, 1433.
8. Only a few who died— Enoch, Moses and Elijah— seem to have bypassed Hades. The latter two were seen on the Mount of Transfiguration.

9. C. I. Scofield Reference Notes state that "the passages in which the word [Hades] occurs make it clear that hades was formerly in two divisions, the abodes respectively of the saved and of the lost. The former was called 'paradise' and 'Abraham's bosom.'"
10. John 3:12.
11. The exact date of the writing of the Apostles' Creed is not known, but an early church father "Ambrose refers to the 'Creed of the Apostles' in 390." Wikipedia
12. Acts 2:31-32.
13. In 2 Corinthians 12:4, Paul says that he "was caught up into Paradise," possibly when he was left for dead in Lystra (Acts 14). This does show that Paradise has been relocated with the resurrection of Christ. Paradise is mentioned once more in the Bible as being in Heaven with the "tree of life" (Rev. 2:7).
14. 1 Peter 3:18-20.
15. Matthew 12:40.
16. Ephesians 4:8-10.
17. Revelation 13:8 NKJV.
18. John 20:17.
19. Revelation 20:14-15.

2.6 Jesus buys wrecks

1. The American Heritage Dictionary, 4th ed., s.v. "salvage."
2. Acts 4:12.
3. 1 Corinthians 1:26-29.

4. Genesis 1:26.

5. If you doubt demon possession exists, just ask a missionary working in a primitive area of the world about the subject. Due to Satan's clever stratagem, demonic possession is not as evident in the West. If it were rampant, thinking people might realize that because evil spirit creatures exist, so must their anti-thesis – angels – and above all, a loving caring God.

6. 2 Corinthians 5:17.

7. 1 John 3:2.

8. Titus 2:14.

9. Unfortunately, not all churches believe the Bible to be the inspired Word of God, nor do they all preach the Gospel—so choose carefully.

10. Hebrews 10:24-25.

11. Ephesians 4:22-24.

12. The American Heritage Dictionary, 4th ed., s.v. "salvage."

13 Acts 16:30-31.

2.7 Where is God when bad happens?

1. The names of my wife's friends have been changed for the story.

2. People have asked me about what it's like to receive a "word of knowledge?" First of all, I'm not a charismatic and I'm not promoting a strange or unique way to receive communication from God. All I'm

doing is reporting two experiences in this book of this happening to me in that manner. The best description that I can give of what it was like is this: it's like getting thumped on the head but having no pain or emotion except perhaps wonderment. I've asked the Lord through the years to do this again for me but up to now He has chosen not to. Furthermore, beware of anyone who comes to you saying they have a "word of knowledge" that conflicts with Scripture. The Word of God is our final authority.

3. What I told Lydia was before the popular saying came about, "If you feel far from God, guess who moved." So I didn't get the words I spoke from this saying which was yet to be popularized.

3.1 The deeper life – what is it?

1. John 3:8.

2. Theo McCully's messages are available at www. voicesforchrist.org/ speakers/mccullytheo.

3. "And I, brethren, could not speak to you as to spiritual men, but as to men of flesh, as to infants in Christ" (1 Corinthians 3:1).

4. "Faith Is a Journey, Not a Destination" A W Tozer, Born After Midnight, Chapter 3.

5. 2 Corinthians 5:17.

6. "But you have come to Mount Zion and to the city of the living God, the heavenly Jerusalem." (Heb 12:22).

7. Galatians 5:16, 22-23

8. Rom 8:28.

9. I'm no longer sure of his exact name.

3.2 I could've had a V8!

1. I still have this problem, but at least in America, one can't be arrested for it – so far.

2. 2 Samuel 12:1-14.

3. 2 Samuel 12:8 NKJV.

4. The game was likely called Sheepshead, but I know it as Sheep Set.

5. Matthew 7:7.

6. James 4:2.

7. Historically, it's questionable that the Director made this assertion, but the attitude is typical of the way we think.

8. Ephesians 3:20.

9. "Come, My Soul, Thy Suit Prepare."

10. Psalm 73:28.

11. James 5:16.

12. After being exonerated by a Turkish judge, I was re-arrested and taken to a jail in Istanbul before being escorted out of the country, as I relate in the chapter titled "Out of Luck and into Grace." However, I did turn around and come back in.

3.3 Out of luck, into grace

1. Romans 12:1
2. Romans 8:28.
3. 1 John 5:19.
4. Jeremiah 29:11.
5. Genesis 45:8.
6. Genesis 50:20.
7. 1 Peter 4:19 NKJV.
8. Romans 8:29.
9. 1 Thessalonians 5:16.
10. 1 Thessalonians 5:18.
11. 1 Peter 5:6-7.

3.4 No more Mr Nice Guy

1. Once I was so far out in the back-country that there wasn't even a bus. Instead, I had to travel with other Turks jammed like refugees into the back of a large open truck, standing on sacks of grain. (But then, I always did love riding in convertibles, at least as a teenager.)
2. It's been a while, so I can't recall my friend's name.
3. John 4:24.
4. Romans 5:12.
5. Psalm 14:1-3.
6. Colossians 2:13.
7. Jesus described the mysterious workings of the Holy Spirit in this way: "The wind blows where it wishes and you hear the sound of it, but do not know where it comes from and where it is going; so is everyone who is born of the Spirit" (John 3:8).
8. Galatians 5:16.
9. 2 Corinthians 5:17.
10. Romans 6:11.

11. Galatians 5:19-24.
12. Ephesians 2:6.
13. Romans 13:14.
14. Galatians 5:16-17.
15. Galatians 2:20 KJV.

3.5 Love is number one

1. This account is reported in Susi Hasel Mundy and Maylan Schurch, A Thousand Shall Fall: The Electrifying Story of a Soldier and His Family Who Dared to Practice Their Faith in Hitler's Germany (Hagerstown, Md.: Review and Herald Publishing Association, 2001).
2. 1 Corinthians 13:4.
3. 1 Corinthians 13:13.
4. Ephesians 5:1-2.
5. 1 Corinthians 13:8.
6. Mark 2:21-22.
7. Acts 2:13 NKJV.
8. Ephesians 4:22-24.
9. Colossians 3:12-14.
10. Galatians 2:20.
11. Galatians 5:16.
12. 1 John 4:16.
13. Luke 6:27-28.
14. Matthew 5:23-24.
15. Romans 12:18.
16. John 4:23-24.
17. Galatians 5:6.
18. Matthew 23:33.
19. Luke 10:37.
20. Carl Lawrence, The Church in China (Minneapolis, Minn.: Bethany House Publishers, 1985), 157.
21. 1 Timothy 1:5.

3.6 Faith 101

1. Hebrews 11:1-2.
2. Philippians 2:13.
3. I often tell people that the only reason I wasn't asked to travel fourth class was that there wasn't any. (Actually, there was an unofficial fourth-class section, but I lacked the agility to ride on top of the train and the lung capacity to hold my breath while passing through smoke-filled tunnels.)
4. Hebrews 11:6.
5. 1 Thessalonians 5:18.

3.7 Overflowing grace and peace

1. John 14:27.
2. My father insisted that I say nothing because he thought that my forgiving the young man would prejudice the case. I sought the counsel of Theo McCully, an elder in our assembly whose son Ed had been one of the five missionaries martyred in 1956 while trying to contact the Auca Indians in Ecuador. Theo advised me to do what my father said, as God knew that in my heart, I wanted to do what was right. As a result, my father developed a deep respect for Theo and was willing to attend Gospel meetings from time to time. Finally, the Lord did allow me to tell the one who took my sister's life

that I had forgiven him, as I describe in Chapter 3.14.
3. 2 Corinthians 12:9 NKJV.
4. Philippians 4:7.
5. Psalm 32:6.
6. 2 Corinthians 9:8.
7. John 1:16.
8. Psalm 84:11.
9. James 4:6.
10. 1 Peter 2:19.
11. "And though you have not seen Him, you love Him, and though you do not see Him now, but believe in Him, you greatly rejoice with joy inexpressible and full of glory" (1 Peter 1:8).
12. Some of you might wonder why I chose to have surgery if the Scripture promised life. I had several reasons. I understood the verse to suggest that the surgery would enable me to live. I also had to consider that because I would soon be without medical insurance, the cost of future treatments would be prohibitive. Finally, I felt grace and peace that I was doing the right thing.
13. Galatians 5:19-21.

3.8 It's not counting to ten

1. Colossians 3:12.
2. 1 Corinthians 13:4.
3. Ephesians 4:1-2.
4. Romans 13:14.
5. Romans 6:4.
6. James 1:3-4 KJV.
7. James 1:19-20.
8. Isaiah 53:7.
9. Romans 6:11.
10. Ephesians 6:12.

11. Luke 12:2-3
12. Hebrews 6:15.

3.9 Worship and the Holy Spirit

1. John 4:23-24.
2. 1 Corinthians 3:16.
3. 1 Timothy 3:15.
4. 1 Corinthians 3:17.
5. 1 Peter 2:5.
6. Ephesians 2:1-5.
7. John 14:18.
8. Galatians 5:16.
9. Ephesians 5:18.
10. A. W. Tozer, Born after Midnight (Camp Hill, Pa.: WingSpread Publishers, 2011, digital). ch. 1.
11. Romans 13:14.
12. Some people believe that speaking in tongues is the ultimate sign of God's fullness although I personally do not believe that. While I have never spoken in tongues, I have friends who claim to have this gift. Where do I stand? Billy Graham once told a story about a politician who, when discussing a touchy issue, stated, "Some of my friends are for it, and some are against it. I'm for my friends." Since all my friends will state, "I'm for what the Scripture says," I, too, maintain, "I'm for my friends."
13. John 4:13-14.
14. John 4:15.

3.10 Pride versus humility

1. Romans 12:3 KJV.

2. Luke 14:10-11.
3. James 4:6.
4. Psalm 138:6.
5. Romans 6:3-4.
6. 1 Peter 5:6.
7. Philippians 2:3.
8. 1 Corinthians 13:4.
9. Philippians 2:5-9.
10. Romans 12:16.
11. Lindy Drake, email to author, 2011.
12. 1 Peter 5:5.
13. 1 Peter 5:8-9.
14. 1 Corinthians 6:7. I'm not suggesting that we should never defend ourselves in court or file lawsuits. Those situations are between you and God. However, Paul does urge Christians not to sue one another.
15. 1 Peter 2:21-23.
16. Jeremiah 17:9 KJV.
17. Colossians 3:12-13.
18. F. B. Meyer, quoted in oChristian.com: Christian Quotes: Humility Quotes (oChristian.com, 2012), Web, 18 June 2013.

3.11 Prayer 101

1. Hebrews 4:16.
2. Please don't think that I have an exclusive "in" with God, because I'm no different than most of you. But we have all been called to pray, and maybe some of you haven't yet by faith accepted the invitation to get serious about prayer.
3. A. W. Tozer, Born after Midnight (Harrisburg, Pa.: Christian Publications, 1959).

4. Psalm 34:4.

5. 1 Corinthians 13:1.

6. Psalm 66:18.

7. Andrew Murray, The Prayer Life (Chicago: Moody Press, n.d.), 31.

8. 1 Peter 3:12.

9. Matthew 18:19.

10. Ephesians 3:20.

11. A. W. Tozer, "Honesty in Prayer," quoted in Mike Balog, "Honesty in Prayer – Tozer," SermonIndex: Discussion Forum: Articles and Sermons (SermonIndex, 26 Sept. 2006), Web, 23 May 2013.

12. Psalm 63:1.

13. Psalm 42:1-2.

14. A. W. Tozer, Born after Midnight (Harrisburg, Pa.: Christian Publications, 1959).

15. This story is from OM International, "Getting to Know the God Who Answers Prayer," OM International (OM International, 2013), Web, 23 May 2013. Zed educates and mentors "forgotten refugees" with no status, no papers and no likely way out of the poverty trap.

16. Proverbs 17:22 NKJV.

3.12 Prayer 102

1. Matthew 6:16.

2. Bill Bright, Seven Basic Steps to Successful Fasting and Prayer (Orlando, Fla.: NewLife Publications, 1995).

3. Ephesians 6:18.

4. 2 Corinthians 13:14.

5. Psalm 145:18.

6. Psalm 34:6.

7. Ephesians 6:12.

8. Daniel 10:12-14.

9. 1 Thessalonians 5:17.

10. 1 Timothy 5:5.

11. 2 Timothy 1:3.

12. Matthew 6:7.

13. Luke 18:1.

14. God also answered my main prayer; the evangelistic event brought many to the feet of Jesus.

15. Psalm 37:4.

3.13 Practicing mercy and grace

1. The Merchant of Venice 4.1.184-197.

2. Luke 6:36.

3. Matthew 5:7.

4. Ephesians 6:8.

5. A video of me driving that electrified VW Bug in 1979 can be found at www.kencetton.com.

6. Hebrews 4:16.

3.15 Don't let anyone give you a haircut

1. A Nazirite was a Hebrew whose life was especially dedicated to the Lord (Judges 13:5).

2. Judges 16:15-17.

3. Judges 16:19-21.

4. 2 Kings 5:9-14.

5. James 1:2-4 TLB.

6. There can be circumstances, such as abusive relationships, in which it would be wise to leave, although it would be best to seek godly counsel first.

7. 2 Corinthians 12:7-10.

8. Judges 16:17.

9. 1 Peter 4:19.

10. Judges 16:22.

11. Judges 16:29-30.

12. Psalm 27:14.

13. 1 Peter 5:10.

3.16 To, from and around the altar

1. The names of the bride and groom have been changed for this story.

2. 1 Peter 5:6.

3. Hebrews 13:4.

4. While we are commanded by Jesus in Matthew 5:28 not to lust, the Bible never strictly forbids "self sex."

5. Joshua Harris, I Kissed Dating Goodbye (Sisters, Oreg.: Multnomah Books, 1997).

6. John 8:11.

7. 1 Corinthians 13:4-7.

8. Ephesians 5:25.

9. Ephesians 5:28.

10. Titus 2:4. Since most marriages in biblical times were arranged, love may not initially have been involved. As a result, Paul prompted older women to be examples of respectful love for younger women to follow.

11. 1 Peter 4:19 TLB.

12. Romans 12:18 NIV.

13. 1 Peter 3:7.

14. 1 John 2:6.

15. 1 Thessalonians 5:15.

16. 1 Corinthians 6:9-10.

13.17 This for that

1. I am always careful not to use God's name disrespectfully, especially in humor. When I do mention Him, as in this story, I intend to teach a lesson that will lead to spiritual growth and thus bring Him glory. In this case, Cindy is acknowledging that the Judge in the booth actually is God.
2. 1 Peter 3:8-9.
3. 1 Peter 2:21, 23.

4.1 The Orient Express – expressing your gifts

1. Agatha Christie wrote the famous mystery novel Murder on the Orient Express in 1934. The popular movie version was released in 1974.
2. When my friend Al and I were smuggling Bibles from Greece into Yugoslavia, the Greek border guard looked at us strangely. The regular tourist season was over, and he was not stationed at a popular exit or entry point. Here in front of him were two single guys, one in a trench coat. Eying us up and down, he muttered with an accent, "James Bond-a." (He thought we looked like spies.) Having read a news magazine article about the current movie craze for the fictional spy, I thought, Sure, pal, you've got that right.

Everything here but the ravishing blonde.
3. 1 Peter 4:10.
4. 1 Corinthians 12:12-26.
5. Romans 12:6-8.
6. Major Bible passages that speak of spiritual gifts include Romans 12:6-8; 1 Corinthians 12:4-11; 1 Corinthians 12:28-30; Ephesians 4:7-12; James 1:17; and 1 Peter 4:10.
7. Several years ago, I had planned to take the Amtrak train from Syracuse, New York, to Milwaukee, Wisconsin. First, I needed to ride the bus from Binghamton, New York, to Syracuse. However, after I was dropped off at the bus station in Binghamton, I discovered the bus schedules had just been changed and I would miss my train if I waited for the next bus. In desperation, I phoned Buddy. He came immediately and drove me more than an hour so that I could catch my train. He then had to return home alone late in the evening. In demonstrating his gift of "helps," he saved me from missing my train.
8. James 1:17.
9. 1 Corinthians 2:14 KJV.
10. I had previously preached at open-air evangelism events. I had also presented a few short Sunday-night messages on holiday weekends when church attendance was guaranteed to be sparse. But I had never before spoken to a sizeable

gathering of possible critics.

4.2 Literature evangelism – its easier than you think

1. This story and chapter are adapted from a much shorter article, which I originally wrote for Billy Graham's Decision magazine in 1991.
2. Romans 10:14.
3. Philippians 1:15, 18.
4. This letter from Bill McCann of Milwaukee, Wisconsin, is used with his permission.

4.3 Whatever happened to Smokey?

1. 1 Corinthians 15:58.
2. Acts 1:8.
3. Daniel 12:3.

4.4 People are dying to meet Jesus

1. The simplest way to do door-to-door evangelism is to bring a brochure about your church and a tract that clearly explains the Gospel. Cheerfully greet the person who opens the door and say, "Hi! I'm (your name) from (name of your church), and I wanted to invite you to our service this Sunday and also to pray for you if you have any pressing requests." Then inquire about the person's needs and look for an opportunity

to share your testimony.

2. The following Christian colleges offer courses in evangelism: Davis College (www.davisny.edu), Moody Bible Institute (www.moody.edu), and Emmaus Bible College (www.emmaus.edu/online).

3. Revelation 3:8.

4. Galatians 6:9.

5. 1 Corinthians 13:12.

6. Luke 8:12.

7. 1 Peter 5:8-9.

8. Maybe Satan is called "the prince of the power of the air" because he's the god of this world (Ephesians 2:2).

5.1 A thumb on your scale

1. 1 Corinthians 1:26-28.

2. The Book of Joshua, written hundreds of years earlier, reports, "Now as for the Jebusites, the inhabitants of Jerusalem, the sons of Judah could not drive them out" (Joshua 15:63).

3. 2 Samuel 5:6 TLB.

4. This affirmation was promoted by Émile Coué, a French psychologist and pharmacist.

5. Psalm 34:4.

6. Psalm 27:8.

7. John 14:23.

8. 2 Corinthians 10:3-4.

9. 1 Chronicles 11:4-5 NIV.

10. Philippians 4:13.

5.2 Finishing well

1. 2 Timothy 4:7.

2. A close friend of mine, Steve Richards, was also ordered to leave Turkey. He told me that the day before his departure, he took his family into downtown Istanbul and handed out hundreds of tracts. Amazingly, he was not arrested. He finished well in that country and continued evangelizing among the Turkish people living in Germany.

3. After the police officer dropped me off at the border, I found another re-entry point and returned to evangelize in Turkey and complete the biblical tourist guide I was writing.

4. 2 John 1:8.

5. 2 Peter 1:10-11.

6. Ephesians 6:10-12.

7. 1 Peter 4:12.

8. 1 Peter 5:8-9.

9. 1 Peter 5:10.

10. Hebrews 4:7.

11. Luke 15:11-32.

12. Patrick K. O'Donnell, Operatives, Spies, and Saboteurs: The Unknown Story of World War II's OSS (New York: Free Press, 2004; reprint, New York: Citadel Press, 2006), 313 (page citation refers to the reprint edition).

13. 2 Timothy 4:7-8.

14. 1 Corinthians 9:24.

5.3 Forever young

1. Not her real name.

2. Daniel 7:9.

3. Wikipedia.

4. John 11:25-26.

5. Acts 10:43 "Of Him all the prophets bear witness that through His name everyone who believes in Him receives forgiveness of sins."

6. Revelation 1:17-18.

7. Mark 12:25.

8. Todd Burpo and Lynn Vincent, Heaven Is for Real: A Little Boy's Astounding Story of His Trip to Heaven and Back (Nashville, Tenn.: Thomas Nelson, 2010), p120-123.